DECISIVE CAMPAIGNS OF THE
SECOND WORLD WAR

DECISIVE CAMPAIGNS
OF THE
SECOND WORLD WAR

Edited by
JOHN GOOCH

FRANK CASS

First published 1990 in Great Britain by
FRANK CASS AND COMPANY LIMITED
Gainsborough House, 11 Gainsborough Road,
London E11 1RS, England

and in the United States of America by
FRANK CASS AND COMPANY LIMITED
c/o International Specialized Book Services Ltd.
5602 N.E. Hassalo Street
Portland, Oregon 97213–3640

British Library Cataloguing in Publication Data

Decisive campaigns of the Second World War.
1. World War   2. Army operations
I. Gooch, John   II. Journal of strategic studies, ISSN
0140-2390
940.5412

ISBN 0-7146-3369-0
ISBN 0–7146–4070 0 (pbk)

This group of studies first appeared in a Special Issue on
Decisive Campaigns of the Second World War of *The Journal
of Strategic Studies* Vol. 13, No.1 published by Frank Cass &
Co. Ltd.

Printed and bound in Great Britain by
Antony Rowe Ltd, Chippenham

CONTENTS

NOTES ON CONTRIBUTORS

John Gooch is Professor of History at the University of Lancaster and co-editor of this journal. Among his recently published works are *Army, State and Society in Italy, 1860–1915* (Macmillan, 1989) and *Military Misfortunes: The Anatomy of Failure in War* (with Eliot A. Cohen) (The Free Press, 1990).

Martin S. Alexander is a lecturer in modern French and British history at the University of Southampton. Educated at Oxford University and at the Université de Paris IV (Sorbonne), he has held a Research Fellowship of the Franco-British Council and was a John M. Olin visiting postdoctoral fellow at Yale in 1988–89. He is co-editor (with Helen Graham) of *The French and Spanish Popular Fronts: Comparative Perspectives* (Cambridge University Press, 1989), and joint general editor (with A.J. Nicholls) of the Longman series 'The Post-War World: Studies in Contemporary History'. A contributor to Peter Paret's new edition of *Makers of Modern Strategy* (Princeton University Press, 1986), he is currently completing a study of General Gamelin, *The Republic in Danger, 1933–1940*, to be published by Cambridge University Press.

Marc Milner has served as an historian with the Canadian Department of National Defence, where he contributed to the official histories of the RCAD and RCN in the Second World War. The author of numerous publications on the Atlantic War, including *North Atlantic Run: The RCN and the Battle for the Convoys,* he has taught military history at the University of New Brunswick since 1986, and is presently Director of UNB's Military and Strategic Studies Program.

Malcolm Smith is a Senior Lecturer in History at St. David's University. He is the author of *British Air Strategy between the Wars* (Oxford University Press, 1984), *British Politics, Society and the State* (Macmillan, 1990), and co-author of *Cinema, Literature and Society: Elite and Mass Culture in Interwar Britain* (Croom Helm 1987). He is currently writing *1940: The Great British Myth* for Routledge.

Lucio Ceva was born in Milan, where he practised law between 1952 and 1987. He has published a large number of books, essays and articles on military history, as well as having presented numerous conference papers. Among his main publications are *Una battaglia partigiana* (1966), *La condotta italiana della guerra* (1975), *Le Forze Armate* (1981) and *Africa Settentrionale 1940–1943* (1982). He teaches the history of military institutions at the University of Pavia, where he has been associate professor since 1987.

Bernd Wegner was educated at the Universities of Tübingen, Vienna and Hamburg, where he took his Ph.D. in 1980. He was a Research Fellow at St. Antony's College, Oxford, in 1979–80 and since then has been a fellow of the Militärgeschichtliches Forschungsamt and a part-time lecturer at Freiburg University. His publications include *The Waffen-SS* (Blackwell, 1990) and a study on the German–Russian war in 1942–43, which will appear later this year as part of *Das Deutsche Reich und der Zweite Weltkrieg*, vol.6 (Stuttgart: Deutsche Verlagsanstalt).

Brian Holden Reid is Lecturer in War Studies, King's College, London, and since 1987 has been Resident Historian at the British Army Staff College, Camberley – the first civilian to work on the Directing Staff for over 100 years. A fellow of the Royal Historical Society and Royal Geographical Society, from 1984–87 he was Editor of the *RUSI Journal*. He is the author of *J.F.C. Fuller: Military Thinker* (1987) and co-editor of *The British Army and the Operational Level of War* (1989) and *New Technology and the Arms Race* (1989) and numerous essays on British and American military history

Louis Allen became Reader in French at the University of Durham, where is now Honorary Fellow of the Northumbrian Universities East Asia Centre. A wartime intelligence officer in South-East Asia, he is the author of many books and articles on Japan and Asia, including *Japan: The Years of Triumph, Sittang – the Last Battle, Singapore 1941–1942, The End of the War in Asia*, and *Burma: The Longest War*, and is at present working on a book on Japanese intelligence.

Decisive Campaigns of the Second World War

Introduction

JOHN GOOCH

Important battles, Clausewitz tells us, are the gold and silver of the strategic budget.[1] Writing in the shadow of Napoleon and greatly influenced by an era in warfare when it had become fairly common for the outcome of a campaign to be decided by a single battle, it was natural that he should hold such a view: contemporary history supported it, and it accorded with the central place occupied by combat in his theory of war. Indeed, it is scarcely possible to study Napoleon's campaigns without recognising that a single decisive battle which could decide the outcome of an entire campaign was generally the Emperor's goal and that he often attained it.

Characteristically, Clausewitz pointed out that a decisive battle was not simply a very large engagement or one which ended in a clear victory for one of the parties involved but that it also depended on other factors, particularly the extent to which both parties had committed the major part of their strength to the duel.[2] Nevertheless he went on to admit that a true commander would probably always try to bring such a battle about. The Prussian victories at Koniggratz and Sedan and the Italian defeat at the second battle of Custoza suggested that campaigns could indeed still be clinched by a single decisive engagement – though French experience at Magenta and Solferino pointed to a rather different conclusion – and almost without exception the generals of the First World War pursued the goal Napoleon had set for them.[3]

Though the decisive battle remained a goal of the German armies during the first three years of the Second World War, on the whole it was not one shared by their opponents. Instead the Allies sought to crush Germany, and then Japan, by exerting overwhelming pressure on them in many places and over an extended period of time. After 1941 Germany was forced to respond in kind as the operational virtuosity of the *Wehrmacht* proved unable to shatter opponents who could mobilise and employ superior resources on a global scale. Japan, inherently much weaker than Germany, succumbed like her Axis partner to the cumulative blows of an opponent who never committed the major part of his strength to a single duel.

France did fall victim to the German armies in only 45 days, to be sure, and Japan was finally brought to her knees largely through the use of two atomic weapons; but for the major combatants – Great Britain, Russia and the United States on the one hand, and Germany, Italy and Japan on the other – the outcome of the Second World War was not determined by any single decisive battle. Nevertheless the lure of such a glamorous quarry has attracted some military historians, though the wiser heads have acknowledged that at best a number of battles can be so described and that no single engagement can receive the laurels as truly 'decisive'.[4]

Alongside the idea of the decisive battle stands that of the decisive moment, either in a single battle or in the war as a whole: the occasion on which the balance was tipped irrevocably in favour of one or other of the combatants. One historian has felt confident enough to identify the turning point in the battle for France as having occurred not merely on a specific day (15 May), but in the afternoon rather than the morning.[5] This may be so, though each historian of that campaign would probably have his or her own preferred moment; but attempts to identify a 'turning point' in the war as a whole have produced a number of candidates without resulting in the declaration of any clear winner.[6] Indeed, the very nature of the Second World War seems to preclude the possibility of a 'decisive' battle or even of a 'decisive' moment. In order to understand both the course and the outcome of the Second World War we need to abandon the Napoleonic model and look elsewhere for enlightenment.

Battles may indeed be the gold and silver pieces in the economy of war, but in order to explain how in war the balance tilts towards victory for one party and defeat for the other we need to look beyond the medium of exchange and examine the management of the economy. A lost battle does not necessarily entail disaster, just as a lost banknote does not necessarily mean bankruptcy. Setbacks of this kind occur to all parties in every war. Ultimately one side or the other overcomes them. But loss of control over a substantial and strategically significant area – be it on land, at sea or in the air – is a major setback from which long-term recovery may be impossible. As such set-backs multiply, the likelihood of victory diminishes and defeat starts to beckon.

Usually many battles have to be fought before control over such vital areas is won and lost – rarely in modern war does the outcome of a single battle decide a campaign. But a campaign won or lost adds much more weight to one side or the other in the scales of victory and defeat. So it is to campaigns that we should look to understand the strategic reasons for the outcome of great wars for, as Bernard Brodie wisely wrote some 40 years ago: 'War is a question not of winning battles but of winning campaigns.'[7]

Campaigns are the building blocks of war. Sometimes a single campaign may bring a decision in and of itself, though this is rare. More often success in a single campaign may not bring victory, although failure might have resulted in defeat: as Marc Milner points out in his study of the North Atlantic campaign, 'It was a struggle the Allies could have lost'.[8] Had they done so the invasion of Europe would have become an impossibility, and much else besides. Most commonly, the outcome of a war is determined as a result of several campaigns which have been conducted simultaneously or sequentially. The defeat of Japan, for example, emerged from at least four campaigns: the twin American island-hopping drives directed by MacArthur and Nimitz, the submarine campaign against Japan's sea lines of communication, and the air campaign of 1944–45 which culminated in the atomic bombing of Hiroshima and Nagasaki. Some campaigns played important supporting roles – the war in the Burmese and Chinese theatres, for example. Others, such as the Aleutian campaign, had virtually no effect on the outcome.

As the example of Japan clearly illustrates, the successful overall direction of the war involves making hard decisions about the allocation of resources among different campaigns and the selection of priorities between them. Such matters are the business of command and as such they are not the subject of this book; but it is worth remarking that the Allies proved very much better at making such decisions than did the Axis and that they did so by learning on the job. In 1943 General George C. Marshall remarked that after having received an education based on roads, railways and rivers during the First World War, he had during the previous two years 'been acquiring an education based on oceans and I've had to learn all over again'[9] The effective distribution of superior resources was in large part the key to the Allies' success in the Second World War, and this in turn rested on their success in jointly maintaining an agreed global view, while Hitler's grip on German strategy ensured that it remained resolutely land-bound and Europe-oriented.

In the vertical hierarchy of strategy campaigns correspond most closely with the theatre dimension rather than with the operational or grand strategic realms which lie below and above it.[10] Theatre strategy is, as Edward Luttwak has pointed out, 'spatial strategy' and in land campaigns, as he suggests, 'some specific territory . . . is the very object of contention . . .'.[11] In sea and air campaigns, however, this is less the case: what is at issue is control rather than possession. The studies by Marc Milner and Malcolm Smith of the North Atlantic and strategic bombing campaigns which follow both demonstrate that the strategic issues in theatres at sea and in the air can be somewhat different from those involved in land war.

At the same time, study of the campaigns in North Africa, Russia and Italy demonstrates the truth of Luttwak's suggestion that the logic of theatre strategy – on land at least – seems to suggest that the farther you advance, the more likely you are to be defeated.[12] Logistics alone may have defeated Germany in North Africa and Russia.[13] They certainly presented the Americans with an enormous challenge in the Pacific: in Louis Allen's well-chosen words, the war against Japan was 'a siege on a continental scale, across a moat of unparalleled dimensions'.[14] In war, force must not only be mobilised and deployed, it must also be sustained. The successful campaign, in any and each of the three dimensions, is characterised by an effort which is maintained across space and over time to a point at which the opponent is unable to continue effective resistance. One of the features of the studies collected together here is that they seek to show how and why one side succeeded in doing exactly this while the other failed.

The contributors to this work were invited to reassess selected campaigns in the light of the most recent scholarship and also to weigh the significance of their campaigns in the overall outcome of the war. No attempt was made to impose a common methodological framework, but nevertheless each author followed his own variant of a general analytical approach to writing campaign history. That approach entails consideration of four different dimensions which together offer a useful model for analysing any campaign: genesis, purposes, operational execution and consequences. Each author gives varying weight to these issues, and some also stress the significance of wider dimensions in explaining their particular subjects.

Martin Alexander's examination of the fall of France in 1940 is shaped by the need to address the charge that France lost that decisive campaign less through military errors committed after 10 May 1940 than through a massive internal haemhorrage of will, itself the consequence of France's response to the events of the 1930s and even perhaps of her reactions to the First World War. No sooner was the campaign over than the charge was levelled: William Shirer, then an American radio correspondent in Berlin, confided to his diary on 27 June 1940, after a tour of the battlefield, the belief that France had not fought. 'The French, as though drugged, had no will to fight, even when their soil was invaded by their most hated enemy. There was a complete collapse of French society and of the French soul.'[15] In substance, this accusation of defeat through internal collapse has often been repeated.

As Dr Alexander demonstrates, an important key to understanding this campaign is a careful examination of the context in which it took place. That context was a complex one, involving as it did the difficulties which hindered French rearmament after 1936, the fragility of the relationship between the western allies, the rejection of strategic alternatives to fighting a campaign in Belgium and France, and the politico-military crisis which smouldered just below the surface of French political life and which flared up with the German attack. Dr Alexander sees premier Reynaud's action in sacking general Gamelin and recalling general Weygand in the midst of the campaign as 'not just a military setback but the prelude to the overthrow of the French Republic . . .'.[16] His essay underlines the importance of evaluating the regime which may be called on to fight a crucial campaign.

Professor Marc Milner's analysis of the North Atlantic campaign – which customary usage insists on labelling a battle, despite the fact that it was prolonged for some three and a half years and went through a number of different phases – focuses on the central issue in the war at sea: the operational execution of theatre strategy. His analysis invites the conclusion that no other campaign surpassed this one in the complexity of the problems to be solved before it could be won; and it is even possible to suggest that in this respect no other campaign even equalled it.

The Allied navies gained the mastery of the North Atlantic, as professor Milner demonstrates, primarily as a result of their success in three fields. One was the development of new technology which outpaced their opponent's abilities to counter with yet newer weapons. A second was their mastery of the techniques of amassing and then using operational intelligence to defeat the U-boat assaults. In the words of a distinguished American historian who witnessed at first hand the naval war on the eastern seaboard of the United States in the first half of 1942, 'The war against the submarine . . . was, in one manifestation, an intellectual exercise demanding the collection, organization, interpretation and dissemination of many different kinds of data.'[17] Skilful organisation and the application of hard critical analysis resulted in an Allied triumph in this field. The third component of victory was the successful development of the doctrine and tactics by means of which to apply the results of intelligence and superiority in weaponry.

Professor Milner also demonstrates that to understand this campaign in depth it is necessary to delve deep into statistics and to compile the graphs which chart the relative strength of Allied and German shipping during the course of the so-called battle of the Atlantic. His conclusions about the downward trend in Allied shipping losses between 1940 and 1942 and his observations about the overall significance of ULTRA in winning the North Atlantic campaign are among the interesting features of this major re-evaluation of the war at sea.[18]

In his re-examination of the Allied strategic air offensive against Germany, Malcolm Smith lays considerable emphasis on the cultural context in which the doctrine of aerial bombardment was developed in pre-war Britain and America. His findings suggest that strategic choices in a campaign such as this may be significantly constrained by strategic preferences which have been established in a peacetime environment as responses to social perceptions rather than to narrowly military calculations.[19] Dr Smith also shows us the importance of the process by which strategy is implemented during a campaign. In this case that process was heavily influenced by the survival of pre-war assumptions up to 1941 and by the important role played by a single individual, Sir Arthur Harris, in the activities of Bomber Command.

As with the war at sea, operational capability probably played the largest role in determining the outcome of the strategic air campaign against Germany. As Dr Smith shows, until the closing stages of the war the Allies lacked the equipment and the techniques necessary to put their preferred strategy into operation with any chance of decisive success. They also lacked full intelligence about the Germany economy, though even if they had it they would very probably have continued to disagree about what to bomb. For many reasons, not least among them the debate as to its overall effectiveness, the strategic air war against Germany is and will probably remain the most controversial Allied campaign of the Second World War.

Lucio Ceva provides a unique insight on the North African campaign, considering it from the point of view of the Italians, the Germans and the Allies. His analysis of the differing purposes the campaign served for the Axis highlights the fact that, while the Italians and the Anglo-American forces treated it as of primary strategic significance, for the Germans it was seen as having only secondary importance. For a brief period between June and November 1940 Hitler flirted with a Mediterranean strategy, but with the decision to go to war with Russia he reverted to the land strategy with which he was most comfortable. The consequences for the North African campaign were momentous, for they meant that Allied strength was matched against Axis weakness.

English-language accounts of the war in North Africa are frequently coloured by a cultural prejudice which at times scarcely bothers with disguise. The denigration of the Italian performance owes some of its virulence to Rommel, who was not above claiming for the Afrika Korps victories which had in fact been won by his ally. Professor Ceva's careful study of the operational aspects of the campaign and his evidence of the improvement in the fighting quality of Italian troops by the end of 1941 will do much to redress this balance. His sensitivity to the human dimensions of the campaign reminds us that, while *matériel* and geographical factors can never be ignored, war is the activity of men who are both its masters and its victims.

Bernd Wegner takes as his subject what is probably the most-studied campaign of the Second World War: the German campaign in Russia in 1941–42. A member of the team of official historians who are in the final stages of writing the definitive German history of the Second World War, Dr Wegner has drawn on his own and his colleagues' research to offer what is undoubtedly the most up-to-date and comprehensive short survey of that decisive campaign. As well as dealing with each of the four main dimensions of campaign analysis, he offers a considered judgement of the overall importance of the German defeat in Russia for the outcome of the war.

Among the many important conclusions embodied in this essay two may perhaps be singled out. First, the Russian campaign had no place for a decisive battle on the Napoleonic model. Between June and September 1941 the Wehrmacht scored victory after victory, taking Russian prisoners by the hundred thousand, and yet as Dr Wegner points out, 'By the end of October [1941] at the latest the blitzkrieg against the Soviet Union had failed, although the German army in the East had not lost a single battle.'[20] Second, the circumstances of the Russian campaign meant that the Germans' neglect of the fundamental principle of concentration of force became a critical error. The stakes on the Eastern Front were high and although losing a single hand did not mean that either party had to leave the table, the Germans had the smaller purse. Their pursuit of competing strategic objectives diminished its value yet further.

Once becalmed in the backwaters of historical scholarship, the Italian campaign of 1943–45 is now emerging as a subject of controversy. In his revisionist essay, Dr Brian Holden Reid argues that its genesis was opportunistic and its purpose unclear since it fulfilled no consistent strategic aim. Its ostensible objective was a diversionary one – to draw German troops away from Russia and then from Normandy – and indeed a decisive success in Italy could never have knocked Germany out of the war. However, in Churchill's mind it took on (if it did not always have) a greater significance as the opportunities for Mediterranean gains seemed to beckon and his struggles to maintain and even expand it, notably at Teheran in November 1943, aroused considerable friction with the Americans. The problems of agreeing on an Allied strategy in a joint campaign are a particularly important feature of this essay.[21]

Brian Holden Reid also gives full weight to the weaknesses in the operational execution of the campaign. On the British side, the fault seems to have lain partly in lack of means as other theatres took priority over Italy and partly in unimaginative methods, exemplified by the battles of attrition at Monte Cassino. Dr Holden Reid identifies a similar unimaginativeness in the operational methods of the Americans, exemplified in their preference for geographical objectives. The failure of the Anzio landings in January 1944 to break the impasse caused by the strength of the German defences in the mountains south of Rome, although undeniably hindered by inadequate resources, may have been just as much a product of American caution and timidity: its commander, General John P. Lucas, later claimed that he was told by General Mark Clark 'Don't stick your neck out Johnny. I did at Salerno and got into trouble.'[22] The importance of generalship, and the shortcomings of field marshal Alexander in this respect, are among the most significant aspects of Dr Reid's essay.

Louis Allen's accomplished *tour d'horizon* of the campaigns in Asia and the Pacific takes in all the dimensions which have already been described and adds to them an important assessment of the place which these campaigns occupied – and occupy – in the Japanese national psyche. This is an aspect of the campaign history of the Second World War which has hitherto been somewhat neglected in English-language studies, and one to which Lucio Ceva also makes reference in his essay. For the historian, this suggests a profitable vein for future research.

All campaigns involve mastering an environment as well as overcoming an enemy; Dr Allen's emphasis on the nature of the theatre in which his chosen campaigns took place, a region where the prevalence of disease and the vast distances over which men and supplies had to be transported were particularly significant factors, is a reminder that all campaigns – and not merely 'small wars' – are to some extent 'campaigns against nature'.[23] The significance of the brief but devastating atomic campaign in bringing about the collapse and surrender of Japan (which Dr Allen was asked to exclude from his study) is in part that it offered a unique means of projecting immense power across these distances and delivering a blow which even an atavistic society like that of Japan was unable to withstand.

The studies which follow, then, provide both specific analyses of individual campaigns in the light of the most recent research and models for further campaign studies. The seven campaigns they examine are by no means the only ones to which the epithet 'decisive' could reasonably be applied: other campaigns could have been chosen and might have appeared to keep company with the selection offered here. But, both separately and together, these case studies provide authoritative guidance in understanding many of the major campaigns whose outcome determined the result of the Second World War.

NOTES

1. Carl von Clausewitz, *On War*, edited and translated by Michael Howard and Peter Paret (Princeton, NJ: Princeton University Press, 1976), p.244.
2. Ibid., p.260.
3. See Lorenzo M. Crowell, 'The Illusion of the Decisive Napoleonic Victory', *Defense Analysis*, Vol.4, No.4 (1988), pp.329–46.
4. For a fine example see Hans-Adolf Jacobsen and Jürgen Rohwer, *Decisive Battles of World War II: The German View* (London: Andre Deutsch, 1965), p.516.
5. Alistair Horne, *To Lose a Battle: France 1940* (London: Macmillan, 1969).
6. See William Richardson and Seymour Freidin (eds.), *The Fatal Decisions* (London: Michael Joseph, 1956).
7. Bernard Brodie, *Strategy in the Machine Age* (Princeton, NJ: Princeton University Press, 1944), p.437.
8. See below, p.45.
9. Jeter A. Isely and Philip A. Crowl, *The U.S. Marines and Amphibious War* (Princeton, NJ: Princeton University Press, 1951), p.3.

10. See Edward N. Luttwak, *Strategy: The Logic of War and Peace* (Harvard, MA: Belknap, 1987), p.xii.
11. Ibid., p.113.
12. Ibid., p.114.
13. For a powerful argument for their primacy in strategy, see Martin van Creveld, *Supplying War: Logistics from Wallenstein to Patton* (Cambridge: Cambridge University Press, 1977).
14. See below, p.165.
15. William S. Shirer, *Berlin Diary: The Journal of a Foreign Correspondent 1934–1941* (New York: Knopf, 1941), pp.437–8.
16. See below, p.32.
17. Elting E. Morison, *Turmoil and Tradition: A Study of the Life and Times of Henry L. Stimson* (Boston, MA: Athenaeum, 1960), pp.467–8.
18. For further consideration of the operational problems to be overcome in winning the North Atlantic campaign, see Eliot A. Cohen and John Gooch, *Military Misfortunes: The Anatomy of Failure in War* (New York: The Free Press, 1990), pp.59–94.
19. For examples of this approach, see Ronald Schaffer, *Wings of Judgment: American Bombing in World War* (New York and Oxford: Oxford University Press, 1985) and Michael S. Sherry, *The Rise of American Air Power: The Creation of Armageddon* (New Haven, CT and London: Yale University Press, 1987).
20. See below, p.113.
21. For a concise summary of this debate, see Michael Howard, *The Mediterranean Strategy in the Second World War* (London: Weidenfeld & Nicolson, 1968); and from a different perspective, Mark A. Stoler, *The Politics of the Second Front: American Military Planning and Diplomacy in Coalition Warfare, 1941–1943* (Westport, CT: Greenwood Press, 1977).
22. General John P. Lucas Diary, Part III, 24 January 1944. U.S. Army Military History Institute, Carlisle, PA.
23. C.E. Callwell, *Small Wars: Their Principles and Practice* (London: HMSO, 1906), p.44.

The Fall of France, 1940

MARTIN S. ALEXANDER*

The fall of France – a shorthand for the political and military crisis for the Allies of May–June 1940 – was the first real upset of the Second World War. It was the first occasion on which the 'form book' of the conflict was overturned. It set the world reeling. Contemporaries struggled to conceive that the collapse was possible, even as it gathered pace around them. They were reluctant to believe the unbelievable, loath to mention the unmentionable – to utter the words 'evacuation', 'defeat', 'armistice', 'surrender'. As the first rumours of the German breakthrough on the Meuse reached Paris on 15 May 1940, the veteran correspondent of the *Manchester Guardian*, Alexander Werth, articulated the general perplexity when he mused: 'what if the French Army turns out to be like the Polish cavalry and the Dutch flooding, and the Albert Canal – just another legend? [But] I can't quite believe it'.[1] The reality became all too horribly apparent just a month later, on 12 June, when the Champs Elysées itself echoed to the tramp of the first of the invader's jackbooted columns.

1940 witnessed the undoing of an entire alliance of the western democracies of Europe, not simply the fall of France. The Netherlands was knocked out of the battle within five days; Belgium followed after a further 13 days, on 28 May. The British were driven from the continent. But it was France's downfall that stunned the watching world. The shock was all the greater because the trauma was not limited to a catastrophic and deeply embarrassing defeat of her military forces – it also involved the unleashing of a conservative political revolution that, on 10 July 1940, interred the Third Republic and replaced it with the authoritarian, collaborationist *Etat Français* of Vichy.

All this was so deeply disorienting because France had been regarded as a great power, certainly a mainstay of the alliance which had resolved to see that the attack on Poland in September 1939 would be the last of Hitler's easy conquests. When the débâcle overtook the western nations in their turn in May 1940, observers could, perhaps, take Belgian and Dutch defeat in their stride. These were lesser powers by any yardstick. The collapse of France, however, was a different case (a 'strange defeat' as it was dubbed in the haunting phrase of the Sorbonne's great medieval historian and Resistance martyr, Marc Bloch).[2] Perhaps some who had monitored her appeasement of Germany in the 1930s may have had nagging doubts about her long-term prospects as a truly front-rank power. But few, even in Germany, had questioned that she remained a first-line military nation and would prove to be a redoubtable and resilient obstacle to Hitler's ambitions. Had not France spent over seven billion francs constructing the Maginot Line to shield the strategic industries of Lorraine between 1930 and 1937? Had not France committed twice that sum in September 1936 for a four-year programme to rearm her land forces? Was it not France that deployed 115 divisions – 91 of them in the North–Eastern theatre facing Germany – on 10 May 1940? Evidently for military might on these dimensions to be simply swept away by the Wehrmacht was bemusing, bewildering, befuddling. Contemporaries, along with those who came later, wanted to know how it could possibly have happened. And so began the inquests, the inquiries, the investigations, from the 1940s to the present time.[3] This essay will seek to identify what has been learned; more specifically, it will seek to give focus to the light that has been shed by modern scholarship on that twilight war and blitzkrieg as the events themselves now slip murkily into the twilight of modern memory.

In 1974, in the *Journal of Modern History*, the Canadian historian John Cairns critically reviewed the literature on the fall of France and concluded that 'the phantom of that defeat eludes us yet. The only certainty is that the problem will continue to have some interest and that a mass of studies of various aspects of the affair will one day come into being'.[4] The succeeding decade-and-a-half more than bore out the prediction. During the 1970s and 1980s books and articles on France's approach to war have continued to make a steady appearance. Nor has the flow of memoirs and the publication of diaries abated (even if it is no longer the torrent of the 1950s).[5] Here, then, all that can be attempted is a mapping of the principal contours of the writings since the mid-1970s, to draw attention to those features on the historiographical landscape that have become most salient in the last 15 years.

Cairns voiced a good deal of disappointment with what had been done down to 1974. He was discouraged not just by the analyses of the fall of France undertaken by French authors but also by the inadequacies of the treatments offered by the British and Americans. In the case of the former, he complained that few professional historians in France had 'seriously taken up the overall challenge of the episode'. There was much justification in the charge: French academics had, Cairns continued, 'to an unusual degree surrendered contemporary history to journalists and politicians'. He opined that the relative neglect by French scholars of the 1940 problem had to be explained, in part, by the uneasy consciences still liable to be stirred in the early 1970s by any evocation of the defeat and the ambiguities of collaboration and resistance that followed. In part, however, Cairns felt that the comparative inattention to the fall of France down to the early 1970s resulted from the politics of French academe itself – and above all from the ascendancy in the 1950s and 1960s of the social history of the *Annales* school over university historians and their research agendas.[6]

Cairns was also critical of the Anglo-Americans who, during the 1960s, addressed the problem of the collapse of France. The books of John Williams, Alistair Horne, William Shirer and Guy Chapman (all published in 1968–69) were extensively reviewed.[7] All were judged wanting on three general counts. These were, 'failure to read the evidence at hand; (2) failure to sort out seriously the political, social, economic and military parts of the problem and to relate them to each other; and (3) failure to think outside the stereotypes and even caricatures of the time itself'. Quite properly, these criticisms were tempered by mention of the fact that none of these writers had access to the unpublished British official documents (Britain's 50-year rule on government archives being liberalised to a 30-year rule only in 1968), or to the corresponding French records (for which a 50-year closure on papers down to the end of the Second World War was lifted in theory by legislation passed in 1969, but implemented in fact only after May 1975).[8]

Despite the many shortcomings that he identified in the historiography that he surveyed, Cairns nevertheless expressed guarded optimism about the future of serious study of the fall of France. The 'inaccessibility of materials', he shrewdly suggested, was probably 'less of a problem than the burden of the past itself'. He voiced a cautious confidence that both these obstacles would be flattened down by the further passage of time.[9]

So, indeed, have things transpired. At a distance of fifty years it does seem possible to say that even for the French, the events of 1939–40 (and, perhaps, the more conscience-troubling experiences of Vichy and the Resistance) have at last become history, rather than burning issues of present political concern. Time has brought dispassionate appraisals on even the controversies which were once most bitter. One example would be the insistence of a director of the French air force historical service for putting it on the published record in 1983 that the British had been completely correct to husband their remaining fighter aircraft in the UK by mid-June 1940 and justified in rejecting entreaties to expend even more Hurricanes and Spitfires than had already been lost in the forlorn fight on the continent.[10]

It has been refreshing, then, to note how the debates that formerly were most impassioned have lost their emotional edge. Equally encouraging has been the correctness of Cairns's prediction that the French sources would become available. The 'signs of greater flexibility regarding access', that were noticeable by 1973, turned out to be the first breaths of a liberal wind that blew through the hitherto stuffy corridors of the record repositories.[11] This new openness was more than welcome. It heralded a conversion to an altogether more relaxed and hospitable attitude towards contemporary diplomatic, political and military historians on the part of the archival custodians and *conservateurs*. In the bracing new climate, French and foreign scholars alike suddenly found help rather than hindrance when they sought out the documentary milestones marking what Cairns, at another time, hauntingly referred to as 'the road back to France, 1940'.[12] Moreover, going hand in hand with liberalised access, appointments were made to directorships of the official French military historical services of officers with well-founded reputations as academic scholars and authors in their own right.[13] From the mid-1970s onwards these in-house research teams increasingly came together with university historians, centres such as the Institut d'Histoire du Temps Présent, and historical commissions (such as the Comité d'Histoire de la Deuxième Guerre Mondiale and the Commission Française d'Histoire Militaire), to co-operate in exploring the great issues of France's recent past.[14]

As far as the study of the 1940 problem is concerned, the 'new' historiography appears to have uncovered four particularly marked features. The first of these is the characteristics of 1940 as an *Allied* defeat rather than as something singularly *French*. The second is a new emphasis on continuities between the Franco-British experiences in the phoney war of 1939–40 and the crisis of the following summer. The third is a recognition that – notwithstanding the military defeat on the continent in 1940 – Franco-British organisation for war displayed an impressive degree of foresight and coherence. Fourthly, there has been a still-unresolved swing back and forth, in regard to the fall of France as a narrower military experience, between interpretations focused on the Allied order-of-battle's intrinsic or 'structural' makeup and those that seek to explain the collapse in terms of the under-performance of Allied generalship.

Taking the first of these features in recent writing, it has become virtually the modern historiographical orthodoxy to argue that the downfall of France can only be satisfyingly explained in the context of the destruction of an entire west European alliance. This case was advanced with verve by the American–Israeli historian Jeffery Gunsburg, writing in the late 1970s.[15] Cairns, however (demonstrating the kind of insight that has made him, since the 1950s, one of the most sensitive and perceptive commentators on recent French history), had already cautioned in his 1974 survey that it was 'unwise to write of this war' without taking advantage of the vast array of available British primary sources, since it 'was very much a Franco-British war on the one side'.[16] The fall of France, continued Cairns, 'was, after all, only the collapse of the most exposed member of the wealthy Atlantic powers, not one of which had provided adequately for its defense after 1918'.[17] And he added (explicitly criticising Chapman's *Why France Collapsed*), this was a point that Chapman discerned but did not always remember as he shaped his book:

> Thus [noted Cairns] the first words in his preface: 'The following pages are concerned with the defeat of the French Army in 1940. They are not concerned with the armies of the Netherlands, Belgium or the British Commonwealth. Those of course appear, but only in relation to the French forces.' This seems very much like acknowledging, on the one hand, the integral nature of the 'allied defeat', while saying, on the other, that it will not be treated. As an approach to the study of the opening phase of a world war it is certainly open to question.[18]

Gunsburg took up the gauntlet that, at least figuratively, had been thrown down by Cairns's strictures before scholars coming after the early 1970s to the problem of the débâcle.

Profiting from access to Belgian and Dutch unpublished sources, as well as British and French, Gunsburg sharply revised older portrayals of France as a tired, lacklustre and ineffectual coalition leader. In a bold, and no doubt sometimes exaggerated, inversion of what had become a historical commonplace, he took the argument that France had disappointed a retinue of faithful followers and stood it on its head. Gunsburg contended, instead, that it was the French political and military chiefs – men such as Edouard Daladier, minister for national defence and war from June 1936 to May 1940, whilst also prime minister from April 1938 till March 1940, and General Maurice Gamelin, head of the French general staff from 1935 to 19 May 1940 – who conscientiously and carefully addressed the problems of defending western Europe. These leaders, affirmed Gunsburg, worked hard and achieved a great deal, especially in refurbishing the French land forces with modern equipment, munitions, mechanised fighting vehicles and motor transport. 'There is', he wrote, 'much to admire in the way Gamelin built a smaller and industrially weaker France into a powerful military machine to oppose Germany'.[19] That this proved insufficient to contain the Germans was in large measure, he argued, because the other western European powers were too reluctant to assist France in preparing a concerted defence and too reticent about making a sufficient commitment of their own money, manpower and material to achieve a common security.[20]

Gunsburg demanded – as did Robert Young in regard to France's broader external policy-making in the 1930s – that historians look anew at the Third Republic's final years. The accomplishment of these writers and others of their stamp has been substantial. They have given credibility to the view that in much of what was attempted by the last governments of the *Troisième* there was competence and conviction, where earlier interpretations had emphasised only irresolution, incoherence and inefficiency – if not corruption, scandal and farce. As a result the portrait of France as the 'sick man of Europe' of the 1930s has been adjusted, changed to one of France as a major power wrestling with age-old dilemmas brought on by relative decline.[21] In the retouched picture it can now be seen that French ministers, and particularly Daladier at the ministry for national defence and war after June 1936, strove determinedly to put France in a position where Hitler would not reckon war to be a game worth the candle. 'The urgency with which an often maligned Daladier expanded the armed forces, developed new weapons and prepared for a war that he . . . looked upon with loathing . . . has seldom been recognised', chided Vivian Rowe, writing 30 years ago.[22] Now, however, these achievements have gained acknowledgement.[23]

Admission by some scholars that France stood up in 1939 not just for herself but also for neighbours who gave little practical help and even less gratitude has come out of the renewed focus on the other western powers in 1940. The so-called minor Allies have been brought back to the centre, rather than the periphery, of explanations of what went wrong. As a consequence, the literature has assumed a greater balance, a greater fairness. Increasingly, research has been devoted to the problems in the later 1930s of the British, the Belgians and the Dutch. Attention has been paid to their efforts at rearmament, their intelligence operations towards Germany, their diplomatic postures, their degrees of political and economic mobilisation. Historians such as Jean Vanwelkenhuyzen, Jean Stengers and Jonathan Helmreich have advanced our understanding of Belgium's reasons for reluctance to join any alliance at all between 1937 and 1940. These writers have demonstrated how far Belgian desires to be independent of France resulted from domestic constraints on the governments in Brussels (socio-economic pressures as well as linguistic–cultural ones) as much as from Belgian foreign office illusions that their country might be left in peace provided it renounced any partnership with Paris.[24]

Likewise, the Netherlands and its policy has been illuminated by the spotlight of modern historical inquiry. No longer is attention confined to the Dutch experience of occupation from 1940–45 (so capably dissected by Dr Louis de Jong and his associates).[25] For, above and beyond that research, there has been attention to Holland's relations in 1939–40 with the Belgians, the British, the French and the Germans. This has revealed more about the immense value to the west of the Dutch connections to anti-Nazi Germans – notably the link between the Netherlands military attaché in Berlin, Major Sas, and the Abwehr deputy chief, Colonel Hans Oster, that gave early warning about German plans for a western offensive during the phoney war.[26] Beyond this even, the work of André Ausems has begun a positive revisionism regarding the Dutch endeavour to improve their army and strengthen their fixed defences before they were invaded.[27]

In respect of Franco-British relations, too, modern authors have shown themselves ready to renounce the older polemical style. In this regard it seems worthwhile to restate that shifts in attitude – not least among historians themselves – have been as crucial an agent for positive change as has the opening since 1975 of most of the archives. (Among those that have become accessible are the papers of the parliamentary commissions, the Quai d'Orsay, the ministries of finance, labour, commerce and industry, and colonies, as well as the documents of arms-manufacturing companies such as Renault and Panhard and the archives of individuals such as Daladier, Gamelin, Paul Reynaud, Léon Blum, Vincent Auriol, Pierre Cot and Raoul Dautry.) The outcome, by and large, has been a more widely-accepted appreciation of how greatly the French authorities in the late 1930s stretched their minds, their muscles and their money to confront Hitler and the dark, dimly-understood horrors that he represented. Furthermore, it has become increasingly appreciated that the exertions of the French did not occur in some eleventh-hour awakening in 1939–40 but were made from at least as far back as 1936. Here, then, is an additional instance where the historians of the last 15 years have successfully taken up another of Cairns's challenges – to show 'awareness of the importance of getting the 1940 events properly situated'.[28]

Admittedly it is the case that even in the late 1970s and 1980s books peddling a more old-fashioned view of pre-war France have still come off the presses. In France, for example, two volumes were authored by Jean-Baptiste Duroselle, one of that country's most eminent and highly-respected modern international historians and successor to Pierre Renouvin, the founder of the Sorbonne's Institut d'Histoire des Relations Internationales Contemporaines.[29] Duroselle's studies appeared under provocative – not to say evocative – titles: *La Décadence* (1979) and *L'Abîme* (1983). The works expounded an unforgiving critique of the makers of French foreign and defence policy in most of the period from 1932 to 1945. They censured a generation of statesmen, soldiers and civil servants for lacking a sense of international morality, a vision for the place of France in the wider fate of Europe, a determination to obtain, by hook or by crook, the means for a stalwart, reputable national policy (and, one instinctively feels, one on which Duroselle himself, in quite a personal sense, would be able to reflect with pride).[30]

Some of this interpretative recidivism has also found its way into modern English-language writings. One prominent example would be the often counter-factual but inventive and interesting *Change in the European Balance of Power*, by Williamson Murray (1984).[31] This book argued that the nations threatened by Hitler's aggressiveness had more interest – if only they had understood – in standing up to Germany in 1938 over the Sudetenland than in 1939 over Poland. Curiously, however, the volume devoted relatively little space to comparing the condition of France in 1938 to that a year later. It did not pay a great deal of attention to exploring the state of French politics, economic and social problems, financial health or armed readiness at the two moments in question. This was an odd oversight, because France, much more than Britain, would have had to stand in the front line to fight Germany in support of the Czechs – just as she had to in 1939–40 for the sake of the Poles. The result was an interpretation that inclined to lay blame rather than seek understanding; one, too, that does not convincingly square with the evidence available in the French archives, demonstrating the steadily more intensive French efforts towards military preparedness and the step by step rise in the effectiveness of French forces as each year went by, from 1935 to 1940.[32]

Yet it was precisely this total context of French political, economic and strategic conditions that made Daladier certain that he had to go – however shamefacedly – to Munich. The French prime minister's parallel responsibilities for national defence and war made him all too familiar with what had been achieved in rearmament at that juncture – and with how much still remained to be done. His journey to meet Hitler was made in the full realisation that he was not negotiating a peace with honour but was simply engaging in a sordid barter for time. All the information available to him in 1938 indicated that French material and moral deficiencies argued decisively for deferring hostilities with the Third Reich. Cheered to the echo at Le Bourget airport by the delirious crowds that greeted him as a peace-maker on his return from Germany, Daladier was impressed by nothing so much as France's psychological unpreparedness for war at that moment. His compatriots, he remarked to an aide, required educating as to the national humiliation to which France's weaknesses had obliged him to submit – and to the tough demands that he would from then on be making of them.[33]

If French leaders such as Daladier and Gamelin appeared ready to postpone the looming trial by arms, this was not least because of their sense of the size of the stakes. As the general put it, when visited at his Vincennes headquarters by Reynaud (then minister of finance), five weeks after the start of the war: 'just at the moment, as at the time of Verdun, what we are witnessing is the world gazing, petrified, on the salute of the gladiators. Once again, it is the duel between France and Germany that is going to decide the fate of the world'. Reynaud responded by invoking other historical images of the glory won against the odds by French arms. 'Never before', he said, had France's situation been this serious. In the days of the 'Patrie en danger' [an allusion to the cannonade of Valmy in 1792 that saved the infant Republic from the Prussian-backed counterrevolution] France was a 'mammoth' opposed to tiny little unorganized nations. Today, it's the 'struggle of the petits bourgeois against the gangsters' . . . And the French army is the world's final barrier against the predators out there. Will it be up to the task of resisting them?[34]

No doubt some scholars who seek to interpret exchanges such as this one, and relate it to the French collapse the following spring, will still insist that France took excessive counsel of her fears. They may still wish to argue that too little heed was paid to the information being gleaned by the 2e Bureau and the Service de Renseignements (the French intelligence agencies), about the difficulties confronting the Germans in the phoney war. Gamelin admitted in his memoirs that he was told how a 'large number of panzers had been destroyed or damaged in Poland', and that the German tank divisions in late 1939 were back behind the Rhine 'apparently undergoing reorganization and reinforcement'. The French awareness that the German army had its problems is confirmed in a dispatch from Belgium's military attaché in Paris, of 21 October, in which it was reported that the '2e Bureau has reliable intelligence telling it that the [German] armoured vehicles have suffered severely in Poland, some having been destroyed in combat but many requiring serious and time-consuming repairs.'[35]

Against this knowledge, however, French commanders had to set their own deficiencies in training and continuing bottlenecks in munitions manufacture. In November 1939 Gamelin instigated an emergency pro-gramme (the 'Five Month Plan') to scrape together seventeen new divisions (of which one was mechanized).[36] In December he ordered the upgrading of the two heavy tank brigades, formed with the formidable but scarce Chars B in September, to divisions.[37] These steps, however, could not improve the Allied armies overnight. Meanwhile, French generals showed the Wehrmacht the respect that it seemed due after its triumph in the east. As the French historian François Bédarida has noted in his study of the Franco-British Supreme War Council (SWC), 'Those responsible for national defence never ceased to be haunted by their knowledge of their inferiority in armaments, especially in aviation.'[38]

There is now a literature, therefore, which credits the governments and military strategists during what we now see as the twilight of the Troisième with purposefulness as well as patriotism, with coherent policies as well as rationally-framed objectives. This interpretation relates to the awareness that has grown up of the historical continuities between the phoney war and the events of 1940.[39]

Whether it be the development of the Allied mobilisation and military build-up that is investigated, or French civil–military relations, or the framing of strategic plans, it makes increasingly good sense to view September 1939 to June 1940 (and perhaps September 1938 to June 1940) as a whole. The problems as well as the progress evident in the alliance by 1940 appear, more than ever, to have been expressions, exacerbations, extensions of a series of knotty questions tabled on the Allied agenda in the preceding months or years. We have already tried to suggest how this was true in regard to inter-Allied affairs. Surely the flaws that opened into gaping chasms of misunderstanding and recrimination, splitting asunder the Allied camp in 1940, resulted from fissures that already ran deeply beneath Anglo-French, Anglo-Belgian and Franco-Belgian relationships in September 1939.[40]

The connections that are evident between trends seen in the phoney war and the events of 1940 themselves are not straightforward, however. This is, in part, because of the two-edged effect of the respite in 1939–40 on Allied morale and military readiness. In the main, historians to date have tended to treat it as axiomatic that Franco-British passivity in the phoney war caused an insidious and eventually-decisive undermining of military as well as civilian belligerence and fortitude. According to this view, the unexpected quiet on the western front for seven months after the fall of Poland induced a false sense of security among the Allies; allegedly, it sapped the staunchness of their fighting spirit. It was argued, in this interpretation, that the Franco-British commanders became deluded that their armies could safely entrench behind the Maginot Line and then simply wait till they overcame Hitler by 'bloodless victories' – squeezing the life out of the German economy by blockading her supplies of essential industrial materials, fuels and foodstuffs.[41]

As a satisfying 'structural' or non-operational explanation for the fall of France, this needs to be treated with extreme caution. Undoubtedly there was something that seemed unreal about the lull in the west at the end of 1939, as disputes between Hitler and his generals, along with deteriorating weather, forced repeated postponements of the projected German offensive.[42] The winter *was* an exceptionally harsh one and Allied commanders did not lightly use it as an excuse for abandoning military preparations and training. But it had the unavoidable effect of inclining the rank-and-file who were huddled along the frontiers to think rather less about war and rather more about their creature comforts. As an officer of Gamelin's staff recollected, the 'overriding preoccupation of our troops was to ensure their immediate security and shelter themselves from the inclement weather.'[43] These problems naturally affected the Germans too, though to a lesser degree because they were not so fearful of being attacked and were thus able to hold many divisions in purpose-built camps behind their lines rather than in rudimentary billets at the front.

For all the phoney-ness of the phoney war, however, the French high command never lost sight of the fact that the winter represented a temporary respite, not a permanent reprieve. This much is apparent from the recently-released evidence in the war diary of Gamelin's headquarters. This document, a detailed day-by-day record of Gamelin's meetings and conversations, demonstrates that nobody was more alive than France's leading soldier to the risks of lowered Allied vigilance. 'Once the real war begins over here', he warned his staff as early as 18 September 1939, 'it will come as a very rude awakening'.[44] During that month and the next he reiterated the importance of watchfulness as well as intensified training for the French and British armies. To oversee this he charged his most experienced subordinates – Generals Georges (responsible for the North-Eastern theatre, facing Germany), Billotte and Prételat (commanding that theatre's army groups), Dufieux (inspector-general of infantry) and Bineau (the *major-général*, or chief of staff, for the North-East). Nor did Gamelin leave everything to these officers and skulk away himself, like some troglodyte, in his Vincennes command post. Three times in the first two months of the war, on 27 September, 7 October and 15–16 October, he personally toured his own armies and the BEF along the frontier. He paid further visits to the front-line formations in March 1940.[45] In the end the campaign in France and Belgium made it plain that his bidding was too often not done well – and, in some instances, apparently not done at all. One of his personal staff officers reflected later that 'At no level of the echelon [of command] were General Gamelin's sage suggestions followed by action. The [subordinate] commanders, who were generally too old, lived on memories of the victory of 1918 and failed to show evidence of the activity that was desired.'[46] Part of the problem was that Gamelin had little concrete evidence on which to base a *limogeage* or clear-out of his generals until the blitzkrieg began – and when he resolved to undertake one in mid-May 1940 he found himself dismissed before he could effect the changes. He was left only to ponder ruefully what would have happened in 1914 if his own mentor, Joffre, had been sacked after the débâcle of the Battle of the Frontiers and not given time to redeploy, appoint new subordinates, and win the Battle of the Marne.[47]

During the phoney war Gamelin was up against the fact that (as he had himself remarked to a contemporary biographer) 'At certain levels of responsibility, it is no longer a matter of giving orders but of persuading'.[48] Nevertheless, it is now apparent that what Cairns called the 'thirty years of open season' for Gamelin hunters is closed. Henceforth 'history will have to try to consider Gamelin as fairly as it considers every commander on whom finally the sun did not shine'.[49] It would appear that a start is at last being made, one historian acknowledging recently that, after all the years of making Gamelin the convenient scapegoat, 'he does not appear to be the weak and characterless man of legend'.[50]

Time and again before May 1940, Gamelin emphasised in conferences with his senior commanders and staff that the Allies would be in perilous danger if they made the mistake of underestimating the Wehrmacht, buoyed up as it was by its success in Poland.[51] Admittedly, Gamelin did not question the prevailing belief in Paris and London that time's passage would help the Allies to increase their strength more than the Germans. Nevertheless, he remained much more sensitive than most Allied leaders to the delicate balance that needed preserving between the point at which prolonged inactivity assisted the Franco-British build-up and the point where it started to sap their will to fight. As regards this psychological dimension to the struggle, the general showed himself to be more perceptive than many inside the French and British governments who reacted to the war's stagnation as if it were a Godsend.

One with this attitude, at any rate during the closing months of 1939, was Reynaud, whose calculations in the autumn and winter appear not to have gone any deeper than 'bean counting'. Whilst his responsibilities, as finance minister, were for the state of the treasury, economic mobilisation and output, Reynaud assessed the costs and benefits of the phoney war in purely material and measurable terms. What was in his sights at this time was the number of men and the amount of munitions that the Allies were accumulating. 'Why risk seeing Hitler under the Arc de Triomphe', Reynaud asked Gamelin when he visited the latter's headquarters in mid-October 1939, 'especially if a few weeks or a few months of respite can lessen the imbalance between France's potential and that of Germany?' Gamelin rejoined that 'It would certainly be good to gain time to continue the material preparation of the country and the units [of the army]' but added, with a note of circumspection, that 'there is the home front to be held too, and that demands high and undivided morale'.[52] Nor was Reynaud alone among the civilians in having boundless confidence in the strength of the Allied strategic position. Fernand Gentin, the minister of commerce and industry, was at this time tenaciously resisting any further encroachment of armaments programmes on the labour and productive capacity still engaged in making civil export goods. 'We need to continue to manufacture for the export market', he insisted, 'in order to hang onto our customers . . . for when the war is over'.[53] French political leaders, in sum, were not so much exercised by what needed to be done to prevent a short-term military defeat as they were preoccupied with safeguarding France's position among the victorious Allies.

The manner in which the 1914–18 conflict had drained French national finances and caused the indebtedness and economic instability of the 1920s haunted government leaders in Paris in 1939–40. Hanging over them was a pervasive belief that, after the earlier war, France had been cheated out of the rewards that ought rightfully to have been hers in return for the disproportionately heavy sacrifices she had borne for the Allies. Hence, in the opening months of the Second World War, French ministers opposed an unrestricted conversion to a war economy; they were too concerned not to be held responsible for 'losing the peace' a second time to countenance anything so drastic. After flying over the Aisne and Somme to Abbeville for the first SWC meeting with Chamberlain, on 12 September 1939, Daladier expressed his shock at seeing the fields still full of unharvested crops and caused a bitter quarrel with Gamelin by pressing for a wholesale demobilisation of farm workers who had been called up at the outbreak of the war.[54] Daladier reflected the view of the politicians that France needed to conserve a sound economy which would enable her to survive the long haul without mortgaging her future standing as a trading nation and international power. As an objective this may, in retrospect, appear to have been extraordinarily naïve in view of the colossal costs of the 1939–45 war to all the belligerents and in relation to the huge changes in the world order that it brought about. But the French ministers were seeking to make the most sensible preparations they could in terms of the grim challenge they faced. The goal was, as Daladier defined it in a directive of February 1940:

> on the one hand to establish a balance between our military effort and our means to meet it . . . on the other, to apportion the effort of France and England judiciously . . . our entire policy must be directed at enabling us to hold on in the long term as much from the viewpoint of our financial resources as from that of our military effort [and] must be framed as though England and France have to win the war by themselves without the aid – even financial – of the United States. A balance . . . will be the best guarantee that we shall be able to keep up our effort until total victory.[55]

When, the next month, Gamelin found Daladier expressing the view that he 'no longer thought there'd be a battle [in 1940] and that men could be sent back to the interior for other duties', the general realised how complacent the politicians had grown about the possibility of a military crisis.[56]

It was Allied soldiers (not just Gamelin but also Lord Gort and Henry Pownall, the BEF commander and chief-of-staff), who kept clear heads about the problems on the French home front and the short-to-medium-term deficiencies of the French and British forces.[57] This in turn served to strengthen their cautious strategic instincts. It also hardened their preference for husbanding resources in the first two or three years of the war, for the military build-up in France.[58] Since he had been one of Joffre's key operations' staff in 1914–16, Gamelin had the temperament, training and experience of a 'westerner'.[59] To him France and Belgium in 1939–40 was – just as it had been 25 years earlier – the principal theatre of war. Not surprisingly, therefore, he strenuously opposed the pressures from British and French political and military quarters to divert some of the accumulating Allied military forces into opening secondary campaigns on the rimlands of Europe, far from the western front. The task of resistance required considerable energy, for there was no shortage of outlandish proposals that winter to widen the war and extend Allied commitments. General Maxime Weygand (Gamelin's predecessor, brought out of retirement in August 1939 to head French forces in Syria and Lebanon), envisioned launching bomber aircraft from Beirut to raid Soviet oilfields in the Caucasus, even though this would have shifted Russia from non-aggression to an active military partner of Hitler against the Allies. He also proposed landing a corps at Salonika in Greece, in a puzzling wish to repeat the indecisive Allied expedition there in 1915. Winston Churchill on the other hand (whom Neville Chamberlain brought back into government in September 1939 with charge of the Admiralty), canvassed the deployment of obsolete battleships into the Baltic to harass Germany's ore trade with Scandinavia. And many Allied politicians were quite serious when they assembled, and almost dispatched, an Anglo-French expedition to assist the Finns after the latter's attack by the Soviet Union in November 1939.[60]

Gamelin was to the fore in dampening enthusiasm for these assorted adventures that captured the imagination of Allied committees in the winter afternoons of 1939–40 when it seemed 'that eventually the war would die of dry rot' (as one Paris-based journalist put it).[61] But if these calls for a more aggressive and risky strategy alarmed Gamelin, so did the siren voices of the unrepentant appeasers. In France enough of these were active, and of sufficient political standing, to have Gamelin and Daladier looking over their shoulders – and to raise some doubts about French steadfastness among British observers. A number of French ministers and ex-ministers were suspected of supporting the idea of a negotiated settlement with Berlin after the defeat of Poland. Admittedly Daladier broadcast an uncompromising rebuff to the overtures that Hitler indeed made in October 1939.[62] But, in the very first month of the war, Gamelin found him privately afraid of being ousted by a cabal of politicians who had laboured on behalf of a *modus vivendi* with Hitler before the war. (Those named were three former prime ministers, Pierre Laval, Pierre-Etienne Flandin and Camille Chautemps, and Georges Bonnet, Daladier's foreign minister in 1938–39, who had been moved to the justice ministry in a cabinet reshuffle ten days after France went to war.)[63] From this point on, Gamelin increasingly doubted the robustness of Daladier's morale and his toughness as a *chef de guerre*.[64] It was an ominous precursor of the breakdown of confidence and consensus between the civilian and military leaderships that would plunge France to such a nadir of division and despair in May–June 1940.

So long as Daladier remained head of the government, the discontents that were seething beneath the surface could be contained. This ceased to be possible once Daladier's position as prime minister became untenable in the second half of March (when parliament, meeting behind closed doors in secret session, used the Finnish–Soviet armistice as a pretext to instigate a critique of Daladier's allegedly over-cautious conduct of the entire war). Heading the long line of inquisitors was the thrusting and ambitious firebrand, Reynaud. He demonstrated how the time-honoured ploy of seeking to disarm rivals by keeping them inside the government might disastrously backfire on a prime minister in a poorly-disciplined system such as the French, which had little attachment to the doctrine of collective cabinet responsibility. On 19 March the battle in parliament reached a climax as Daladier moved a motion of confidence in his administration in the Chamber. 239 deputies expressed their support, against just two openly hostile votes. But three hundred abstained. Daladier concluded that after the acerbic debates of the preceding days, those who were not explicitly for him had to be counted against him. The next day he visited the Elysée and tendered his government's resignation to President Albert Lebrun. Reynaud was immediately summoned and invited to form a ministry of his own. Presented for the Chamber's approbation on 21 March, the new government was invested by the narrowest possible majority of just one vote.[65]

Reynaud's margin of authority could not have been more wafer-thin. Yet, after accusing Daladier of pusillanimity and procrastination, the new prime minister perceived a need to cloak some substance round his self-styled image as a 'man of action'. It was not possible for him to begin by another attack on Daladier. For the latter's participation in the new government (where he stayed on as minister for national defence and war), had proven to be essential to the parliamentary arithmetic of the slender majority cobbled together on 21 March.[66] Instead, Reynaud seized on a strategy of indirect approach, turning his fire against the performance of 'the high command' (a euphemism or code which, everyone understood, really meant Gamelin). If he were to succeed in ousting Gamelin, Reynaud knew that he would achieve two objectives in one. For not only would he be able to install a soldier more attuned to his own impetuous personality and beholden to him for his appointment, he would also neutralise Daladier's influence in the direction of the war effort by eliminating his protégé and strategic *alter ego*. Reynaud's understanding was that (as one commentator has put it), 'Gamelin was, and remained, Daladier's "man"' and to try to differentiate between their military outlooks was as purposeless as 'trying to distinguish between Tweedledee and Tweedledum'.[67]

As a result of Reynaud's determination to force the issue with Gamelin, a civil–military relationship that had already become unsteady degenerated precipitately into an unrestrained brawl. Reynaud's intentions were first intimated on 3 April when he revealed that – without so much as notifying Daladier and Gamelin – he had recalled Weygand from Beirut to Paris, to give a special briefing to the war cabinet convened that evening at the Quai d'Orsay. Gamelin was 'surprised' and Daladier 'furious' at a decision which so provocatively bypassed their authority. The critical reaction of most military figures the next day showed they regarded Weygand as an unwelcome interloper. The 'meeting yesterday was heartbreaking', thought Gamelin; 'General Weygand's behaviour was maladroit. His entire briefing was a critique of our action and our foreign policy'. Even Darlan (whose conservative politics might have been expected to put him on Weygand's side) complained sarcastically at having 'been required to make a 180 kilometre round trip just to listen to Weygand deliver a lecture like they get at the Collège des Hautes Etudes de Défense Nationale'.[68]

On 8–9 April the French leaders were suddenly given a whole new cause over which to wage their private wars. For Hitler had ended the phoney war game of cat and mouse by launching Operation *Weserübung* – the invasion of Denmark and Norway to head off Allied plans to mine the northern waters and cut Germany's sea-borne Scandinavian ore supplies. The extension of the conflict gave Reynaud a new pretext for stepping up his pressure on Gamelin. For whereas he enthusiastically supported Allied contingency plans to intervene by major landings at Norwegian ports, the general preferred that the Allies restrict themselves to a smaller and mostly British expedition and naval riposte. The two Frenchmen's positions were not in practice as far apart as they were made to appear. Gamelin did not disagree that a military operation should be mounted to attempt to deny the Germans a clean sweep in Norway. What was at issue was not the principle of an intervention but its nature and especially its scale. Long and rancorous meetings occurred throughout 9 and 10 April as the French political, military and naval leaders discussed the timetable and the availability of forces to support the troop convoys that the British had already dispatched for Norway on the 8th.[69]

The concern uppermost in Gamelin's mind was to prevent an over-reaction to *Weserübung*. His wish was to limit what he feared would be the diversion of Allied military resources away from the main front to a secondary theatre – one he suspected might become a hopeless cause anyway. The tension between Gamelin's and Reynaud's views was given particular point since, during the first week of April 1940, French intelligence had received a series of warnings from reliable sources that the German attack in the west was imminent, with Holland and Belgium the most likely invasion route.[70] Gamelin suspected that *Weserübung* was, at least in part, a stratagem to distract the Allies. As one of his personal staff explained later, Gamelin felt duty-bound to demand that the intervention in Norway not cause any weakening of the Franco-British situation on the western front. The 'drama of our participation in the Scandinavian operations', wrote this officer, lay in the fact 'that at the moment when the support of our forces was sollicited, these forces were still hardly adequate to guarantee our own frontiers. . . . The dispatch of an expeditionary corps to so distant a locale entrained, *ipso facto*, a weakening of the principal theatre of operations.'[71] The deliberations among the French leaders over how far to assist the British in Norway were agitated and acrimonious. After more meetings on 10 April, Gamelin rejoined his staff at Vincennes late in the evening and exclaimed: 'We're swinging from one extreme to the other. After Daladier, who couldn't manage to make a decision at all, here we are with Reynaud who makes one every five minutes.'[72]

The Norwegian affair, without question, held a strategic significance in its own right for the later course of the war. But its importance for the Allies in immediate terms was in the way it plunged French civil–military relations to a new low. The Reynaud–Gamelin feud assumed its most naked guise in the context of the dispute as to appropriate responses to *Weserübung*. But the underlying issue concerned the relative powers of politicians and professional military chiefs over the conduct of the war effort. It was, reflected Gamelin's staff officer quoted previously, 'to be noted how far the war in Norway was detrimental to the harmony and understanding that ought to have existed among those in France responsible for the direction of the country'.[73] The quarrelling in the spring of 1940 was a prolongation – as well as a personalisation – of the unresolved questions about the extent of civilian competence and supremacy in military policy that had bedevilled the French state at least since the 1870s. Around this central concern, furthermore, there revolved the ongoing and immediate political trial of strength between Reynaud and Daladier (the latter being the real target of the former's guerrilla campaign against Gamelin).[74]

By 12 April the general had no doubt left what was in the offing. 'We're no longer waging war', he told his adjutant, Major Christian de l'Hermite, that day; 'we're seeing pure cinema. *Ce Reynaud, c'est un fantôche.*' Leaving a further meeting of the war cabinet held at the Quai d'Orsay that evening, Gamelin offered a terse summary of the situation as he perceived it, to Captain Lorenchet de Montjamont (his ordnance officer). The crisis, he thought, was fast coming to a head. 'I truly believe that president Daladier is going to resign', he said. 'He'd have done better for himself if he hadn't remained part of this [ministerial] combination', ventured the aide. 'On his own account', rejoined the general, 'that's right, but he has covered the high command'.[75] Reynaud, he realised, wished to lever him out.

Gamelin bridled, not surprisingly. He gathered that what was afoot was a calculated manoeuvre to sacrifice his career and reputation to the ego and ambition of an untried prime minister. The fact that he was being made a stalking horse in Reynaud's grander design to discredit and be done once-and-for-all with Daladier put in better perspective his disillusionment with the latter's conduct as a war leader in the closing months of 1939. This, he now appreciated, had been caused by the inevitable frictions of war, not by conflict over fundamentals. With the new prime minister at both their throats, Gamelin recalled the common cause he and Daladier had made on the army's behalf since 1933. In particular, he remembered the minister's key role in bringing about re-equipment and rearmament after June 1936.[76] And, since Reynaud appeared bent on menacing his professional survival, Gamelin found it expedient to see how Daladier and his bloc of Radical deputies in the Chamber might serve to protect his own position.

For Gamelin had long since learnt the crucial part that lay in mastering the art of Republican politics in order to advance – and afterwards defend – a career in the army. He had learnt in 1916, seeing his own mentor, Joffre, become a scapegoat for ministers disgruntled at the failure of the Allies to break the German lines on the western front. He had learnt in the Levant in 1925–26, watching the government in Paris sacrifice the high commissioner, General Sarrail, because the depleted local forces proved unable at the first attempt to quash the revolt of the Druzes. He had learnt by observing the favour shown him because of his own consensual style by politicians of such contrasting hues as the conservatives André Tardieu and Jean Fabry, the independent socialist Joseph Paul-Boncour, and Radicals such as Maurice Sarraut, his brother Albert, and Daladier himself. Gamelin was a 'political' general in this sense that he understood how it was the skills of the military manager, rather than the bravery of the boots-and-spurs commander, that had become essential in the complex world of twentieth-century military leadership. He was, perhaps, the first of a line of the most senior generals, admirals and air marshals who found in 1939–45 that, for men in uniform at the very top, the conduct of war now lay in a grey, blurred world where grand strategy overlapped with politics. This was noticed by the more astute observers even at the time. (The novelist Jules Romains, for example, after interviewing Gamelin at Vincennes in December 1939, wrote that 'those who tell you that Gamelin has made his successful career thanks to the politicians . . . forget that high-ranking military men always have to reckon with politicians. Recognizing that this is so is neither to pronounce for nor against the military worth of these officers.')[77] Some modern historians have begun taking a not-dissimilar view, Douglas Porch recently arguing that 'Gamelin had . . . great finesse. . . . Simply because he was a "political" general and declined to pound the table and shout as had his irascible predecessor, General Weygand, this did not mean that he lacked character.'[78]

As the crisis in Paris in April 1940 intensified, Gamelin resolved to fight for his professional life. He did so with no holds barred, displaying his considerable accomplishments as a past-master in the arts of French military politics. Unlike Reynaud, he had built himself a handsome bank of parliamentary patronage down the years. The moment had arrived, he realised, to draw deeply on its reserves; for all that it was Reynaud who was the professional politician, the new prime minister had chosen to play in a game for which his own skills were not nearly as finely-honed as those of the general. After the war cabinet in the evening of 12 April, Gamelin unveiled his strategy to his ordnance officer:

> As long as Daladier remains part of the ministry, I shall stay on. If he resigns without the Reynaud Cabinet falling, I shall resign too. I cannot tolerate for a moment longer being treated as I have been by Reynaud. This is not a question of personal pride, it's the general interest that's at stake. The commander-in-chief cannot have his prerogatives trampled on in this fashion.[79]

Furthermore, through an anonymous interlocutor's 'indiscretion', Gamelin had been told that Reynaud had for some time been toying with 'a Weygand–Georges replacement team'. Since it seemed that the climax of the struggle was approaching, Gamelin sensed that it was time to mobilise some heavy political firepower on his own account. Accordingly, late that evening, he had one of the section heads of his personal staff, Lieutenant-Colonel François Guillaut, telephone Maurice Sarraut, one of the general's oldest and most trusted friends and political allies, 'to bring him abreast of the situation'. Sarraut, among the most senior Radicals in the Senate, was also owner of the major provincial paper, La Dépêche de Toulouse. His power in south-western France was so great that it gave him an almost baronial domination over the parliamentarians elected in that region. He did not disappoint Gamelin's call for support, replying 'that he was going to throw himself into action immediately and consult his brother' Albert, who had been Daladier's minister of the interior till 20 March (and had twice been prime minister in his own right earlier in the 1930s).[80]

During the next day, 13 April, Gamelin took further measures to bluff or apply pressure to those whose political backing he needed for survival. Early in the morning he sent a message to tell Daladier of the decision he had reached to resign if Daladier himself quit the government. Also in the course of the day Guillaut (who had telephoned Maurice Sarraut) arranged to see Albert Sarraut to present Gamelin's viewpoint on his running battle with the prime minister. By now, as the general's war diary noted, the dissensions between himself and the head of the government had boiled over into the 'acute phase of the Daladier–Reynaud conflict'. Following a meeting of the French comité de guerre at the Elysée in the afternoon, Gamelin was visited by another long-standing political ally, Jean Fabry. Once the general's superior (when war minister, in 1935–36), Fabry was a leading figure in the Democratic Alliance (one of the two main French conservative parties). Although sitting in the Senate since late 1936, Fabry retained extensive influence throughout parliament for he had chaired the

Chamber's army commission between 1928 and 1935 and was widely regarded as an authority on defence issues. Though it was hardly a warning that Gamelin needed to be given by this stage, the purpose of Fabry's visit was to tip off his old friend, and 'he did not hide the fact from him that Reynaud looked on him with disfavour'.[81]

As April went on the Allied operations in Norway had some success at sea but were in deepening trouble ashore. In both cases German air superiority gave Hitler's forces an edge. From varied quarters in London and Paris it was proposed to cut Allied losses and withdraw. Reynaud, however, vehemently opposed all talk of evacuation. It would, he claimed, paint Franco-British political determination and military competence in a very bad light in the eyes of the neutrals. In reality, Reynaud was afraid of the personal consequences of a pull-out. On the French side, the intervention was largely undertaken at Reynaud's insistence. The commitment of French troops alongside the British was an expression of the new French government's supposedly more pugnacious approach to the war. On the campaign's outcome rested a good deal of Reynaud's prestige and, perhaps, the future of his ministry.[82] But, as far as Gamelin was concerned, Reynaud was guilty of putting his individual fortunes above French strategic interests. En route to another *comité de guerre* on 16 April, the general turned to his adjutant and exclaimed, in alarm as well as exasperation: 'This M. Reynaud is deranged. If he goes on, he'll lead France to her ruin . . . he must not be left where he is.'[83]

In the closing days of April and first days of May the situation of the Allied bridgeheads in Norway deteriorated so much that withdrawal became not an option but an urgent necessity. The evacuation was completed – except for the force at Narvik – by 3 May. But if the military disengagement was accomplished without disaster, the political after-effects in both London and Paris were considerable. In France both the Senate and the Chamber reconvened in secret session. Daladier as well as Reynaud was interpellated about the course of the campaign and about the reasons for the Allied reverses. Reynaud learnt – as had Daladier before him – that the opposition was having no truck in this war with any 1914-style *union sacrée*, or parliamentary truce. The inactivity of the phoney war had not eradicated the partisanship of French politics. It had merely put it under a temporary anaesthetic. Coming on the heels of the Finnish embarrassment, the failure to thwart the Germans over Norway was quite enough to re-infuse French politics with their accustomed bile. Moreover, not only were the French inveighing against one another, the Allies were now trading recriminations between themselves with an unhealthy zest.[84]

Under these circumstances, the SWC meetings that took place on 22–3 and 26–7 April 1940 were uncomfortable affairs. Chamberlain's continuation as prime minister was increasingly under pressure in London. Reynaud, likewise, appeared to be tottering on the brink. As a British diplomat in the Paris embassy noted in his diary on 1 May: 'P.R. will almost certainly fall .... But the rot may go further. Laval is active in the background. P.R. is in a nervous state and inclined to blame us and Gamelin and the two General Staffs for what has happened.'[85]

Over the first week of May French intelligence (partly exploiting its decrypts of intercepted German air force ENIGMA signals), again reported firm indications that Hitler's attack on the west was imminent. So far as Gamelin was concerned, the Norwegian expedition had succeeded only in diverting Allied forces – and distracting Allied leaders' attentions – from the much more critical German threat close to home. On 3 May he offered a forecast to his adjutant that, with hindsight, appears to have had a grim clairvoyance: 'France [he prophesied] is going to experience one of the hardest summers of her history.'[86]

The scene was thus set for the climactic final act of the tragicomedy between Reynaud and Gamelin, on the very eve of the blitzkrieg. The setting was the notorious meeting of the full cabinet which the French prime minister, with the theatrical touch of a political showman, called without warning for the morning of 9 May. Since this was a meeting of the government, rather than of the *comité de guerre*, neither Gamelin nor the other professional military chiefs was present. The proceedings have been vividly captured in the diary-style memoir of one eyewitness who was a little away from the eye of the storm, the minister of public works, Anatole de Monzie. Convened in an elegant *salon* at the Quai d'Orsay, the meeting opened in an atmosphere of unusual solemnity and tension. The arriving ministers found Reynaud sitting before a number of bulky dossiers spread out on the conference table. 'Gentlemen', he began, 'I have to talk to you about the state of the command.' He proceeded to launch into a detailed and minutely-documented history of his relations with Gamelin. It was, noted de Monzie in astonishment, an 'indictment rather than a chronicle'. Reynaud spoke for over an hour, the monologue punctuated only when he paused from time to time to extract another paper from the files of letters, directives and instructions that he had exchanged with the general over the previous seven weeks. Nobody else spoke; nobody moved. Presented so one-sidedly, without contradiction, the case made against Gamelin appeared devastating. 'This is an execution' whispered the minister of finance, Lucien Lamoureux, in de Monzie's ear. Finally, Reynaud shut his dossier and concluded. 'I do not agree', replied Daladier weakly. The room fell silent. Morally-speaking, thought de Monzie, at that moment the French army no longer had a leader. 'So long as the enemy doesn't benefit from ... this disavowal of the commander ...', he ventured to the minister for the merchant marine as they departed.[87]

It did not take Gamelin long to learn that at the meeting he had been the object of a 'violent attack' by the prime minister, but that Daladier had stood by him, having remarked that 'the matter appeared to be his concern, since he was still the minister for national defence'. Reynaud was reported to have rejoined that, feeling unable to collaborate with Gamelin any longer – and in view of the general's support from Daladier – he felt obliged to tender his resignation (a decision that was not made public at the time, however). Daladier had actually argued that Norway was primarily a British responsibility, a matter for the Admiralty in London. Gamelin, he had insisted, was not to be blamed for the Allied misadventures in Scandinavia.[88] More than a quarter of a century later, Daladier's view remained unchanged. As he reflected from that distance on his fidelity towards Gamelin during the spring crisis, he wrote that 'If I disapproved of the general being relieved of his command, in the meeting on the morning of 9 May 1940, it was because he had my confidence. And I thought that, with the German attack [in the West] imminent, General Gamelin had taken what military measures were necessary'.[89] Before dawn the next day, the German blitzkrieg began. Gamelin had warded off the stigma of being relieved of command as a result of losing the prime minister's confidence, only to suffer the humiliation of being dismissed ten days later as the price for disintegration of the Allied front.

Gamelin received the news of his replacement late in the evening of 19 May, in a short note delivered to Vincennes by an officer from Reynaud's *cabinet*. Accompanying the 'thanks of the government for the services that you have rendered the country in the course of a long and brilliant career' were copies of decrees naming Weygand commander-in-chief of all theatres of operations.[90] The succession, however, had an importance that went far beyond closing Gamelin's career. For, in seizing the moment to score this final and singularly vindictive triumph over Gamelin, Reynaud opened the way for his own political defeat over the armistice question at Bordeaux on 16 June and for the Republic's demise at Vichy on 10 July. In replacing Gamelin with Weygand, a general who kept faith in ultimate Allied victory was substituted by a man totally without a vision of the war's global context – and a grave-digger of the regime to boot. In the terse exchange that marked the handover of command at Vincennes on the morning of 20 May, Gamelin caught an unnerving glimpse of what was coming to France. 'All this politics', suddenly exclaimed Weygand, 'that's got to change. We've got to be done with all these politicians. There's not one of them worth any more than the others.'[91] Five days later, when ministers assembled for a *comité de guerre* on 25 May, Weygand said, to general consternation, that if his improvised defensive line along the Somme failed to hold the next phase of the German offensive, he could see no further way for France to continue in the war at all.[92]

Weygand was not, after all, the never-say-die spirit that Reynaud had believed. But Reynaud made this discovery when it was too late: the alternatives had been eliminated. Gamelin was disgraced; Georges had collapsed under the strain on 14 May; Billotte died on 22 May after his staff car had crashed; Giraud was surprised and taken prisoner by a German patrol; Huntziger, although briefly considered, was too discredited by his Second Army's defeat at Sedan. In reality, Weygand had been placed in an unassailable position. Reynaud's misjudgement in recalling him (and in appointing Pétain deputy prime minister on 18 May), ensured that the failure of the Allied armies was not just a military setback but the prelude to the overthrow of the French Republic, to the 'fall of France'.[93] As de Monzie noted sceptically on the day Pétain was brought into the government, a strategic crisis was being met by symbolic gestures to try to jolt France back onto her feet. 'The search after psychological shocks', mused the minister, 'occupies Paul Reynaud's mind whether he's at the finance ministry or the *présidence du conseil*. He mistakes himself for a psychiatrist.' France's tragedy was that in this case the Reynaud therapy killed off the patient.[94]

The foregoing discussion provides only one of the numerous instances where the fall of France cannot be understood without relating the continuities of the phoney war to the politico-military crisis of 1940 itself. Such an integrated analysis is required in order to respond to Cairns's point that 'it is hard to discuss sensibly the war of 1939–40 and the *French* conduct of that war, in particular, without evaluating the regime.'[95]

Nor can military history be presented in a vacuum when consideration is given to the third focal point in recent historiography: the Franco-British organisation for war in 1939–40. This, it is apparent, was characterised by far-sighted anticipation of what the Allies would require, logistically and institutionally, to win the Second World War. It was 'no good thinking this is going to end soon with the internal collapse of Germany', Britain's military attaché in Paris accurately predicted in September 1939; 'It's going to be a long, hard business and one must plan as well as one can on that basis'.[96] This planning was, as modern scholarship has demonstrated, remarkably sophisticated and systematic by 1939–40. It ranged from the establishment of permanent committees and reciprocal liaison missions to coordinate the Anglo-French military efforts, to the initiatives taken since as early as 1937 to rationalise the application of the economic resources of the two powers in accordance with each's economic requirements.[97]

In much of what was accomplished, the blueprint that was followed was the organisation for managing an industrialised war that the French and British had laboriously learned to fabricate twenty years earlier. The French and British had retained the lessons learnt by 1917–18 about the part that a genuinely joint conduct of the conflict could play in securing victory. In the approach to war with Hitler's Germany, therefore, they did not wait till 1939 before setting teams of officials to work to plan the pooling of the two nations' resources, or the fashioning of the administrative apparatus to balance each's financial and military burdens. As far as they could, the leaders of France and Britain prepared in 1939–40 to wage the war against Hitler in unison, meshing their two empires into one grand alliance. Notwithstanding the blow that the fall of France administered in the short term to these designs, the governments of Chamberlain and Daladier, their officials and military staffs, had correctly devined the shape of the Second World War.[98]

When one turns, finally, to the narrower military side to the events of 1940, the recent historiography is rather less sure of its interpretative direction. One trend has been the shift away from the detailed attention given in the past to the battles themselves – away from the exploits of commanders and combatants. In its stead a greater interest has arisen in the part ascribable in victory and defeat to the different doctrine and training of the German forces on the one side, the French, British and Belgians on the other.[99] There have been, also, some illuminating investigations of the planning processes, the military reasoning and the political influences that produced the opposing strategies of *Fall Gelb* and the Dyle-Breda manoeuvre.[100] Nor has concern with the operations themselves, with chronicling particular portions of the fighting, by any means entirely disappeared. The gallantry of individual formations, the performance of commanders (especially subordinate generals destined for greater heights, such as Alan Brooke, Alexander and Montgomery with the BEF), these have still found their historians in the 1980s – and perhaps always will.[101]

At least one old legend, that the Germans simply swept through France in 1940 because of their material superiority, has been conclusively interred. As far back as 1947, in the *Revue de Défense Nationale*, the notion that the Allies suffered from a quantitative inferiority in armoured vehicles was exposed as a myth by Charles de Cossé-Brissac. A seminal article in 1970 by an American, R.H.S. Stolfi, entitled 'Equipment for Victory in France in 1940', in the British journal *History*, went a stage further by persuasively attacking the shibboleth that the western powers were even qualitatively outclassed in the tank balance.[102] Modern scholarship has also demonstrated that by April, May and June 1940 the Franco-British war industries were manufacturing greater amounts of munitions each month than were the Germans. Thus the French air force, greatly outnumbered though it was by the Luftwaffe at the outset of the campaign, actually had more serviceable aircraft (though fewer trained aircrew) when the armistice was signed on 22 June than it had put into line on 10 May.[103] In sum, a consensus has emerged that the Allies were, on a material calculation alone, sufficiently equipped to have avoided defeat – if not yet sufficiently to have tried to win the war. As Gary Sheffield, writing in 1988, put it:

'Superior doctrine and tactics, not superior technology, decided the battle for France.'[104]

In conclusion, it may be worth attempting to signpost some of the paths that study of 1940 seems likely to travel in the future. In the first place, it appears that the drawing up of the more favourable *bilan* or ledger-sheet in respect of Franco-British provision with armaments will redirect attention to more contingent factors, to the strategic planning and the operational decisions of each side. In other words, it can be expected that the human rather than the material shortcomings of the Allies will receive further reappraisal. There will probably be more of a focus, too, on the reasons for the ineffectiveness of Allied methods of combat at the level of the division and below. There may be renewed emphasis on Franco-British deficiencies in air–ground support and in combined-arms tactics, together with a more systematic investigation of the long-term modes of thought and methods of instruction that produced such unimpressive Allied middle and junior leader cadres. In a central place in the historians' spotlight, then, will be the decisiveness of the initial deployment and missions of the Allied order-of-battle on 10 May; the poor training of so many Allied formations (especially French B-series reserve divisions); the calamitous consequences of having Allied generals who were aware of new military technologies but had not understood that these made possible a three or fourfold increase – a revolution – in the pace of warfare.[105]

Bound up with the question of changes that had transformed the speed at which battles could be fought were the crucial issues of command, control, communications and intelligence. These – C[3]I as they are termed in strategic studies – constitute the second area to which future historians of the 1940 campaign must give more attention than did those of the past. As it is, the research so far done by John Ferris into the shortcomings of the BEF's signals apparatus and security, together with that of Robert Doughty into the similar deficiencies of the French, indicates the promising avenues for inquiry that may be followed through this terrain. A deeper understanding of the nature and impact of the Allied C[3]I limitations bids fair to provide some major new insight into what brought about their undoing on the battlefield in 1940.[106] The Allied communications' systems were defective at virtually every level. 'Gamelin's command post', recalled an officer of his *cabinet*, 'had neither a wireless telegraph office nor even carrier pigeons'. It was completely dependent on telephone landlines. 'It was [therefore] impossible for it to receive information direct from the front, or intercept radio messages broadcast by the armies and air force formations. As a result, from the first hours of the battle, the *cabinet* of our most senior general found itself relegated to the fringe of an insufficiently centralized communications network.'[107] As another commentator added, this 'outmoded equipment contributes partially to explaining the slow reactions of Billotte, of Georges, of the staff, of Gamelin'.[108] The position lower down the chain of command proved to be every bit as flawed. 'At divisional level, taken as a whole, communications by wireless telegraph failed to give the results for which we were looking. The apparatus in the hands of our small units proved defective, the encoding complicated; the communication posts and their equipment had no protection against low-flying aircraft.' Some French tanks, it is true, were fitted with radio sets; but too many were not, or had either a transmitter or receiver but not both.[109] Throughout the Allied forces there was a disastrous mismatch between the types of communications systems commonly available and the fast, flexible type of war which the Germans made them fight.

These are matters which historians have only recently begun to tackle in earnest. Yet they have already yielded sufficiently significant findings to mark them out for additional work. Might the overwhelming of the Allied forces – as distinct from France's political collapse and withdrawal from the war – have remained a 'strange defeat' for so long if scholars in former times had taken half the pains with the unglamorous subject of military communications that they lavished on studying the generalship of Rommel and Guderian?

Thirdly, the politics of both the Franco-British alliance and the closing months of the Third Republic require further attention. In this respect there are encouraging signs in, for example, the renaissance in France of the scholarly political biography – so long a Cinderella of the French historical genre – and the production of specialist monographs on the French political parties.[110] Despite progress in these directions, however, the gaps that remain are important. There is still no biography of Chautemps, thrice prime minister in the 1930s and a key figure in resolving the French to explore armistice terms in 1940, nor of Pierre Cot and Guy La Chambre, the air ministers between 1936 and 1940; still no book on one of France's two main conservative parties, the Democratic Alliance.

Finally, it may be asked whether the fall of France merits inclusion as a 'decisive campaign' of the Second World War? An answer can be provided at several levels. Militarily, despite a good measure of recovery under the Fifth Republic, France has never been able fully to regain the status or strength that were swept away in 1940. In this sense, de Gaulle was only partially correct when he courageously prophesied that France had lost the battle but had not lost the war. Militarily, too, the 1940 campaign sounded the death knell of British as well as French hopes that the overthrow of Germany could be accomplished without resort to the giants waiting in the wings – the USA and the Soviet Union.[111] For Hitler, also, the fall of France had decisive repercussions, since it deluded him and most of his senior commanders into the disastrous overestimation of Wehrmacht power that encouraged them to turn against Russia the following summer. Hitler, it would appear, became ensnared in an illusion of his own invincibility after 1940, so surprised and delighted was he at the speed of the Allied collapse. But he, just like the French leaders gathered around Gamelin's lunch table in October 1939, had overestimated the significance of the 'Franco-German duel' in this war. No longer did the familiar contest between these two gladiatorial adversaries hold the world's destiny in its grip: the world outside their arena had changed in ways that neither had sufficiently noticed. 1940 was not so much the final act of a change in a *European* balance of power as it was the prelude to a bigger change in the whole world order.[112]

NOTES

*The author is indebted to the University of Southampton for special leave and to Yale University for electing him to a John M. Olin postdoctoral fellowship for 1988–89, which facilitated the work for this article. He is likewise grateful to Generals Delmas and Bassac along with their staff at the Service Historique de l'Armée de Terre (SHAT), and to General Robineau and his colleagues at the Service Historique de l'Armée de l'Air (SHAA), Vincennes, France. Thanks are owing also to Jean Vanwelkenhuyzen, Jean Stengers and Jacques Willequet for helping locate Belgian sources bearing on 1940, and to Mlle. F. Peemans, archivist at the Ministère des Affaires Etrangères et du Commerce Extérieure, Brussels.

1. Alexander Werth, *The Last Days of Paris: A Journalist's Diary* (London: Hamish Hamilton, 1940), p.40.
2. Marc Bloch, *L'Etrange Défaite: Témoignage écrit en 1940* (Paris: Edns. Franc-Tireur, 1946); *Strange Defeat: A Statement of Evidence Written in 1940* (English-language ed. trans. Gerald Hopkins, New York: W.W. Norton, 1968).
3. Pétain's Vichy regime conducted its own show trial of six former leaders of the Third Republic at the town of Riom between late 1940 and spring 1942. See Henri Michel, *Le Procès de Riom* (Paris: Albin Michel, 1979). After the war the Fourth Republic conducted an inquiry: see *Commission d'Enquête parlementaire sur les évènements survenus en France de 1933 à 1945* (Paris: Presses Universitaires de France, 1951–52, 2 vols. of report; 9 vols. of testimony and annexed documentation).
4. John C. Cairns, 'Some Recent Historians and the "Strange Defeat" of 1940', *Journal of Modern History* 46 (March 1974), 60–85 (quote from p.84).
5. For example, Col. Paul de Villelume, *Journal d'une Défaite. Août 1939 – juillet 1940* (Paris: Fayard, 1976); Sir John R. Colville, *The Fringes of Power: Downing Street Diaries, 1939–1955* (London: Hodder & Stoughton, 1985); Charles de Gaulle, *Lettres, Notes et Carnets. Tome II: 1919 – juin 1940* (Paris: Plon, 1980); Jacques Rueff, *De l'Aube au Crépuscule* (Paris: Plon, 1977); Jean Daridan, *Le Chemin de la Défaite, 1938–1940* (Paris: Plon, 1980); Charles Rist, *Une Saison Gâtée* (Paris: Fayard, 1984); Hervé Alphand, *L'Etonnement d'être: Journal, 1939–1973* (Paris: Fayard, 1977); Michel Debré, *Mémoires. Tome I: Trois Républiques pour une France* (Paris: Plon, 1985); Charles Ritchie, *The Siren Years: A Canadian Diplomat Abroad, 1937–1945* (Toronto: Macmillan of Canada, 1974 and Laurentian Library, 1977); Orville H. Bullitt, *For the President: Personal and Secret: Correspondence between Franklin D. Roosevelt and William C. Bullitt* [US ambassador to France, 1936–40] (London: André Deutsch, 1973); Miles Reid, *Last on the List* (London: Leo Cooper, 1974).
6. Cairns, 'Some Recent Historians', 67–71. French journalists, however, still remain encamped in force in the field of recent French history. See, for example, Claude Paillat,

Dossiers Secrets de la France Contemporaine (Paris: Laffont, 7 vols., 1979–86); Henri Amouroux, *La Grande Histoire des Français sous l'Occupation, 1939–1945* (Paris: Fayard, 6 vols., 1977–83); see Rémy (pseud. of Gilbert Renault-Roulier), *Chronique d'une Guerre Perdue* (Paris: France-Empire, 5 vols., 1979–82) [Rémy was an important wartime France Libre agent and Resistance leader].

7. The works were John Williams, *The Ides of May: The Defeat of France, May–June 1940* (London: Constable, 1968); Alistair A. Horne, *To Lose a Battle: France 1940* (London: Macmillan, 1969); Guy Chapman, *Why France Collapsed* (London: Collins, 1968); William L. Shirer, *The Collapse of the Third Republic: An Inquiry into the Fall of France in 1940* (New York: Simon & Schuster, 1969).

8. Cairns, 'Some Recent Historians', 63; for a comparison between British and French record-conservation and record-access policies and practices see Julia G.A. Sheppard, '"Vive la différence!": An Outsider's View of French Archives', *Archives: The Journal of the British Records Association* 14, No. 63 (Spring 1980).

9. Cairns, 'Some Recent Historians', 73.

10. Gen. Charles Christienne, 'La R.A.F. dans la bataille de France au travers des rapports Vuillemin de juillet 1940', in *Recueil d'articles et études (1981–1983)* (Vincennes: Service Historique de l'Armée de l'Air, 1987), pp.313–32. (The article began as a paper under the same title, delivered to the Franco-British historians' colloquium on 'Relations between France and Great Britain from 1935 to 1940', fifth meeting: 'La rupture franco-britannique, mai–juillet 1940', London, 14–16 Dec. 1983.) 'It is said', wrote Christienne,

> that Air Chief Marshal Barratt [commander of Britain's Advanced Air Striking Force in France in 1940], an outspoken defender of French standpoints moreover, observed one day 'that the R.A.F. could not win the war if the French infantry had lost it'. I have not been able to prove the veracity of the remark but I find myself compelled to admit its force . . . . Today, with the passage of time, problems take on a different light and one cannot but offer thanks that Fighter Command managed to convince the politicians not to make it a useless sacrifice in a hopeless cause (ibid., pp.328, 330).

11. Cairns, 'Some Recent Historians', 69 (n.33).

12. See idem, 'Along the Road back to France, 1940', *American Historical Review* 64 (April 1959), 583–603.

13. These included Gen. Jean Delmas, head of the SHAT, 1978–86; General Christienne (SHAA head, 1974–85) and his successor, Gen. Lucien Robineau, as well as the chiefs of the SHAT *section d'études* from the late 1970s to the mid-1980s, Cols. Michel Turlotte and Henry Dutailly – to all of whom I am grateful for co-operation and scholarly comradeship over many years.

14. See Henri Dubief, *Le Déclin de la Troisième, 1929–1938* and Jean-Pierre Azéma, *De Munich à la Libération, 1938–1944* (Paris: Seuil, 1979, 1980) now in English translation as volumes in the *Cambridge History of Modern France* (Cambridge: Cambridge University Press, 1984–86); René Rémond, *Histoire de France. Tome 6: Notre Siècle, 1918–1988* (Paris: Fayard, 1988); Jean Doise and Maurice Vaïsse, *Politique Etrangère de la France, 1871–1969: Diplomatie et Outil Militaire* (Paris: Imprimerie Nationale, 1987); *Pour Une Histoire Politique* sous la dir. de René Rémond (Paris: Seuil, 1988). The IHTP, directed by Professor François Bédarida, is located at 44 rue de l'amiral Mouchez, 75014 Paris, and produces the quarterly journal *Vingtième Siècle* (launched 1985). The CHDGM has been reorganised as the Institut d'Histoire des Conflits Contemporains, under Professor Guy Pédroncini of the Sorbonne. Its periodical, the *Revue d'Histoire de la 2e Guerre Mondiale* was founded in 1951 and renamed, in 1983, the *Revue d'Histoire de la 2e Guerre Mondiale et des Conflits Contemporains*.

15. Jeffery A. Gunsburg, *Divided and Conquered: The French High Command and the Defeat of the West, 1940* (Westport, CT: Greenwood Press, 1979).

16. Cairns, 'Some Recent Historians', 64, n. 18. Cairns's other relevant publication include 'International Politics and the Military Mind: The Case of the French Republic, 1911–1914', *Journal of Modern History* 25 (Sept. 1953), 272–85; 'Great Britain and

the Fall of France: A Study in Allied Disunity', *Journal of Modern History* 27 (Dec. 1955), 365–409; 'A Nation of Shopkeepers in Search of a Suitable France', *American Historical Review* 79 (1974), 710–43.

17. Cairns, 'Some Recent Historians', 75. See the remark by Richard D. Challener ('The Third Republic and the Generals: The Gravediggers Revisited', in Harry Coles [ed.], *Total War and Cold War. Problems in civilian control of the military* [Columbus, OH: Ohio State University Press, 1962] pp.91–107) that: 'In the memoirs of General Weygand . . . France emerges as the advance guard of a world coalition which had not as yet fully mobilized' (p.92). The same line was argued earlier in respect of Germany's initial conquest of Poland, by the head of France's air liaison mission in Warsaw in 1939, General Jules Armengaud, who tried to comfort the defeated Poles, saying: 'The battle of Poland was only the first battle of the war. . . . The Polish army was only the advance guard of the armies of the coalition' (*Batailles Politiques et Militaires sur L'Europe: Témoignages, 1932–1940* [Paris: Editions du Myrte, 1948] pp.133, 138).

18. Cairns, 'Some Recent Historians', 75–6.

19. Jeffery A. Gunsburg, 'General Maurice-Gustave Gamelin, 1872–1958', in Patrick Hutton (ed.), *Historical Dictionary of the Third Republic* (Westport, CT: Greenwood Press, 2 vols., 1986), I, pp.412–13.

20. Idem., *Divided and Conquered, passim.*

21. See Robert J. Young, *In Command of France: French Foreign Policy and Military Planing, 1933–1940* (Cambridge, MA: Harvard University Press, 1978). The influence of the 'revisionist' case for 1930s France is generally visible in such modern syntheses as Philip M.H. Bell, *The Origins of the Second World War in Europe* (London: Longman, 1986), pp.90–100, 135–8, 166–74, 208–12, 233–4; Paul M. Kennedy, *The Rise and Fall of the Great Powers: Economic Change and Military Conflict from 1500 to 2000* (London: Unwin Hyman, 1988), pp.310–15, 335–9. See also Robert J. Young, 'A.J.P. Taylor and the Problem with France' in Gordon Martel (ed.), *The Origins of the Second World War Reconsidered: The A.J.P. Taylor Debate after Twenty-five Years* (London: Allen & Unwin, 1986), pp.97–118.

22. Vivian Rowe, *The Great Wall of France: The Triumph of the Maginot Line* (London: Putnam, 1959), p.94.

23. See Susan Bindoff Butterworth, 'Daladier and the Munich Crisis: A Reappraisal', *Journal of Contemporary History* 9 (July 1974), 191–216; René Rémond, Janine Bourdin (eds.), *Edouard Daladier: chef de gouvernment* and *La France et les Français en 1938–39* (Paris: Fondation Nationale des Sciences Politiques, respectively 1977, 1979); J. Kim Munholland, 'The Daladier Government and the "Red Scare" of 1938–1940', in John F. Sweets (ed.), *Proceeding of the Tenth Annual Meeting of the Western Society for French History*, 14–16 Oct. 1982 (Lawrence, KA: The Regents' Press of the University of Kansas, 1984), pp.495–506; idem, 'Between Popular Front and Vichy: The Decree Laws of the Daladier ministry, 1938–40', unpublished paper read at the Fourteenth annual meeting of the Western Society for French History, Baltimore, MD, 19–22 Nov. 1986. A full reassessment of Daladier awaits the forthcoming book, *Edouard Daladier et la sécurité de la France*, by Elizabeth du Réau of the Université du Maine, Le Mans.

24. See Jean Vanwelkenhuyzen, *Neutralité armée: la politique militaire de la Belgique pendant la drôle de guerre* (Brussels: La Renaissance du Livre, 1979); idem, *Les Avertissements qui venaient de Berlin, 1939–1940* (Paris and Gembloux: Duculot, 1983); idem., 'L'Alerte du 10 janvier 1940. Les documents de Mechelen-sur-Meuse', *Revue d'Histoire de la 2e Guerre Mondiale* 3, 12 (Sept. 1953), 33–54; Jean Stengers, *Léopold III et le Gouvernement: aux origines de la Question Royale belge* (Paris and Gembloux: Duculot, 1980); Jonathan E. Helmreich, *Belgium and Europe: A Study in Small Power Diplomacy* (The Hague: Mouton, 1976). Cf. Daniel H. Thomas, *The Guarantee of Belgian Independence and Neutrality in European Diplomacy, 1830s–1930s* (Kingston, RI: D.H. Thomas Publishing, 1986), pp.553–98.

25. Louis de Jong, *Het Koninkrijk der Nederlanden in de tweede wereldoorlog* ('s-Gravenhage: Martinus Nijhoff for the Rijksinstituut voor Oorlogsdocumentatie, 1969–86, vols.1–11 c).

26. See Vanwelkenhuyzen, *Les Avertissements, passim.*

27. André Ausems, 'The Netherlands Military Intelligence Summaries 1939–40 and the Defeat in the Blitzkrieg of May 1940', *Military Affairs* 50, 4 (Oct. 1986), 190–99; idem., 'Ten Days in May: The Netherlands and Fall Gelb', unpublished Master's dissertation, San Diego State University, 1983.

28. Cairns, 'Some Recent Historians', 67.

29. This convened major international history colloquia, holds research seminars at the Université de Paris I (Panthéon–Sorbonne) and sponsors the important periodical, *Relations Internationales*, founded in 1972.

30. Jean-Baptiste Duroselle, *Politique Etrangère de la France, 1871–1969: La Décadence, 1932–1939* (Paris: Imprimerie Nationale, 1979); idem, *L'Abîme, 1939–1945* (Paris: Imprimerie Nationale, 1983).

31. Williamson Murray, *The Change in the European Balance of Power, 1938–1939: The Path to Ruin* (Princeton, NJ: Princeton University Press, 1984). See its critical appraisal by Wesley K. Wark, 'Williamson Murray's Wars: A Review Essay', *Intelligence and National Security* I, No.3 (Sept. 1986), 472–81.

32. Murray has entire chapters on German strategic problems (pp.3–49) and British (50–92), analysing political structures, economic constraints and rearmament. France, however, is relegated to a survey section on 'The Rest of Europe' and allotted barely 18 pages (93–110). Further, though still limited, attention to French perspectives occurs at pp.162–9, 190–3, 197–8, 211–2, 241–3, 262–3, 274–8, 348–51, 364–5. A weakness throughout is the tendency to evaluate French policy according to *British* sources from the 1930s. More satisfying are the essays in *La Puissance en Europe, 1938–1940*, sous la dir. de René Girault et Robert Frank (Paris: Publications de la Sorbonne, 1984).

33. See Anthony P. Adamthwaite, *France and the Coming of the Second World War* (London: Frank Cass, 1977), pp.224–5; also the special issue of the *Revue des Etudes Slaves* (1979), devoted to a fortieth anniversary assessment of 'La France et la crise de Munich'.

34. Cabinet Gamelin – Journal de Marche, 9 Oct. 1939, Fonds Gamelin 1K 224 Carton 9, SHAT. I am indebted to M. Pierre Uhrich, Lt. Col. Jacques Uhrich and the late M. Paul Gamelin for permission to use the Gamelin archives.

35. General Maurice Gamelin, *Servir* (Paris: Plon, 3 vols., 1946–7), III: *La guerre: Septembre 1939–19 Mai 1940*, p.115; L'Ambassade de Belgique en France. L'Attaché militaire et de l'Air, No.1 O.D./ 5836/ 210 c: le Colonel Maurice Delvoie au Lieutenant-Général . . . chef d'état-major général de l'armée, 2e section: 21 Oct. 1939 (Archives du Ministère des Affaires Etrangères et du Commerce Extérieure, Brussels: microfilmed copy of the dispatches of Belgian military attaché in France, 1937–39).

36. See Fonds Gamelin 1K 224, Carton 7, Dossier labelled 'Le Problème des Effectifs, 1939–40', sub-dossier III 'Le Plan de Cinq Mois', SHAT; Minart, II, pp.51–78; Gamelin, *Servir*, III, pp.228–44.

37. General Gaston Billotte, 'Etude sur l'emploi des chars', No.3748 S/3, 6 Dec. 1939 [sent to Gamelin and Georges], Archives Daladier 4 DA 7, Dossier 1, sub-dossier a, FNSP; see Gamelin, *Servir*, III, pp.275–81.

38. François Bédarida, *La Stratégie secrète de la drôle de guerre. Le Conseil Suprême interallié, septembre 1939–avril 1940* (Paris: Centre Nationale de la Recherche Scientifique, 1979), p.553.

39. See Brian Bond and Martin S. Alexander, 'Liddell Hart and De Gaulle: The Doctrines of Limited Liability and Mobile Defense', in Peter Paret (ed.), *Makers of Modern Strategy: From Machiavelli to the Nuclear Age* (Princeton, NJ: Princeton University Press, 1986), pp.598–623. Cf. Bradford A. Lee, 'Strategy, Arms and the Collapse of France, 1930–40', in R.T.B. Langhorne (ed.), *Diplomacy and Intelligence during the Second World War: Essays in Honour of F.H. Hinsley* (Cambridge: Cambridge University Press, 1985), pp.43–67.

40. For Anglo-French relations see Eleanor Gates, *End of the Affair: The Collapse of the Anglo-French Alliance, 1939–40* (London: Allen & Unwin, 1981); Nicholas Rostow, *Anglo-French Relations, 1934–36* (London: Macmillan, 1984); Philip M.H. Bell, *A Certain Eventuality: Britain and the Fall of France* (Farnborough: Saxon House, 1974); on Belgian diplomacy, Fernand Vanlangenhove, *L'élaboration de la politique étrangère de la Belgique entre les deux guerres mondiales* (Gembloux: Duculot, 1980).

41. See recent variations on this theme in Murray, pp.347–53, 361, 369.
42. See Harold C. Deutsch, *The Conspiracy against Hitler in the Twilight War* (Minneapolis, MN: University of Minnesota Press, 1968).
43. Col. Jacques Minart, *P.C. Vincennes: Secteur 4* (Paris: Berger-Levrault, 2 vols., 1945), I, p.48. See Brian J. Bond (ed.), *Chief of Staff: The Diaries of Lieutenant-General Sir Henry Pownall* (London: Leo Cooper, 1972; Hamden, CT: Archon Books, 1973, 2 vols.), I, pp.249, 279, 283. The *poilu*'s experience emerges in Robert Felsenhardt, *1939–40 avec le 18e corps d'armée* (Paris: Editions La Tête de Feuilles, 1973); Georges Sadoul, *Journal de Guerre, 2 septembre 1939–20 juillet 1940* (Paris: Les Editeurs français réunis, 1977); Jean-Paul Sartre, *Carnets de la drôle de guerre: novembre 1939–mars 1940* (Paris: Gallimard, 1983), English edn., *The War Diaries of Jean-Paul Sartre: November 1939–March 1940* (London: Verso, 1984), trans. Quintin Hoare.
44. Gamelin – Journal, 18 Sept. 1939, 1 K 224/9, SHAT.
45. The formations visited and subordinate commanders briefed are listed in ibid., 27 Sept., 7 Oct., 15–16 Oct. 1939. The later missions were to the French 7th, 1st and 9th armies and the BEF (8–9 March 1940), and to the French 2nd and 3rd armies (22 March 1940). See Colonel Roderick Macleod, Denis Kelly (eds.), *The Ironside Diaries, 1937–1940* (London: Constable, 1962), pp.231–3; Gamelin, *Servir*, III, pp.116–7, 292.
46. Minart, I, p.77.
47. Gamelin, *Servir*, I: *Les Armée Françaises de 1940*, pp.15–16; III, pp.405, 414–9, 427–33; Minart, II, pp.176–7, 189–92.
48. Quoted in Maurice Percheron, *Gamelin* (Paris: Editions Documentales Françaises, 1939), p.27.
49. Cairns, 'Some Recent Historians', 81.
50. Douglas Porch, 'French Intelligence and the Fall of France, 1931–1940', *Intelligence and National Security*, 4, 1 (Jan. 1989), 28–58 (quote from p.45). See also Jeffery A. Gunsburg, 'Coupable ou non? Le rôle du général Gamelin dans la défaite de 1940', *Revue Historique des Armées*, 4 (1979), 145–63; Martin S. Alexander, 'Soldiers and Socialists: The French Officer Corps and Leftist Government, 1935–7', in Martin S. Alexander and Helen Graham (eds.), *The French and Spanish Popular Fronts: Comparative Perspectives* (Cambridge: Cambridge University Press, 1989), pp.62–78. A full appraisal of Gamelin will occur in Martin S. Alexander, *The Republic in Danger: Maurice Gamelin, The Defence of France and the Politics of French Rearmament, 1933–1940* (Cambridge: Cambridge University Press, forthcoming).
51. See Gamelin – Journal, 9, 10, 14, 21 Sept. 1939, 7 Oct. 1939; *Servir*, I, pp.294–6; III, pp.61–4, 88–91, 94–7, 101–5; Pierre Le Goyet, *Le Mystère Gamelin* (Paris: Presses de la Cité, 1976), pp.235–9.
52. Gamelin – Journal, 9 Oct. 1939.
53. Commission du Commerce et de l'Industrie: Chambre des Députés. Audience de M. F. Gentin, ministre, le 18 Octobre 1939: procès-verbal, pp.13–14 (Archives de l'Assemblée Nationale, Palais Bourbon, Paris).
54. Gamelin – Journal, 12 Sept., 18 Sept. 1939. Cf. Gamelin, *Servir*, I, pp.215–20; III, pp.65–8, 224–8; Minart, II, pp.41–9.
55. Présidence du Conseil: 'Directives de la politique économique française: Programmes de production et d'achat pour 1940', 24 Feb. 1940, pp.2–4, Archives Edouard Daladier, Fondation Nationale des Sciences Politiques, Paris: 3 DA 5, Dossier 2, sub-dossier c.
56. Gamelin – Journal, 11 March 1940; cf. *Servir*, III, p.125.
57. See Bond, *Chief of Staff*, I, p.292 (Pownall diary, 21 March 1940); Sir John R. Colville, *Man of Valour: The Life of Field-Marshal the Viscount Gort* (London: Collins, 1972), pp.170–80.
58. See Robert J. Young, 'La guerre de longue durée: some reflections on French strategy and diplomacy in the 1930s', in Adrian Preston (ed.), *General Staffs and Diplomacy before the Second World War*, (Totowa, NJ and London: Croom Helm, 1978), pp.41–64.
59. Le Goyet, pp.18–38; General Maurice Gamelin, *Manoeuvre et Victoire de la Marne* (Paris: Grasset, 1954); René-Gustave Nobécourt, 'Gamelin et la bataille de la Marne (septembre 1914)', *Bulletin de la Société d'Histoire de Rouen*, 10 Nov. 1973, 181–7; idem, 'Gamelin, 1914–1918' (unpublished typescript consulted through the generosity of M. Nobécourt).

60. Especially illuminating for French perspectives on these projects are, Charles O. Richardson, 'French Plans for Allied Attacks on the Caucasus Oil Fields, January–April 1940', *French Historical Studies* 8, No.1 (Spring 1973), 130–56; R.A.C. Parker, 'Britain, France and Scandinavia, 1939–40', *History* 61 (1976), 369–87; Jukka Nevakivi, *The Appeal that was Never Made: The Allies, Scandinavia and the Finnish Winter War, 1939–1940* (London: Hurst, 1976); Patrice Buffotot, 'Le projet de bombardement des pétroles soviétiques du Caucase en 1940', *Revue Historique des Armées* No.4 (1979); François Kersaudy, *Stratèges et Norvège, 1940: Les Jeux de la guerre et du hasard* (Paris: Hachette, 1977); Duroselle, *L'Abîme*, pp.87–94, 108–16; Villelume, pp.90–104, 114 ff., 262–327; Martin Gilbert, *Winston S. Churchill: Finest Hour, 1939–1941* (London: Heinemann, 1984); Ronald Wheatley, 'La guerre russo-finlandaise, les plans d'intervention alliés et les relations britanniques avec la Russie'; René Girault, 'Les relations franco-soviétiques après septembre 1939'; François Bédarida, 'Convergences et divergences stratégiques franco-britanniques'; Philippe Masson, 'La préparation de la campagne de Finlande', all in *Français et Britanniques dans la drôle de guerre: Actes du colloque franco-britannique tenu à Paris du 8 au 12 décembre 1975* (Paris: Centre National de la Recherche Scientifique, 1979), pp.245–61, 263–79, 359–77, 583–7.

61. A. J. Liebling (Paris correspondent for *The New Yorker*, 1939–40), 'Paris Postscript', *The New Yorker Book of War Pieces: London 1939 to Hiroshima 1945* (New York: Schocken, 1988 [reprint of 1947 original]), pp.39–53 (quote from p.49). See Gamelin – Journal, 15 Sept., 20 Sept., 22 Sept. 1939; Armengaud p.201; Bond, *Chief of Staff* I, pp.268–72, 293.

62. Bell, *Origins*, pp.269, 271–2.

63. Gamelin – Journal, 19 Sept. 1939, 3 Oct. 1939. Cf. Bullitt, p.373; Jean-Louis Crémieux-Brilhac, 'L'opinion publique française, l'Angleterre et la guerre (septembre 1939–juin 1940)'; Philip M.H. Bell, 'L'évolution de l'opinion publique anglaise à propos de la guerre et de l'alliance avec la France (septembre 1939 – mai 1940)'; Guy Rossi-Landi, 'Le pacifisme en France (1939–1940)'; Philippe Masson, 'Moral et propagande', all in *Français et Britanniques dans la drôle de guerre*, pp.1–79, 123–51, 163–71; Guy Rossi-Landi, *La Drôle de Guerre: la vie politique en France, 2 septembre 1939–10 mai 1940* (Paris: Pedone, 1971).

64. See Gamelin – Journal, 14 Sept. 1939, 18 Oct. 1939, 11 March 1940.

65. See John Harvey (ed.), *The Diplomatic Diaries of Oliver Harvey, 1937–1940* (New York: St. Martin's Press, 1971), pp.339–40; Paillat, *Dossiers Secrets: La Guerre Immobile*, pp.411–43.

66. See Anatole de Monzie, *Ci-devant* (Paris: Flammarion, 1941), pp.173, 176–7, 182–3, 188–9, 190–92, 194–5, 198, 200–201, 203–7; Gamelin, *Servir* III, pp.187–205, 287–90.

67. Challener, p.96; cf. Harvey, pp.341–2; Minart, I, pp.167–89.

68. Gamelin – Journal, 3–4 April 1940; *Servir*, III, pp.292–311. On the CHEDN, established as an inter-service college for senior officers and civil servants by Daladier in 1936, see Eugenia C. Kiesling, 'A Staff College for the Nation-in-Arms: The Collège des Hautes Etudes de Défense Nationale, 1936–1939' (unpublished Ph.D. dissertation, Stanford University, 1988).

69. Gamelin – Journal, 8, 9, 10 April 1940; *Servir*, III, pp.312–18; Minart, I, pp.189–99; Le Goyet, pp.257–8; Harvey, pp.346–8.

70. Gamelin, *Servir*, III, pp.312–14; Gamelin – Journal, 31 March 1940; Paul Paillole, *Notre Espion chez Hitler* (Paris: Laffont, 1985), pp.173–81; Minart, I, pp.139–49; Porch, 48–9.

71. Minart, I, p.225. Cf. Armengaud, p.205.

72. Gamelin – Journal, 10 April 1940; see Monzie, p.209; Gamelin, *Servir*, III, pp.315–30; Le Goyet, pp.271–4, 292–7; Bédarida, *Stratégie Secrète, passim.*

73. Minart, I, p.229.

74. See Harvey, pp.348–9; Pertinax (pseud. of André Géraud), *Les Fossoyeurs: Défaite militaire de la France. Armistice. Contre-révolution* (New York: Editions de la Maison Française, 1943: 2 vols.), I, pp.192–233.

75. Gamelin – Journal, 12 April 1940.

76. See Philip C.F. Bankwitz, *Maxime Weygand and Civil–Military Relations in Modern*

France (Cambridge, MA: Harvard University Press, 1967), pp.95–105, 165–7.

77. Jules Romains, *Sept Mystères du Destin de L'Europe* (New York: Editions de la Maison Française, 1940), pp.99–100. Cf. A. J. Liebling, *The Road back to Paris* (New York: Paragon House, 1988), pp.25–33.
78. Porch, 52.
79. Gamelin – Journal, 12 April 1940; *Servir*, III, pp.336–8.
80. Ibid.; on the origins of Gamelin's political friendships and alliances see *Servir*, II (*Le Prologue du Drame, 1930–Août 1939*), pp.xxvii–xxx.
81. Gamelin – Journal, 13 April 1940; *Servir*, II, pp.3–4; III, pp.338–52; Paul Baudouin, *Neuf Mois au gouvernement, avril–décembre 1940* (Paris: La Table Ronde, 1948), pp.22–34; translated as *The Private Diaries of Paul Baudouin, March 1940–January 1941* (London, 1948).
82. Harvey, pp.349–50.
83. Gamelin – Journal, 16 April 1940; *Servir*, III, pp.352–5. Cf. Minart, I, pp.191–210; Pertinax, I, pp.212–7, 229–38; Le Goyet, pp.258–9.
84. See de Monzie, p.216; Bond, *Chief of Staff*, I, pp.296–303; Colville, *Fringes*, pp.96–104.
85. Harvey, p.354; Colville, *Fringes*, pp.105–15; Bond, *Chief of Staff*, I, pp.304–5; Gamelin, *Servir*, III, pp.356–79.
86. Gamelin – Journal, 3 May; cf. ibid., 30 April 1940: 'Au cours de la nuit, plusieurs coups de téléphone annoncent de très bonne source l'attaque allemande à l'ouest pour le 1er ou le 2 mai'. See *Servir*, III, pp.380–82; Paillole, p.183 (which describes Allied consternation when ULTRA fell silent on 2 May, the Germans having abruptly changed their ENIGMA settings; Bletchley broke back into the new codes on 22 May but by then the débâcle in France was well under way). See also General Louis Rivet [chief of French secret intelligence, 1934–40] 'Le camp allemand dans la fièvre des alertes (1939–1940)', *Revue de Défense Nationale RDN*, 5e année, IX (juillet 1949), 33–48; idem, 'Etions-nous renseignés en mai 1940?', Part I, *RDN* 6e année, X (juin 1950), 636–48, Part II, *RDN*, 6e année, XI (juillet 1950), 24–39; Gerd Brausch, 'Sedan 1940: Deuxième Bureau und strategische Überraschung', *Militärgeschictliche Mitteilungen* 2 (1967), 15–92; General Maurice-Henri Gauché, *Le Deuxième Bureau au Travail* (Paris: Amiot-Dumont, 1953), pp.206–13.
87. De Monzie, pp.218–19; Harvey, p.355.
88. Gamelin – Journal, 9 May 1940; cf. *Servir*, III, pp.382–3; Pertinax, I, pp.238–9; Paul Reynaud, *La France a sauvé L'Europe* (Paris: Flammarion, 1947, 2 vols.), II, pp.22–43, 51–4; Le Goyet, pp.300–301.
89. Daladier, letter dated 20 May 1966 in response to Colonel Adolphe Goutard's article, 'La surprise du 10 mai', *Revue de Paris*, 10 May 1966, in Archives Daladier, 4 DA 7 Dossier 1, sub-dossier a, FNSP.
90. Gamelin, *Servir*, I, pp.6–8; III, pp.427–34; Gamelin – Journal, 19 May 1940; Minart, II, pp.183–98; Pertinax, I, pp.95–6. On the question of the extent of Weygand's powers and whether they extended (as Gamelin's had not) to command of all French naval and air forces as well as the armies, see Colonel Robert Villatte, 'Le changement de commandement de mai 1940', *Revue d'Histoire de la 2e Guerre Mondiale* II, 5 (Jan. 1952), 27–36; André Reussner, 'La réorganisation du Haut Commandement au mois de mai 1940', ibid. III, 10–11 (June 1953), 49–59.
91. Gamelin, *Servir*, III, p.436. See Bankwitz, *Weygand and Civil–Military Relations*, pp.290–96, 328–37; idem, 'Maxime Weygand and the Fall of France: A Study in Civil–Military Relations', *Journal of Modern History* 31 (Sept. 1959), 225–42.
92. Bankwitz, *Weygand and Civil–Military Relations*, pp.296–305; Pertinax, I, pp.258–70.
93. Minart, II, pp.196–7; Bankwitz, *Weygand and Civil–Military Relations*, pp.299–300, 312.
94. De Monzie, p.231; cf. Harvey, pp.360–68, 372–3; Colville, *Fringes*, pp.132–44, 151–68; Henri Michel, *La Défaite de la France. Septembre 1939–Juin 1940* (Paris: Presses Universitaires de France, 1980), pp.96–101, 106–17.
95. Cairns, 'Some Recent Historians', 76.
96. Colonel William Fraser, letter to his wife, 17 Sept. 1939. I am indebted to Colonel Fraser's son, General Sir David Fraser, for permission to consult this correspondence.

97. See, for example, the arrangements made from 1938 onwards to replace French imports of high-grade coal from Germany with British supplies in the event of war: de Monzie, pp.67–8, 93, 124–5, 139, 178–9, 196–8, 200, 208. Also Robert Frankenstein, 'Le financement français de la guerre et les accords avec les Britanniques, 1939–40' and L.S. Pressnell, 'Les finances de guerre britanniques et la coopération économique franco-britannique en 1939 et 1940', in *Français et Britanniques*, pp.461–87, 489–510.

98. See Alphand, pp.25–39; Jean Monnet, *Mémoires* (Paris: Fayard, 1976), pp.13–36, 59–89, 137–78 (English edn., trans. Richard Mayne, *Memoirs* [London: Collins, 1978]); Lord [Arthur] Salter, *Memoirs of a Public Servant* (London: Faber & Faber, n.d.), pp.254–67; John McVickar Haight, *American Aid to France, 1938–1940* (New York: Athenaeum, 1970); idem, 'Jean Monnet and the American Arsenal after the Beginning of the War', in Evelyn M. Acomb, Marvin L. Brown (eds.), *French Society and Culture since the Old Regime* (New York: Holt, Rinehart & Winston, 1966), pp.269–83. A key part was played by Méric de Bellefon, commercial counsellor at the French embassy in London, in arranging the coal supplies mentioned above, as well as requisitioning and pooling of Franco-British merchant shipping. (See *Documents Diplomatiques Français, 1932–1939* [Paris: Imprimerie Nationale, 1963–85, two series], 2nd ser., XV, Docs. nos.19, 39, 284, 399, 517.) For embryonic coordination of arms procurement see the documentation in the files of the French military attaché in London: EMA/2 Grande-Bretagne, cartons 7N 2815–19 (Sept. 1938 to Feb. 1940), SHAT; in Fonds Gamelin 1K 224 carton 7, Dossiers labelled 'Correspondance avec les Britanniques' and 'Problème des effectifs, 1939–40', SHAT; and in Archives Daladier, 3 DA 2 Dossier 3, sub-dossier c; 3 DA 5 Dossier 2, sub-dossier c; 4 DA 23 Dossier 1, sub-dossier b, FNSP.

99. See Williamson Murray, 'The German response to victory in Poland: a case study in professionalism', *Armed Forces and Society* 7, No.2 (Winter 1981), 285–98; idem, *Change*, pp.338–40; Charles W. Sydnor, Jr., *Soldiers of Destruction. The SS Death's Head Division, 1933–1945* (Princeton, NJ: Princeton University Press, 1977), pp.37–119; Colonel Henry Dutailly, *Les Problèmes de L'Armée de Terre Française, 1935–1939* (Paris: Imprimerie Nationale, 1980), pp.175–204; Robert A. Doughty, *The Seeds of Disaster: The Development of French Army Doctrine, 1919–1939* (Hamden, CT: Archon Books, 1985); idem, 'De Gaulle's Concept of a Mobile, Professional Army: Genesis of French Defeat?', in Lloyd J. Matthews, Dale E. Brown (eds.), *The Parameters of War* (London and McLean, VA: Pergamon–Brasseys, 1987), pp.243–56; De Fabribeckers, *La Campagne de L'Armée belge en 1940* (Brussels: Rossel, 1973).

100. See especially, John J. Mearsheimer, *Conventional Deterrence* (Ithaca, NY and London: Cornell University Press, 1983), pp.67–133; Donald W. Alexander, 'Repercussions of the Breda Variant', *French Historical Studies* 8, No.3 (Spring 1974), 459–88.

101. Examples include Pierre Le Goyet and Jean Fussureau, *Calais: 1940* (Paris: Presses de la Cité, 1980); Brian Bond, *France and Belgium, 1939–1940* (London: Davis-Poynter 1975; to be reprinted by Pergamon–Brasseys, 1990); Michael Glover, *The Fight for the Channel Ports, Calais to Brest 1940: A Study in Confusion* (London: Leo Cooper, 1985); Roy Macnab, *For Honour Alone: The cadets of Saumur in the defence of the Cavalry School, France 1940* (London: Hale, 1988); Paul Huard, *Le Colonel de Gaulle et ses blindés: Laon, 15–20 mai 1940* (Paris: Plon, 1980); General Sir David Fraser, *Alanbrooke* (London: Collins, 1982); Nigel Nicolson, *Alex: The life of Field-Marshal Earl Alexander of Tunis* (London: Weidenfeld & Nicolson, 1973); Nigel Hamilton, *Monty: The Making of a General, 1887–1942* (London: Hamish Hamilton, 1981); also the forthcoming biography of Field-Marshal Lord Ironside being written by Professor Wesley Wark of the University of Toronto.

102. Lt. Col. Charles de Cossé-Brissac, 'Combien de chars français contre combien de chars allemands le 10 mai 1940?', *RDN* (Juillet 1947), 75–89; R.H.S. Stolfi, 'Equipment for Victory in France in 1940', *History* 55 (Feb. 1970), 1–20.

103. Jeffery A. Gunsburg, 'L'Armée de L'Air versus the Luftwaffe, 1940', *Defence Update International* 45 (1984), 44–53; Herrick E. Chapman, 'Reshaping French Industrial Politics: Workers, Employers, State Officials and the struggle for control in the aircraft industry, 1928–1950' (unpublished Ph.D. dissertation, University of California, Berkeley, 1983; microform edn., University Microfilms International, Ann Arbor, MI, 1984),

pp.345–63; Jean Truelle, 'La production aéronautique militaire française jusqu'en juin 1940', *Revue d'Histoire de la 2e Guerre Mondiale* 19e année, No.73 (Jan. 1969), 75–110; General Charles Christienne, 'L'industrie aéronautique française de septembre 1939 à juin 1940', in *Français et Britanniques*, pp.389–410.

104. Gary D. Sheffield, 'Blitzkrieg and Attrition: Land Operations Europe, 1914–45', in Colin McInnes and G.D. Sheffield (eds.), *Warfare in the Twentieth Century: Theory and Practice* (London: Unwin Hyman, 1988), pp.51–79 (quote from p.69).

105. Some of these issues will doubtless be addressed in the forthcoming book on the battles for the Meuse crossings, 10–15 May 1940, by Colonel Robert A. Doughty, head of the military history department at the US Military Academy, West Point.

106. John Ferris, 'The British Army, Signals and Security in the Desert Campaign, 1940–1942' (revised typescript of a paper delivered at the Third US Army War College Conference on Intelligence and Military Operations, May 1988), 10–22; Robert A. Doughty, 'The French Armed Forces, 1918–40', in Williamson Murray, Allan R. Millett (eds.), *Military Effectiveness* (London: Unwin Hyman, 1988, 3 vols.) II, pp.39–69; Anthony P. Adamthwaite, 'French Military Intelligence and the Coming of War, 1935–1939', in Christopher M. Andrew, Jeremy Noakes (eds.), *Intelligence and International Relations, 1900–1945* (Exeter: Exeter University Publications, 1987), pp.191–208; Robert J. Young, 'French military intelligence and Nazi Germany, 1938–1939', in Ernest R. May (ed.), *Knowing One's Enemies: Intelligence Assessment before the Two World Wars* (Princeton, NJ: Princeton University Press, 1984), pp.271–309; Jean Stengers, 'Enigma, the French, the Poles and the British, 1931–1940', in Christopher M. Andrew, David Dilks (eds.), *The Missing Dimension: Governments and Intelligence Communities in the Twentieth Century* (London and Basingstoke: Macmillan, 1984), pp.126–37; F.H. Hinsley (with E.E. Thomas, C.F.G. Ransom, R.C. Knight), *British Intelligence in the Second World War: Its Influence on Strategy and Operations* (London: HMSO, 1979–83, 3 vols.), I, pp.89–158.

107. Minart, II, p.103.

108. Pertinax, I, p.92.

109. Minart, II, p.79 (n. 3).

110. For example Fred Kupferman, *Laval* (Paris: Fayard, 1987); Serge Berstein, *Edouard Herriot ou la République en personne* (Paris: Fondation Nationale des Sciences Politiques, 1985); Marc Ferro, *Pétain* (Paris: Fayard, 1987); William D. Irvine, *French Conservatism in Crisis: The Republican Federation in the 1930s* (Baton Rouge, LA: Louisiana State University Press, 1979); Serge Berstein, *Histoire du Parti Radical* (Paris: Editions de la FNSP, 2 vols. 1980–82). See Thomas Ferenczi, 'Le retour du politique: La profession de foi d'une nouvelle génération d'historiens', *Le Monde* (18 Nov. 1988). A biography of Reynaud is currently being written by Dr Julian Jackson of University College, Swansea.

111. See Maurice Matloff, 'Allied Strategy in Europe, 1939–1945', in Paret, pp.677–702.

112. For the greater though still imperfect extent to which the changes and their consequences were grasped by Britain's leaders see David Reynolds, 'Churchill and the British "Decision" to Fight on in 1940: Right Policy, Wrong Reasons', in Langhorne, pp.147–67; cf. Colville, *Fringes*, pp.150–77; David Dilks, 'The Twilight War and the Fall of France: Chamberlain and Churchill in 1940', *Transactions of the Royal Historical Society*, 5th ser., 28 (1978), 61–86.

The Battle of the Atlantic

MARC MILNER

The Battle of the Atlantic was one of the decisive campaigns of the Second World War. Without secure use of the sea Anglo-American land and air campaigns could not have been mounted and sustained, and without pressure on the Germans from the west and sea-borne aid the Soviet Union's successes on the eastern front would not have been possible. Over the long haul everything depended, ultimately, on the Atlantic. But there the simplicity ends. The Atlantic campaign was the longest and most complex of the whole war. The popular perception of it as largely naval in character obscures its significance to the war in general and the factors which decided its outcome. This perception obscures as well the totally dissimilar nature of the 'battle' of the Atlantic from those fought on land or in the skies of Europe, or even the battle of Midway and other distinct naval engagements. Rather, this was a six-year struggle to ensure that the men and resources needed to achieve final victory through force of arms were assembled and sustained. It was a struggle the Allies could have lost, but to win it they had to overcome more than the Germans.

The Second World War was ultimately about the management and accumulation of resources, and this posed tremendous problems for both sides. The Germans, of course, had a continent to exploit and their spider's web of communications – road, rail, canal and coastal shipping – proved a difficult system to disrupt effectively, as Bomber Command discovered. In contrast, the tap-root of the Western Alliance, particularly after the fall of France, looks singularly vulnerable: merchant shipping. Virtually all the men, weapons and supplies for the West's campaigns against Germany had to be moved into place by sea. For the Allies this involved two related tasks; securing the sea lanes through naval and air operations, and ensuring that a sufficient volume of men and goods arrived the pursue to war effort. Achieving these two goals involved a very broad range of interested parties with forces at sea only a part – albeit an important part – of the equation.

Historians have tended to define securing of the sea lanes in terms of naval battles, a pattern of writing which was set early in the Admiralty's wartime 'Naval Staff Histories' and in the first volume of the American official history which appeared in 1947.[1] In these, and subsequent naval accounts, the ebb and flow of the Atlantic war is interpreted in terms of the naval war. Most of the writing on the Atlantic is about what warships did – and usually in relation to other warships.[2] Implied in this is the notion that naval forces and battles were the decisive elements of the war at sea: to suggest otherwise approaches heresy for a 'naval' historian. But one needs to be reminded of Sir Julian Corbett's injunction to foreswear battles and to remember that naval 'war is not made up of them'.[3] This is particularly true when assessing the 'decisiveness' of the war at sea from 1939 to 1945. The naval war was indeed hard, long and vital to the success of Allied arms on all fronts, and has been the stuff of many good histories. Yet German capacity for disrupting or destroying Allied shipping was not limitless. For most of the war the key to securing the sea lanes was sound organisation and good intelligence, which allowed shipping to be routed safely clear of enemy dispositions. Put in a nutshell, the principle means of *defending* shipping in the Second World War was avoidance of the enemy. This was done through a complex but highly efficient global naval intelligence and naval control of shipping (NCS) system initially centered at the Admiralty in London and by mid-1942 shared by the USN in Washington. The NCS and intelligence system developed by the British before the war had regional centres throughout the World, such as Cape Town, Ottawa, Hong Kong and Kingston Jamaica, responsible for passing along information on shipping movements in their areas, and a feed-back system from London with intelligence to permit the safe routing of local shipping based on a global plot. The NCS network also functioned as the link between operational forces, which provided the close escort or the distant cover for shipping movements, and the civilian agencies which regulated the movement of goods, scheduling of shipping and handling at ports. Matching available ships with available cargos, tackling port congestion, and capacities of railways proved, in the end, more difficult problems to solve than those resulting from enemy action.[4]

In assessing the influence of the Atlantic war on the war in general it is important therefore to distinguish between delays and complications caused by enemy action and those which resulted from administrative or organisational shortfalls. Many argued at the time, and some since, that the complex arrangements for protecting shipping through convoy systems and evasive routing wasted available tonnage by extending voyages and delays in harbour. There is some truth to this, although it cannot be proven that the lost carrying capacity was greater than that preserved from loss by enemy action. Moreover, close regulation of movements was crucial to the efficient management of ports. In the end, the object of the exercise in the Atlantic was safe and timely arrival of the ships and for most of the war the best way to do this was to avoid trouble. Unfortunately, our perception of this issue is usually backwards, fostered by a combination of Mahanist naval historians and the essential wartime myth that presented the sailor on watch as the first line of defence against the enemy's attack on trade. The whole affair becomes more comprehensible if one remembers that the close escort of a convoy was the *last* line of defence, and it fought if all else failed.

It was the Germans, of course, who determined that there would be a 'Battle of the Atlantic' and for the most part the ebb and flow of the naval war was set by their initiatives. The German navy was utterly unprepared for a war in the west in 1939, and was reduced to a strategy of tying down British naval forces while the Luftwaffe and Army tackled the major opponents. The daring stroke into Norway in April 1940 gave Germany a dramatic victory, but the success of the campaign was largely dependant upon German air superiority while the Kriegsmarine, which performed very well indeed, suffered serious losses. However, until the fall of France German naval strategy lacked a unifying focus: there was too much to do with too little. The isolation of Britain by June 1940 simplified German strategic planning problems immensely, since British dependance upon shipborne imports provided a clear target for decisive action. Unfortunately, in 1940 the Germans had a strategy without a means. Donitz observed in 1939 that he needed at least 300 U-boats to knock Britain out of the war, and the unfulfilled Z-Plan, upon which the German Navy was banking for war with Britain, would have given him most of the ships.[5] But they were not available in 1940. In fact, Dönitz began his blockade of Britain in mid-1940 with fewer than 60 U-boats, only a third of which could be kept on station at one time.[6] Co-operation with the Luftwaffe was and remained abysmal, and the main units of the German fleet were largely held in check by the RN.

The burden of the attack on trade none the less fell on the U-boats, whose innovative tactics from August 1940 onward produced impressive results. Attacking on the surface, at night and in packs the U-boats struck terror into the hearts of mariners and sank shipping as fast as the torpedo tubes could be reloaded. But to have been successful in what Churchill ultimately described in March 1941 as the 'Battle of the Atlantic' – and the German submariners as their first 'Happy Time' – the Germans had to strip Britain's tonnage away faster than the U-boat fleet was capable of doing. It was, in some measure, for Britain a 'death of a thousand cuts' inflicted slowly enough to permit wounds to heal before the accumulation could be fatal.

Much of the interest and emotion in this phase of the war at sea stems from the problems the British had in dealing effectively with a radically new form of submarine attack and in the high drama of convoy battles. Historians ascribed Britain's survival of this trying period to a number of things. Naval writers traditionally point to the misguided nature of the RN's initial A/S doctrine, its fruitless 'offensive' sweeps for elusive targets, the habit of abandoning escort duties to pursue U-boat contacts thereby leaving the convoy open to the next attacker, the ineptness of early Coastal Command aircraft and practices, lack of a good surface warning radar to find the U-boats at night, the need for permanent escort group compositions, permanent senior officers of groups and trans-Atlantic A/S escort of convoys. Developments in the spring of 1941, particularly the establishment of Western Approaches Command, closing the gap in trans-Atlantic A/S escort between Newfoundland and Iceland, the defeat of the surface raider threat in May (with the destruction of *Bismarck*), tackled many of the outstanding problems posed by wolf-pack tactics. On the face of it, Britain was saved because she began to get her A/S forces properly organised, the surface raiders were beaten and the attack on Russia in June 1941 distracted the Germans.[7] It only remained to close the gap in air patrols, as aircraft reaching out from bases in Britain, Iceland and Newfoundland still left a funnel shaped area in the mid-Atlantic free of Allied aircraft.

To be sure all of these improvements had a profound impact on the development of the naval war. But the German campaign against trade over the winter of 1940–41 could only have been successful had a total blockade of Britain been established, and that was an extremely difficult thing to do. Simply sinking ships was not enough. Even the British did not know with certainty just how much they needed to import in order to survive and pursue the war. They estimated in 1939 that Britain imported about 60 million tons of goods per year, but really required only about 47 million tons per year to get by. British registered shipping it was believed was sufficient to carry the 47 million essential tonnage while neutral shipping, available through charter, could easily provide for surplus war needs. As it turned out, British estimates erred greatly. By 1940 they had discovered that they had less shipping to hand than previously thought but more surprising was the realisation by 1942 that Britain could live and fight – just – on about 26 million tons, less than half the level of prewar imports.[8]

There was, then, considerable 'fat' in the British import situation in 1940–41, and the German attack forced them to cut it. As the U-boats whittled away at tonnage by about 250,000 tons per month over the winter of 1940–41, the British reviewed their whole programme of imports, ship scheduling and port management. The review was prompted, in part, by the chaos resulting from the need to abandon Britain's east coast and channel ports to large-scale movements after the Fall of France and the Low Countries. Whatever the reason, to a considerable extent losses to enemy action were made good by the end of 1941 through reductions in port congestion and a rationalisation of the import and shipping programmes. Martin Doughty has estimated that the savings from these developments amounted to approximately three million tons.[9] Losses to U-boat attack over the same period equalled 2.1 million, from a total to all causes of 3.6 million. The savings accruing from more efficient management coupled with 1.2 million tons of new merchant shipping constructed actually left Britain slightly better off by early 1942 in terms of available tonnage than she had been at the end of 1940.[10] In addition, as part of the lend-lease agreement reached with the Americans in early 1941 Britain had contracted for a massive shipbuilding programme in the US.[11] In the end the British would see little of it, but the ships were available to the Allies by 1942 and new construction on an enormous scale would be completed in 1943. The essential point here is that the German attack developed slowly enough for the British to take effective countermeasures, and for the improving situation generally to have a decisive influence. One American scholar has observed recently that the shipping situation changed favourably for the British in the Atlantic in mid-1941 *despite* their efforts to influence specific problems areas, such as lack of air support and an excessive backlog of damaged merchant shipping awaiting repair.[12]

The interpretation of developments in 1941 has been clouded somewhat by recent Ultra revelations. The British only began to use Ultra to assist in routing convoys following the capture of *U110* in June 1941 and, with some delays, used it effectively until February 1942 when an 11-month blackout of Atlantic U-boat cyphers began. Jurgen Rohwer has estimated that Ultra saved 300 ships in 1941 and that these ships ultimately influenced the development of Allied strategy later in the war (a point to be pursued shortly).[13] It is clear, however, that Ultra did not decisively influence the German attempt to knock Britain out of the war in the winter of 1940–41. That campaign failed because the U-boats were too few, the weather improved and, by the fall, the U-boats were drawn off the trade routes to the Mediterranean in response to British advances in the desert and to Norway in response to Hitler's machinations.

The winter of 1940–41 was the only time in the war when the German Navy had a good chance of achieving a decisive result against Britain. From then on their only hope was seriously to impede the development of Allied offensive strategy by sinking ships, and in this they enjoyed a modicum of success. However, it is arguable that factors other than enemy action in the Atlantic were more decisive in determining Allied strategy in Europe after 1941, and a brief dip into Leighton and Coakley's *Global Logistics and Strategy* reveals how difficult it is to ascribe decisive influence to U-boat depredations.[14] But before looking at the impact of shipping on Allied strategy in 1942 it should be noted that the first year of global war brought with it horrendous shipping losses. In each of 1940 and 1941 the Axis had sunk roughly 2.1 million tons of Allied shipping. In 1942 U-boats alone accounted for 6.1 million, most of it in the Atlantic.[15] It is a staggering figure, but in the end does not seem to have materially affected Allied strategy: the bottlenecks were elsewhere.

In the broadest strategic sense the Allies tackled three objectives in 1942, all of which required shipping: stemming the Japanese tide in the Pacific, the build-up of American forces in Britain (Operation BOLERO) for an invasion of north-west Europe, and a major landing in North Africa. The preferred Allied strategy (particularly the preferred American strategy) was a quick build-up in the UK followed by a decisive thrust to the heart of Germany through northern France.[16] As Leighton and Coakley observe BOLERO was dependent upon availability of shipping *and American army formations.* The latter were still being mobilised during 1942, and much of their essential equipment had yet to be manufactured. Planners trying to move the US Army to Britain also discovered in early 1942 that its scales of equipment were excessive, methods of loading wasteful and inefficient. It was estimated, for example, that it required no less than 200,000 tons of cargo capacity to lift one US Armoured division. Vehicles of all sorts, for example, planners expected to ship fully assembled, taking an enormous amount of space for little weight. At the same time ships carrying steel plates, beams and ingots were loaded to their plimsol lines and then sailed with great empty spaces in their cargo decks. The British protested the American Army scales of equipment, but at the same time were prepared to curb their own imports in order to get BOLERO going. Combat troops could be lifted quickly, if given priority on the giant troopships, but they could not train effectively in the UK without their equipment, and the formations were of questionable value without their support troops. Losses to shipping, Leighton and Coakley argued, made it 'very difficult to arrive at precise answers' on the question of available cargo space over the balance of the year. Some would be available, but how much was unclear.[17]

In March 1942 it appeared that BOLERO was strapped by lack of *predictable* cargo capacity and that at best only one infantry and half of an armoured division would be battle ready in the UK by September 1942 – hardly enough to take on the Germans. By April planners had conceded that D-Day could not take place before 1943, and in May, even with some 'sweating down' of equipment scales, it appeared that there would still be a shortfall in shipping for BOLERO of four million tons over 1942. No sooner was that conclusion reached than the temporary abandonment of the Russian convoys produced a potential windfall surplus of shipping of some one million tons over the July–August period. Through May and June then a scramble ensued among planners to find something to fill those 'empty' ships, a problem compounded by lack of precise knowledge of the size and availability of the ships themselves: where they would arrive, when, what size they were, and how many berths would be needed. By the time additional cargo was found for the anticipated million-ton windfall the surplus had evaporated. Rommel had advanced to the gates of Egypt by mid-summer, and much of the British shipping earmarked for BOLERO in 1942 went to the Mediterranean. The decision to invade North Africa, operation TORCH, taken in the summer and executed in November, swallowed up what remained of surplus shipping in 1942.

Such was the nature of the struggle to build up forces for D-Day and keep Britain supplied that they were profoundly influenced by events in the Western Desert and the Pacific, but such is the nature of global war. The North African campaign would, in fact, lead to a major disruption in British supplies and BOLERO and precipitate one of the great crises of the war. To mount and sustain TORCH it was necessary to introduce major disruptions in shipping patterns throughout the Atlantic, with significant losses in carrying capacity as the result of longer turn-around times. The SL series of convoys, UK to West Africa, were temporarily abandoned to free the escorts needed for TORCH, and all UK bound shipping was routed through the convoy system of the western hemisphere. This was a major diversion, which sharply reduced British imports. The import and war reserve situation in Britain was also exacerbated by a much larger drain of resources to TORCH over those anticipated. For example the British initially estimated that TORCH would need a maximum of 66 ship sailings per month from UK ports in order to sustain operations. In fact, by the end of 1942 the average was 106, with a corresponding drain on British resources. Major losses in cargo carrying can be attributed to Rommel's success in North Africa, German success in Russia that forced the Western allies to do something on the ground in 1942 and in December to resume the Russian convoys, and the use of escort vessels to support TORCH which restricted the movement of trade convoys. The resulting import crisis in Britain by the end of the year was therefore directly the result of Allied military operations.[18]

Historians have done a poor job of knitting it all together. Naval historians seldom discuss the impact of global strategic development on the Atlantic war, except where it affects operations, while scholars of strategy and shipping stick firmly to their lasts and seldom reflect on other areas: which is perhaps mute testimony to their assessment of the significance of the Naval war. Rohwer contends that without the shipping saved by Ultra in 1941 the invasion of Normandy might well have been pushed back into 1945.[19] Presumably it was this same shipping that made the military operations of 1942 possible. Ironically, some historians have seen the development of a Mediterranean strategy as a massive distraction of Allied effort which ultimately delayed D-Day beyond 1943.[20] In the end, many of the arguments for delays or for possible improvements in BOLERO are predicated on the belief that there was something to ship. Yet there is little indication that sufficient resources were available in 1942 to build-up much of a force in Britain. The US army was simply not ready for war in 1942. What could be put into the field was already in action in North Africa and the Pacific, and it was a very small portion of the 90-division army envisaged in the American mobilisation plan. There is no doubt that more might have been done in 1942, but how it could have been done is not clear. Shipping was tight, to be sure, and the losses made *planning* hard.

But there was considerable 'fat' in the American management system and the cycle of rationalisation and regulation tackled by the British in 1941 had begun anew in 1942. The success of the German attack on trade in the Atlantic 1942 was dramatically better than any other year of the war, at 6.1 million tons (80 per cent of the global total), and yet American yards were now completing ships faster than the Germans could sink them. By the end of the year the net loss in shipping (losses compared to new construction) was the lowest it had been since 1939. This was part of a trend in evidence since 1940, when the Allies ended the year with a 3.1 million ton deficit, in 1941 it was 2.4 and by the end of 1942 deficit was 1.0 million tons, with the curve of new construction already surging past losses.[21] In the end the Americans were never as efficient at shipping usage as the British, and it is estimated that they lost about nine million tons of shipping through misuse annually by the end of the war – three times their entire merchant shipping losses for the whole war.[22]

The tonnage-shipping-cargo availability shell game points to the difficulty of attempting to define what was decisive about the Atlantic war and what decided it. In the process one moves a long way from the conning towers and bridges of the shooting war. Viewed from the lofty heights of strategic planning, the battle at sea become something of a self-regulating system of checks and balances, with each advance in German attack met and stalemated by Allied forces. And so it was with 1942, with the trends in U-boat successes seen even then as anomalies. The biggest anomaly of them all was the tremendous carnage off the US Eastern seaboard from February to August. In the first six months of the year some 2.34 million tons of shipping was lost in the western hemisphere, most of it off the US Atlantic and Gulf coasts. Indeed, in May and June alone over a million tons were sunk in US waters – half the German score for all of 1941 in just two months.[23] It was recognised at the time, and by historians since, that these prodigious losses were almost entirely avoidable, and that the failure of American authorities to take sensible and simple precautions gave the Germans their second 'Happy Time' and cost the Allies an enormous volume of precious shipping. The crisis off the US east coast in early 1942 was followed by a British import crisis at the end of the year and, in early 1943, a decisive defeat of Germany's wolf-packs. It would be appropriate at this point briefly to reassess these milestones in the Atlantic war in light of some recent scholarship.

The Americans based their 'defence' of shipping in the western hemisphere in early 1942 on concepts long discredited by British experience: 'patrolled' routes, offensive A/S sweeps, independent routing of ships, and the like. In short, defence was based not on the avoidance of the enemy but rather on the dubious notion of protecting shipping by finding and destroying an enemy whose primary task was to avoid the confrontation being sought.

The British, who had shared all their hard won information on convoying and ASW, could only wring their hands and grind their teeth as shipping escorted safely to Halifax was lost to the south. The Americans protested that they could not establish convoys until they were ready, particularly until they had sufficient escorts. The British could not see the reasoning then, nor since,[24] and astonishingly no major American scholarship on the catastrophe of early 1942 has appeared since Morison's first volume in 1947.

Recent scholarship on the Canadian Navy sheds some light on this enduring and long neglected problem. The Canadian naval and air forces formed a major portion of the Allied effort in the Atlantic. By mid-1942 half of the naval escorts and a quarter of the aircraft involved in convoy movements north of New York were Canadian. Historians have been negligent in not dealing with the RCN and the RCAF as independant actors in the Atlantic, and have failed to look closely at the Canadians' influence on the pattern of the war at sea. For example, it was the Canadian Navy's Trade Division that operated a network of Naval Control of Shipping agents in the neutral US from 1939 to 1941. These 'Consular Shipping Agents' not only managed the movement of British shipping in the US, but by 1941 they had begun to instruct the nascent USN NSC system in the basics of trade movement. Confidential Books and Special Publications on trade matters were supplied to the USN from Ottawa in 1941, and by the time of Pearl Harbor the Agents and American 'Port Directors' were working in harness. American–Canadian trade liaison had been underway since 1940, when a USN attaché was appointed to Ottawa to develop contacts, and a Canadian naval liaison officer specialising in trade matters was appointed to Washington in 1941. The trade and intelligence network operated by Ottawa was so efficient that it took control of shipping west of 40° and north of the equator from December 1941 until July 1942, while feeding the developing USN trade directorate with daily intelligence summaries from the British system. It is not stretching the point beyond credulity to say that the Canadians could have instituted a convoy system off the US coast in early 1942 – with a little help from the locals. The British of course were well aware of all this and it no doubt fuelled their despair at the USN's slow march to a convoy system.[25]

In the end it seems the delay was due less to problems of organisation than to a USN desire to ensure that its coastal convoys received a measure of escort usually reserved in British experience for trans-Atlantic passages. The American contention that they lacked sufficient escorts to establish a convoy system was baffling to the British and Canadians, who had built their coastal convoy systems around a myriad of miscellaneous vessels. They knew from experience that the object of trade defence was safe and timely arrival and that this was best done by simply shepherding convoys from port to port. Anti-submarine defence could be concentrated around the

U-boat's objective, forcing him to fight for targets and risk counter-attack. If the U-boat failed to press home attacks the trade got through and the submariner failed in his mission. Moreover, convoys and evasive routing were particularly successful in areas where constant air patrols prevented the development of wolf-pack operations. The long shipping route along the North America Atlantic seaboard provided an excellent 400 mile wide corridor within which to route convoys under sustainable air support, and yet it was wide enough to make an individual German submariner's search problem well-nigh insoluble. Even chance interceptions could be expected to produce no more than a single attack.

The British could not understand why the Americans missed this point in 1942. They would have been less baffled had they looked more closely at American experience in the Atlantic in the fall of 1941. From September to December 1941 the Americans served alongside the RCN in the Newfoundland to Iceland stretch of the main trade routes.[26] These operations included a number of pitched convoy battles around the slow convoys escorted by the Canadians. The RCN was in the very preliminary stages of its wartime expansion, and its performance in these battles was alarmingly bad. Canadian crews were utterly untrained and inexperienced, their equipment was poor and frequently broke down, leadership was dubious and the level of overall efficiency deplorable. It was this expansion fleet that Donald Macintyre would immortalise in his memoir as being wildly incompetant and a menace to those they sought to protect.[27] Unfortunately, Macintyre missed the point about operations in 1941, about the hasty nature of Canadian deployment to the Newfoundland to Iceland route – at Admiralty request – and about the importance of routing. The Americans saw in these ill-fated Canadian operations their worst fears about poorly escorted convoys and vowed to have none of it. The USN's Board on the Organization of East Convoys, which reported in March 1942, strongly advised against 'weakly escorted' convoys. No jury-rigged groups of motor launches, yachts, trawlers and clapped-out vessels for the USN: its coastal convoys were to have destroyer escorts or none at all.[28]

The American experience in the North Atlantic in late 1941 alongside the struggling RCN clearly shaped their handling of the 1942 campaign off their own coast. Obviously in this case experience counted for more than shared information from an erstwhile rival. The Board on Convoys was correct in its assessment of the impact of a pack attack on a weakly escorted slow convoy beyond the range of effective airpower, but apart from the speed of the convoy none of these conditions obtained off the US east coast. In time a proper convoy system, supported by air patrols, made the US east coast an unprofitable theatre of operations but not before millions of tons of shipping had been lost. In this instance the Canadians had a profound – and pernicious – influence on the pattern of the war at sea. It remains to be seen if some future historian of the USN over this period will find the same connections in American documents. In the meantime new Canadian scholarship modifies other aspects of the 1942–43 period as well, ultimately affecting previous interpretations of the crisis of the U-boat war in 1943 and these are worth pursuing briefly.

It was the RCN's contribution of escort forces to the Newfoundland to Iceland stretch of the convoy route that closed the gap in A/S escort in 1941. And it was Canadian forces who assumed the burden of USN commitments in the western Atlantic north of New York in 1942, when the war spiralled out of control. In Sir Dudley's Pound's words, the Canadians solved the problem of the North Atlantic convoys. But in doing so the Canadians were stretched to the limit by late 1942, their forces operating in the air gap were by far the weakest link in the chain. The operational crisis of 1942 which drew Canadian forces south to Boston, New York and the Carribean stripped Canadian mid-ocean groups of surplus ships, training time, refits and even the opportunity to fit essential new equipment such as 10cm radar and HF/DF. The Canadians also continued to escort the bulk of slow convoys in late 1942, the result of an earlier agreement with the USN.[29] Canadian sailors were now experienced North Atlantic veterans but their groups were small, leadership still unsteady and equipment outdated. Escorting the slow convoys made them an easy mark for prowling wolf-packs. In the last six months of 1942, with only four of the 11 escort groups in the Mid-Ocean Escort Force Canadian, RCN convoys lost 60 of the 80 vessels sunk by U-boats. It was another season of Canadian misfortune – ON 127 7 ships, SC 107 12 ships and ONS 154 14 ships.[30] The Admiralty's *Monthly Anti-Submarine Report* for January 1943 observed that the Canadians bore the brunt of U-boat attacks in the last half of 1942: no one has noticed since.

The Canadian crisis sheds light on the whole campaign over the winter of 1942–43. The British were so disturbed by the apparent inability of the RCN adequately to defend convoys that in December 1942 they convinced Canadians of the need to 'withdraw' their escorts from the mid-ocean. The RCN therefore 'missed' the bitter battles of February and March 1943, and enjoyed a cautious re-entry in April and May. As a result, the fleet with nearly half of the escorts along the main convoy route accounted for only two of the 50-plus U-boat kills by warships during those decisive months. The victory over the wolf-packs was thus overwhelmingly British in flavour.

Canadian misfortunes of late 1942 were largely passed off by the British as more Canadian bungling. In reality, the nationality of the escorts' sailors had little to do with the alarming losses. Slow convoys, escorted by poorly equipped groups, battling ten to 20 U-boats in the air gap for days on end were simply a recipe for disaster.[31] The Admiralty's cautious steps towards dealing with problems endemic to the escort arrangements themselves gained a pace when the RN took over responsibility for the slow convoys in early 1943 and got savagely mauled in the process. The Canadians could have told them as much.

Part of the difficulty the Canadians faced in late 1942, and what would confront the British early in 1943, was the inability to avoid being overwhelmed by increasingly large and more numerous wolf-packs that operated in the mid-ocean air gap. The problem of the air gap had been foreseen, but so long as U-boats were busy elsewhere there was no pressure to close it. That pressure mounted by the end of 1942. U-boats driven from other areas by the extension of convoys and air power now concentrated in the mid-Atlantic where the absence of Allied aircraft allowed them to operate with impunity. It also put them astride Britain's only link to the rest of the world. Dependence on a single embattled route, declining imports, rising exports to North Africa, increasing losses and shaky morale within the merchant marine itself all pushed Britain towards a crisis. New construction of merchant shipping did surpass losses by late 1942, but virtually all of that new tonnage was American while virtually all of the losses in the Atlantic were British. The Americans were not entirely sympathetic to Britain's plight. When the issue of declining British oil stocks was raised with the Americans in December Roosevelt attempted to calm Churchill by pointing out that Britain's reserves were no worse than those in Australia, Newfoundland, Greenland and Noumea. As Churchill observed, the Americans failed to appreciate that Britain, too, was a major base for the production and trans-shipment of material to theatres of war around the world.[32]

American interest in sorting out the Atlantic's problems at the end of 1942 stemmed from their concern over the fate of BOLERO, and so it was decided at Casablanca in January 1943 that the Atlantic would finally get first priority. The British already had a clear idea of how to tackle the U-boats in the air gap. The renowned operational scientist PMS Blackett demonstrated convincingly in early 1943 that closing the air gap would result in a 64 per cent decline in losses, and that increasing the size of naval escorts from six to nine would reduce losses by 25 per cent. He also concluded that increasing the average size of convoys would reduce losses further by limiting the opportunities for U-boat attack.[33] The notion of larger convoys was not an immediate success with operational staffs, but increased air and naval support was. Following the disaster around SC 118 in early February authorisation was received to remove one destroyer from each escort group and transfer several Home Fleet destroyers into a new force of Support Groups, whose task was to reinforce convoy escorts as they transited the air gap. Air support was forthcoming from two areas. The small escort carriers long considered ideal for the mid-ocean had been diverted to support TORCH, but some were now freed to tackle the wolf packs. More importantly, Liberator Very Long Range patrol aircraft were found to permit sustained air operations in the depth of the air gap. It was a very small increment of strength, but it was enough.[34]

Ultra played an important role in allowing the Allies to use these forces to the maximum, but it is doubtful if the final result would have been much different without it. Most of 1942 had been fought without the aid of Ultra intelligence in the Atlantic. Given the roving, independant nature of U-boat operations in the western hemisphere in the early part of the year it would have been of limited use. So long as U-boats signalled frequently on HF and the Allies could read the codes of other German naval commands the general patterns of German operations were easy to follow. Enthusiasts of special intelligence frequently forget that in an era when navigation was as much an art as a science even knowing all details of the enemy's estimated position did not mean it was easy to connect. Air records, in particular, are replete with 'convoy not met' notations. In the German case difficulties of navigation at sea made coordination of U-boat and Luftwaffe operations impractical,[35] with aircraft reports of convoy positions often out by 50 miles. Shipboard navigation was more reliable, but often after days – or a week – of plotting movements by dead reckoning a convoy could be miles away from its signalled position.

It is true none the less that the fall of 1942 campaign in the air gap would have gone better had Ultra been available to effect routing. Losses would also have been substantially lower had the Canadians been properly equipped, and had the Germans not been reading the Allied convoy cypher![36] Another complicating factor in the scenario is that winter was always a difficult time for both convoys and escorts, particularly those facing the wolf packs over the winters of 1940–41 and 1942–43. Darkness covered German movements more effectively, and the rougher seas masked attacking U-boats better from both numbed watch-keepers and early radars. The advantage of going north in the winter to seek more effective air support in the narrow portion of the air gap was often offset by the more favourable U-boat operating conditions and by slower passages due to winter storms. Taking a southern route in winter offered better weather and therefore an easier passage for men and ships, but the air gap in the south meant a long and hazardous passage, as the Canadian escorted ONS 1543 discovered in December 1942 losing 14 ships in a five-day transit of the gap just north of the Azores.

Avoidance of the U-boat packs was the key to success in the trans-Atlantic convoys, but by early 1943 avoidance was no longer a certainty for the main routes. Dönitz's strategy, driven by the amount of tonnage sunk per U-boat day at sea, had forced him to concentrate his effort in the mid-ocean air gap so that by early 1943 it was literally filling up with submarines. Very precise intelligence was now crucial to routing and that intelligence could only be provided by Ultra. Through January and February Ultra provided the information, but the Germans were reading the Allies' daily estimates of U-boat positions and anticipated their movements. The battle for ONS 166 in late February, in which 14 ships were lost in a six-day battle with 18 U-boats, was fought with both shore staffs reading the other side's signal traffic. Unfortunately for the Allies, the situation only got worse. At the end of February the Germans changed the weather code which had served as the key to Allied penetration of the operational code used by U-boats.[37] A three-week gap in Ultra information ensued in early March and every Allied convoy in the North Atlantic was intercepted. Over half were attacked, and 22 per cent of trans-Atlantic shipping in those convoys was lost. It was physically impossible for the Germans to do more.[38]

The crisis of March 1943 has been the subject of several books, and much has been written about it in others. There is a tendency to credit the restoration of Ultra intelligence in late March with reversing the tailspin in the air gap. This goes too far. The air gap was the problem, and its elimination would have put an end to wolf-pack attacks with or without Ultra. The singularly decisive influence of airpower on the battle of the Atlantic was well understood at the time, at least by sailors. It was airpower, after all, which shaped the pattern of the U-boat war. Submerged U-boats, driven down by aircraft, lacked the speed, range, endurance and tactical effectiveness to tackle convoys in the broad ocean. Until 1945 targetting data could only be effectively obtained either through the periscope or through the fire control system mounted on the conning tower and used while on the surface. When forced to submerge U-boats were, as diesel electric submarines are today, little more than smart mines waiting for targets of opportunity. Active target acquisition, and on a decisive scale, could only be done on the surface, and strategic range was entirely predicated on surface cruising.

The real significance of the U-boat as a raider was its ability to penetrate Britain's surface and air blockade of Europe and to escape retribution by submerging when counter-attacked. But simply getting out to sea and returning safely was not enough. Without the benefit of either long-range air reconnaissance or sensors, the Germans could only locate convoys reliably by organising and controlling long patrol lines of submarines laid-out perpendicular to the axis of the convoy route. Contacts were typically visual with details of position, course and speed passed by HF to U-boat headquarters. Shore staffs then orchestrated the pack's concentration on the convoy through extensive HF traffic. The shadower continued to feed corrections to the shore staff, and broadcast a homing beacon on MF to aid the pack in its final assembly. The need to move freely on the surface and to transmit routinely made the wolf-pack extremely vulnerable to Allied air and naval forces.[39]

Naval escorts, better equipped with 10cm radar, HF/DF and more destroyers acquitted themselves well during 1942, and with the help of support groups could probably have fought the U-boats to a draw. It was airpower that proved decisive. Its speed and range had largely driven wolfpacks 400 to 600 miles from the coasts on either side of the Atlantic by 1942 and had made the operations of solitary U-boats unprofitable. There were some anomalies however. Wolf-packs did operate on the Grand Banks of Newfoundland under the noses of Canadian and US aircraft, taking advantage of the almost perpetual fog generated by the mixing of the Labrador Current and the Gulf Stream. The fog, of course, could be penetrated by radar, but the early sets could not distinguish between a towering iceberg – carried down from Greenland on the Labrador Current – and a U-boat, and it was only the foolhardy who plunged to sea level through thick fog to classify a contact. Prevailing westerly winds also reduced the 'Prudent Limit of Endurance' of Newfoundland-based aircraft such as the Catalina to about 400 miles, while the British were able to coax 600 miles of range out of similar types in the eastern Atlantic. The recently published volume of the Royal Canadian Air Force's official history adds a wealth of new material on the role of airpower in combatting the U-boats, a subject mainstream air enthusiasts ignore utterly and naval historians treat only in passing.[40]

The failure of the Allies to close the air gap before 1943 remains one of the great unsolved historical problems of the war. In some measure the reluctance stems from the fact that the aircraft needed, the Liberator, formed a major portion of the burgeoning American strategic bomber offensive and was widely employed by the USN in patrolling the vast reaches of the Pacific Ocean. The other aircraft used in maritime patrol operations, apart from those like the Catalina and Sunderland types designed for maritime work, were all unsuited for front line operations over enemy territory: Hudsons, Whitleys, Wellingtons, Digbys and the like. None of the standard inventory of maritime patrol aircraft in 1942 had the range to conduct patrols in the depths of the air gap. Modifications to some early marks of Liberators by 120 Squ, RAF, in 1942 showed what the aircraft could do. Their presence in the depths of the air gap, 800 miles from Iceland and 300 miles further afield than the pattern in 1941, came as a rude shock to the Germans in August 1942. However, with only a few VLR aircraft nothing could be done by 120 Sqn. in 1942 materially to alter the campaign itself.[41]

In the end about 40–50 Liberators were needed to close the air gap – permanently: the same number of Liberators lost from the first Ploesti raid alone. And since the maritime patrol aircraft loss rate was minimal most of those airplanes were still doing the same job in 1945. For many historians of the Atlantic war the myopia of the airmen who drove the strategic bomber offensive seems incredible. The very strategic bombing campaign upon which airmen staked their reputations, and the outcome of the Allied war effort, was dependant upon securing the Atlantic and easing the task of planners. Once determined that the aircraft were needed the issue of allocation of VLR Liberators to the North Atlantic revolved around two sticky points. The aircraft themselves were first rate, modern, tremendously capable machines, eyed jealously by the USN and the US Army Air Force. It was no easy matter to decide who would fly them, the US Army, the US Navy, the RAF – or the Canadians. As Alec Douglas points out, it proved hard for the senior partners to accept that the Canadians, with their breadth of experience in Atlantic air operations, crews, air fields, staffs and experienced squadrons, could handle the B-24. By April, however, the aircraft began to arrive and RCAF and RAF aircraft were soon intervening decisively in the depths of the mid-Atlantic. The air gap was eliminated, and when it disappeared so too did the final area for free-wheeling U-boat operations.

Ultra played a role in helping this happen by allowing the Allies to concentrate their efforts. If U-boats could not be avoided, they could be destroyed. It helped that the escorts themselves were, by 1943, well equipped, that they were manned by battle-experienced veterans of the Atlantic and that the level of their skill in dealing with wolf-packs was reaching its peak. In contrast, the U-boat fleet was in the throes of its major expansion, crews were inexperienced, captains new to the job and losses had begun to rise. Ultra revealed the state of the U-boat fleet and allowed the Allies to push hard when it would achieve the greatest effect.[42] The despair of March, when it looked like the North Atlantic trade routes were untenable, gave way to a major offensive against the wolfpacks by April. Unable to route all convoys clear of trouble, those standing into danger were reinforced by support groups and given additional air support. Extra escorts allowed commanders to build double screens around convoys and permitted escorts the time to pursue contacts to a conclusion while the remainder of the escort sailed on with the convoy. U-boats could still concentrate around convoys, but once there the advantage lay with the defender. So many U-boats (a total of 40) groped through the Newfoundland fog for ONS 5 in early May 1943 that two collided, sinking one of the submarines. The convoy lost 11 ships but the escorts, using their 10 cm radar, found and attacked 15 U-boats and sank *four* in a single night.[43] By the end of May wolf-pack operations in the mid-ocean had become untenable and Dönitz ordered his submariners to withdraw. Moreover, it speaks volumes for the limited tactical and strategic capabilities of a submarine offensive built on surface mobility that the U-boats could only stay and take the pounding: the soft theatres were all gone by 1943. As Sir Julian Corbett observed, the great moments of naval history have to be worked for.

If a few words were needed to describe the Allied approach to the wolfpacks in the spring of 1943 they would be, flexibility, coordination, sophistication and professionalism. It was not perfect, but it was enough.

By mid-summer evasive routing had given way to a 'tram line', essentially a fixed route long preferred by the Americans. U-boats approached this route at their peril, as convoy battles had become a means of punishing the German fleet. The Germans returned to the fray in the summer, attempting to fight their way through the oppressive airpower in the Bay of Biscay transit area with heavier anti-aircraft weapons, only to suffer grievous losses. They came back to the mid-Atlantic in September with an acoustic homing torpedo, gained modest success in a novel battle against the combined convoys ONS 18/ON 202.[44] Towed noise-makers were ready for escorts in a matter of weeks and the U-boat packs failed to achieve more than qualified success in the face of withering naval and air power. Over the same summer the USN destroyed Germany's U-boat replenishment fleet, using Ultra intelligence to guide carrier support groups to rendezvous, catching the 'Milch Cows' and their clients.[45] By the end of the year the U-boats had all but abandoned surface movement and regular radio traffic. The wolf-pack had been beaten.

The victory over the U-boat in 1943 was a dramatic event in the naval war; whether it had a decisive influence on the war itself is a moot point. From 1940 to 1943 Dönitz had been able to exploit the limited range and disorganisation of Allied countermeasures to achieve dramatic results through an innovative use of submersible torpedo boats. It could not last. When airpower finally forced U-boats to act like true submarines neither their technology nor their crews were up to it. Their defeat in 1943 was the culmination of a long process of progressive denial of freedom of movement for massed and surfaced attacks. The U-boats were, after all, kept in check throughout 1944 and early 1945 despite the fact that Ultra proved very difficult to employ. Ironically, had the Allies succeeded in sorting out the airpower problems in 1941 or 1942 the wheel of submarine development may well have turned early enough – all other things being equal – for the first true submarines, the German types XXI and XXIII, to have launched the Atlantic into another crisis.[46]

What then, apart from the fate of the wolf-packs, did the Allied naval victory of 1943 accomplish, and what influence did it have on the course of the war? Arguably, little. The shipping situation generally was improving by leaps and bounds at the end of 1942. New construction in 1942 amounted to seven million tons, during 1943 it doubled to over 14 million tons. Shipping was freed with the opening of the Mediterranean over the summer and the mid-ocean remained, until April–May, the only serious drain in terms of losses. This drain seriously threatened Britain's import programs, and ultimately the build-up for D-Day. By March, with staggering losses in the Atlantic to shipping engaged in the UK trade, the British threatened to withdraw all their commitments to BOLERO in order to concentrate on their own imports. American chiefs of staff protested, preferring to see British imports further reduced in order to pursue the D-Day build-up (echoes of the December 1942 position on oil, which failed to consider Britain's legitimate role as a principal Allied producer and sustainer). It took the direct intervention of the American President in May 1943 to divert new shipping to British use, thereby restoring the British import situation and allowing BOLERO to get back on track.[47]

In the end, the real problem in 1943 was a happy one: what to do with all the surplus shipping available by the middle of the year. Here victory over the U-boats was a contributory factor, but not decisive. By all accounts the Allies could have sustained shipping losses at 1940–41 rates and still proceeded with a spring 1944 invasion of France. Although shipping losses made it very difficult to *plan* effectively for BOLERO in early 1943, it would undoubtedly have been less so had American planners allowed for the redress of British losses with new US-built ships earlier on. It must be admitted as well that difficulty in planning early in the year probably contributed to the inability of the Allies to fill the shipping they had available by the fall. By then the bottleneck was not shipping, but men and material to move.[48] BOLERO met its objectives in 1943, and could have surpassed them had it been possible to deliver goods to and remove them from ports on either side of the Atlantic. In the end priority for BOLERO over all other Allied operations was only achieved when a firm date for D-Day of spring 1944 was agreed to at Tehran in November 1943. With that decision the final, frantic build-up in the UK was possible. In the end that final build-up was complicated by the decision to increase the size of the initial assault to five divisions and the consequent need to amass more assault shipping – especially LSTs. The best that could be said for the U-boat campaign was that without it D-Day might have happened a month earlier.

Historians have treated the last two years of the Atlantic war as a denouement, and in so far as its impact on the course of the war itself is concerned that is an accurate assessment. Following the defeat of 1943 Dönitz waged a holding battle against the Allies in the Atlantic, striving to tie down resources and husbanding his fleet to meet the invasion. The holding action worked, although the scale of Allied resources committed to the Atlantic began to decline by 1944 in part because more effective equipment and procedures were adopted. The much-feared attack on assault and follow-up shipping in the English Channel failed to materialise, and those submarines which did attempt to attack were dealt with roughly. The adoption of schnorkels for the U-boat fleet and widespread fitting of radar detectors capable of sensing 10 cm sets improved the lot for U-boats slightly. Schnorkels allowed them freedom of movement at a much reduced pace, and a measure of success inshore was achieved in the last year of the war. The schnorkels were difficult to locate, and sharply reduced the effectiveness of airpower for offensive ASW. But most U-boats could detect the aircrafts' search radar on the detector mounted on the schnorkel head, and the need constantly to react to the presence of a searching aircraft made life hard for U-boats crews. Moreover, passage to distant theatres, such as North America, became laborious and seriously reduced time on station. Aircraft may not have sunk as many U-boats after 1943, but they remained the principal reason for the submariners' quiescence.

Historians have also looked upon the final phase of the war at sea as a success for the Allies. Strictly speaking it was. Losses to merchant shipping were inconsequential and the Allies were able to develop their plans with little interference from enemy action. In the end, it was a stalemate. U-boats were not able materially to affect the total available tonnage and, once the U-boats were equipped with schnorkel and radar detectors, the Allies had a hard time finding and destroying submarines. For the Germans the buy-down in resources was well worth the effort. By April 1945 it was estimated that 25 U-boats operating or in transit from their bases to British waters were tying-down 400 surface vessels and 800 aircraft. More importantly, this was the old U-boat technology with minimal adaptation. Waiting in the wings at the end of April were 100 of the new type XXI ocean-going true submarines, for which the Allies had no sure cure. The Allies' only hope was that the 'fat' in the shipping situation was sufficient to allow them to learn how to fight the new U-boat. It was a daunting proposition. The A/S ships and technology developed during the war were designed to exploit the old U-boat's reliance on the surface. How the Allies would have dealt with a deep diving, very fast U-boat which did not need to surface to fire its torpedoes remains a mystery – one of the great what ifs of the war.[49]

The 'Battle of the Atlantic' is a misnomer for the longest, most complex and dynamic campaign of the Second World War. The perception of it as a battle, in the same sense as those for Normandy, Cassino or even in the air over Berlin, was fostered by the essential wartime propaganda that portrayed the men at sea – accurately enough – as the backbone of the system. The operational focus of writing on the Atlantic was sustained by the official historians of Allied naval forces, whose purpose was to record the activities of services at war. Subsequent historians have followed their lead, and with good reason. Men in battle makes for good reading, and there is a rich and dramatic operational history to record. It would be absurd to suggest that the shooting war was unimportant, or that the losses to shipping were inconsequential. Without the German submarine campaign the Western Allies could have moved ships at will, and the steel, money and men consumed in the naval and air forces poured into other areas – just as Allied aerial bombing would have been conducted with greater facility and precision had the Germans not developed their air defences.

Dönitz knew full well how limited was his capacity for decisive action and how fragile was the sword he wielded from 1940 to 1943. The war at sea was not within his capacity to win, although the Allies – like Jellicoe at Jutland – might have lost it through utter incompetance. It is only when one moves away from the battles and begins to look at the essential issues in the Atlantic war, shipping and cargoes, and how these influenced the crucial land and air campaigns that the scope of the problem faced by Allied, and Axis, service and civilian planners and managers becomes evident.

That problem remains as a challenge to historians. Despite all that has been published on the Atlantic, its historiography still requires modern, scholarly accounts of both the Royal and United States Navies. Recent enthusiasm for Ultra has left us with a welter of books on 'special' intelligence but we still lack a thorough account of how naval intelligence as a whole functioned. And despite the pioneering work of Behrens, Leighton and Coakley's neglected work on 'logistics' and Doughty's recent scholarship we have only begun to map the perimeters of the struggle for shipping and a viable strategy. Sir Julian Corbett admonished historian to remember that war at sea is more than battles, and as an historian with a firm grasp of Britain's wars against continental powers he knew whereof he spoke.

NOTES

1. Copies of the Naval Staff Histories open to scholars can be found at the Public Record Office [PRO], Kew, England, and at the Directorate of History [DHist] NDHQ Ottawa. S.W. Roskill's, *The War at Sea*, 3 vols. (London: HMSO, 1954–61), drew heavily from these histories. S.E. Morison's first volume of the USN official history, *The History of US Naval Operations in the Second World War* (Boston, MA: Little, Brown, 1947), dealt with the Atlantic up to the defeat of the wolf-packs in 1943.
2. Roskill's *The War at Sea* is the most balanced of all the official naval histories, but his purpose was to recount *all* RN operations worldwide. The late Adm. B.B. Schofield, who served as Director of Trade at the Admiralty through much of the war, confided to the author his dissatisfaction with the brevity and lack of depth in Roskill's handling of the Atlantic war.
3. Sir Julian Corbett, from *England and the Seven Years' War*, I, p.3, as quoted in D.M. Schurman, *The Education of a Navy* (London: Cassell, 1965), p.165.
4. The best recent account of this neglected problem is Martin Doughty, *Merchant Shipping and War*, (Royal Historical Society: London, 1982), and see also CBA Behrens, *Merchant Shipping and the Demands of War* (London: HMSO and Longmans Green, 1955).
5. Karl Dönitz, *Memoirs: Ten Years and Twenty Days* (London: Weidenfeld & Nicholson, 1959), discusses the failure of his U-boat plans in Ch. 5, see especially p.41.
6. T. Hughes and J. Costello, *The Battle of the Atlantic* (New York: Dial Press: 1977), p.102.
7. See, for example, Roskill, Vol. I, Ch. XVII and XXI, and Donald Macintyre's *The Battle of the Atlantic* (London: B.T. Batsford, 1961).
8. Behrens, pp.36–7 and Appendix X, p.71, see also p.185 where Behrens claims Britain got by on 30.5 million tons in 1940.
9. Doughty, p.9.
10. Figures drawn from the tables on pp.304–5 in Hughes and Costello which, in turn, were

compiled from Roskill's *The War at Sea*.

11. Behrens, pp.284 and 290, and Appendix XXVII, p.292.

12. Max Schoenfeld, 'Winston Churchill as War Manager: The Battle of the Atlantic Committee 1941', *Military Affairs*, Vol. 52, (July 1988), 122–7.

13. Jürgen Rohwer and Roger Sarty, 'Intelligence and the Air Forces in the Battle of the Atlantic 1943–45', paper to the XIIIth International Colloquy on Military History, Helsinki, 31 May–6 June 1988.

14. Richard M. Leighton and Robert W. Coakley, *Global Logistics and Strategy*, 2 vols., United States Army in World War II (Office of the Chief of Military History, Department of the Army, Washington, DC, 1955–1968).

15. Hughes and Costello, pp.304–5.

16. Maurice Matloff, 'Allied Strategy in Europe, 1939–1945' in Peter Paret (ed.), *Makers of Modern Strategy* (Princeton, NJ: Princeton University Press, 1986), pp.677–702.

17. Leighton and Coakley, I, pp.356–58.

18. This conclusion is supported by Doughty's work, see pp.39–40, and in R.M. Leighton's 'U.S. Merchant Shipping and the British Import Crisis', in K.R. Greenfield (ed.), *Command Decisions* (Office of the Chief of Military History, Department of the Army, Washington, DC, 1960), pp.199–223.

19. Rohwer and Sarty, op. cit.

20. For the most extreme view see John Grigg, *The Victory that Never Was*, (London 1980), while a more balanced assessment can be found in R.M. Leighton's 'Overlord versus the Mediterranean at the Cairo–Teheran Conferences', in K.R. Greenfield, op. cit., pp.255–85.

21. Hughes and Costello, pp.304–5, see also Roskill, Vol. II, p.379, for a graphic representation of the new construction/loss rate curves.

22. Morrison, Vol. XV, p.164, supports the British contention that the US failed to manage its shipping effectively.

23. Morison, I, Appendix I(4), pp.413–14.

24. See, for example, Roskill, Vol. II, pp.95–9, Macintyre, p.124, and Patrick Beesley's *Very Special Intelligence* (London: Hamish Hamilton, 1977), p.148.

25. For more details of RCN/RN trade activities in the US prior to 1942 see the brief account in M. Milner, *Canadian Naval Force Requirements* (Operational Research and Analysis Establishment, NDHQ, Extramural Paper, No.20, Ottawa, 1981).

26. The best account of the USN's 1941 North Atlantic convoy operations is Patrick Abazzia's, *Mr. Roosevelt's Navy* (Annapolis, MD: US Naval Institute; 1975).

27. Donald Macintyre, *U-Boat Killer* (London: Weidenfeld & Nicholson, 1956), see especially the first ten pages of Ch. 7.

28. The Board's report, undated, can be found in the Public Record Office, Kew, Surrey, England, Adm 205/19. The USN's insistance on destroyers was confirmed by Dr Phil Lundeberg of the National Museum of American History, Washington, who served on Morison's staff.

29. When the USN began planning to assume responsibility for A/S escort in the Western Atlantic an agreement was reached with the RCN to have the faster USN destroyer groups escort the fast convoys (the HX and ON [odd numbers]). 'History of North Atlantic Convoy Escort Organization . . .' RCN Plans Division narrative, 1 May 1943, DHist., Ottawa. When the USN groups withdrew in early 1942 and the stop-over in Iceland abandoned most of the USN's responsibility for fast convoys was assumed by the RN. See the chart 'Deployment of the Ocean Escort Groups, April 1942 to May 1943' in Jürgen Rohwer, *The Critical Convoy Battles of March 1943* (Annapolis, MD. US Naval Institute, 1977), p.39.

30. This period is dealt with in depth in Marc Milner, *North Atlantic Run: The Royal Canadian Navy and the Battle for the Convoys* (Toronto: University of Toronto; 1985), Chs. 5–8.

31. The fortunes of the token USN group in the North Atlantic, A.3, are dealt with in Milner, *North Atlantic Run*, and are covered in greater detail and with personal insight in J.M. Waters, *Bloody Winter* (Princeton, NJ: van Nostrand, 1967).

32. The exchange, with one of Churchill's famous 'pray' memoes attached, can be found in

PRO, Mt 63/70.
33. Blackett's famous memo can be found in his, *Studies of War* (London: Oliver and Boyd, 1962), or in PRO, PREM 3, 414/1.
34. For recent scholarship on the VLR debate – and a major contribution to the historiography of the war at sea – see W.A.B. Douglas, *The Creation of a National Air Force: The Official History of the Royal Canadian Air Force*, Vol. II (Toronto: University of Toronto Press, 1986), see especially section IV which deals with the Atlantic war.
35. Dönitz, p.139.
36. F.N. Hinsley, *British Intelligence in the Second World War*, Vol. II, (Cambridge: Cambridge University Press, 1981), Appendix I, p.636, and Appendix I, pt. II.
37. Ibid, pp.561–8.
38. Rohwer, *The Critical Convoy Battles of March 1943*, and Martin Middlebrook, *Convoy* (London: Allen Lane, 1976).
39. Donitz, pp.127–54, explains how the system worked – and how it could be undone.
40. The difference between mid-ocean ASW and 'inshore' ASW is discussed in M. Milner, 'Inshore ASW: The Canadian Experience', in W.A.B. Douglas, *et al*, *The RCN in Transition* (Vancouver: University of British Columbia, 1988), pp.143–58, and Douglas' *The Creation of a National Air Force . . . .*
41. Douglas, *The Creation of a National Air Force . . .* discusses the operations of 120 sq, RAF.
42. See Hinsley, II, pp.567–8.
43. See especially V-Adm Sir Peter Gretton's, *Crisis Convoy* (London P. David, 1974).
44. The latest accounts of ONS 18/ON 202 can be found in Douglas, *The Creation of a National Air Force*, and Jürgen Rohwer and WAB Douglas, 'Canada and the Wolf Packs, September 1943', in Douglas (ed.), *The RCN in Transition*, pp.159–86.
45. A recent account is provided by William Y-Blood, *Hunter Killer* (Annapolis, MD: US Naval Institute, 1983).
46. See M. Milner, 'The Dawn of Modern ASW: Allied Responses to the U-Boat 1943–1945' in *RUSI Journal* (spring 1980).
47. Leighton and Coakley, I, pp.680–702.
48. Ibid., II, pp.240–43.
49. Milner, 'The Dawn of Modern ASW . . .'.

The Allied Air Offensive

MALCOLM SMITH

Just a few minutes after the British declaration or war, air raid sirens were heard over London. It was a grimly fitting end to the 'low dishonest decade' of unemployment, fascism and appeasement. Fittingly, too – given the inflated contemporary estimates of the potential of air power – that first air raid warning proved to be a false alarm. It was to be almost a year before Britain came under sustained air attack; it was to be almost two years before Britain could begin to mount one of her own, and almost three before that attack could be sustained. Yet, in the early months of the war, the bombing of Warsaw and then of Dutch cities kept alive the fear of bombing that had been so dominant an element in the popular culture of the interwar period. It was not as clear in the early years of the war as it may be now that the bomber had failed to live up to its reputation as the ultimate weapon. Indeed, faith in the air weapon continued to sustain not simply airmen, but also newsreelmen and other journalists, as well as Prime Ministers and Presidents, in the view that the contribution of the air war would be the major factor in the outcome of the war as a whole.

Since the end of the war, the balance of opinion on the value of the Allied air offensive has been heavily on the critical side. Perhaps the most favourable view has been that it is inconceivable that the war as a whole could have been won without victory in the air. On the other hand, it has not been at all clear to most historians that the bombers were applied as efficiently, and therefore as effectively, as they might have been. Working on the assumption that the bomber was qualitatively different from other weapon forms, aircraft were called upon to perform tasks which they were simply incapable of fulfilling. The bomber could not win the war on its own: it was only one piece in a jigsaw of strategies which integrated all three media of war. The destruction of Hamburg and Dresden only showed that bombers were capable of inflicting enormous damage; they did not show that the terms of warfare had changed irretrievably. The historiography of the Allied air offensive has mostly focused on this gap between the aspirations and the achievements of the airmen, in particular on the failings of the apocalyptic concept of air power which underlay the attacks on cities such as Hamburg and Dresden. Yet, fundamentally justified though this approach may have been, it has itself often created difficulties in perspective, a narrowing of vision. To argue that the airmen did not actually achieve what they set out to achieve, and to leave it at that (as the earliest and most polemical critics of the air war did, at least)[1], is to undervalue the real importance of Allied performance in the air. Such a position obviously underrates the aims and achievements of those who planned and executed the offensives against oil and transport in Germany, for example, in the latter part of the war. Moreover, as John Terraine has pointed out, to separate strategic air power from tactical air power – and to concentrate so much historiographical emphasis on the former – is not only to fall into the trap into which the more immoderate prophets of air power themselves fell, it is also to undervalue the contribution of air power to the war on land and on sea[2]. A realistic judgement of the role played by strategic air power, in other words, can only be made within an overall assessment of the function of air power in the Second World War.

Part of the problem in reaching a balanced view of the Allied Air Offensive has been the tradition among military historians of seeing history in terms of its major personalities. Air Chief Marshal Sir Arthur Harris has become the Douglas Haig of the Second World War, apparently impervious to the evidence that a policy of city-busting, the equivalent of attrition through trench-fighting in the Great War, was not having the desired effect and was preventing precious resources being spent on more profitable targets. Harris himself undoubtedly contributed to the 'Great Man' view of military history in an autobiography, published shortly after the war, in which he dismissed alternative uses of air power as misguided. He was also quite unrepentant in his justification of his claim that the bombers could have won the war on their own, if only he had been given the resources he needed.[3] Certainly, Harris's personality cannot lightly be dismissed in any overview of the Offensive. He possessed a single-mindedness or, alternatively a myopic strategic vision, which made the conduct of the British offensive different in kind from that of the American offensive. As Director of Plans at the Air Ministry in the 1930s, too, he could be said to have contributed more than most to the preparation as well as to the execution of the Offensive. It was Harris, more than any man, who associated strategic bombing in the historical imagination with general area bombing. Finally, however, the Offensive was shaped by – and finally needs to be judged alongside – the economic, political and even cultural circumstances in which it developed. Harris's views did not spring fully-formed out of his own head. He was a product of inter-war reactions to what had happened between 1914 and 1918. Strategic air bombardment grew out of a serious attempt to understand and to deal with the factors at work in keeping an enemy going in twentieth-century warfare. Given the disastrous misunderstandings of these forces in the Great War, which had led to the bloodbath on the Western Front, the aspirations of the strategic airmen were at least necessary and perhaps even laudable, even if the airmen in turn grossly miscalculated. They hoped they had found the strategic stiletto which would pierce the tough and complex armour which sustained advanced industrial nations in war. In fact, finding the weak points in this armour proved to be a great deal more difficult than the early theorists believed. By the end of the war, however, they may well have found them and, in so doing, they may well have accelerated the collapse of Germany. What has been significant about much of the recent writing on the strategic air war is the way in which, as the events themselves have receded into the past, and as the moral contentiousness of the early debate on the offensive has dissipated, the very complicated nature of these socio-economic and cultural factors has assumed more prominence in the argument.

The theory of strategic air power itself was, after all, a product of particular historical circumstances. Militarily, the rationale lay in the need to discover a means by which to avoid the trench deadlock of the Great War.[4] The lesson of 1914–18 appeared to be that advanced industrial nations had developed the capacity to soak up huge military punishment, that military confrontation had become simply the sharp end of a much deeper conflict between economies and societies. Victory depended no longer on the defeat of enemy armed forces *per se*, but rather on the testing of the very infrastructure of the enemy nation, as the collapse of Russia in 1917 and Germany in 1918 seemed to prove. Attrition of these resources, through trench warfare, was only an indirect and inefficient means of defeating the enemy nation. The original attraction of the notion of strategic air power was that aircraft could literally leap over the trench deadlock and aim directly for the industrial resources and for the civilian will to war, upon which the enemy ultimately relied to keep the war effort going. In the latter stages of the Great War, the German Gotha offensive and then the RAF's Independent Air Force appeared to presage a revolutionary breakthrough in military technique. The very fact that the idea had not been fully tested by 1918 only added to its appeal. Along with the tank, the bomber became the Great White Hope of those inter-war radicals who accused Haig and his contemporaries in High Command of a misunderstanding of the real significance of the new technology. What gave this idea particular force in the interwar period, however, was the lessons that could be drawn from the apparent instability of industrial societies in the era of the Great Depression. The supposed ability of the bomber to bring a war directly to the home front, and to win the war there rather than in simply military conflict, made frightening sense in a period of economic dislocation, mass unemployment and political dissent. It was no mere coincidence that Stanley Baldwin chose the year of the General Strike to ask the House of Commons: 'who does not know that, if another war comes, our civilisation will fall with as great a crash as that of Rome?' Civil Defence preparations in Britain were even kept secret until the second half of the 1930s, for fear that the very phrase 'Civil Defence' would spark off a public panic. British pre-war preparations for evacuation and post-raid welfare reveal that government believed that in the next war, if there had to be one, the people themselves would be the real enemy. 'Civil Defence', indeed, was expected to be a policing activity, to control an inherently panicky, even revolutionary, population.[5] Popular literature, as well as film, almost revelled in the fright of the prospect: no less than 133 books were published in English in the inter-war period on the war of the future, the large majority prophesying social revolution as an inevitable consequence of renewed conflict.[6] The bomber, in short, was moulded by the Great Depression. It could even be described as a paradigm of that crisis: technology, like Frankenstein, had produced a monster that would destroy its maker.

Such evidence, of the cultural context in which the notion of air power developed, casts an important sidelight on the central reasoning of the air power theorists – in Britain, at least. The idea that the bomber would be the decisive weapon in any renewed war rested on a depressed faith in the future of advanced industrial society, with its economic recessions and social divisions. If industrial economies were indeed inherently unstable, how could they withstand a rain of high explosive? It was easily argued that an attack on important sectors of the economy could bring the entire structure crashing down under the cumulative weight of its interdependence. Similarly, how could civilian morale take the strain of bombardment, when societies were barely surviving the divisive effects of mass unemployment? One of the only optimistic results that was to emerge from the experience of bombing in the Second World War was the evidence of the extraordinary resilience both of industrial systems and of civilian morale. Although there certainly were to be signs that the civil structures in some bombed cities momentarily faltered under bombing, there is no evidence that this ever came anywhere near being decisive.[7] Rarely did bombing cause more than, at most, a three-month hiccup in production in a city; defeatism among bombed civilians was easily hushed up by the media or police, and rarely continued once the city had ceased to be a target.[8]

Pre-war theorists had underestimated the strengths of the inter-reinforcing networks that underpinned advanced industrial societies, as well as the power of the modern state under threat to weld together a tenacious political consensus. For the British, the fact that they themselves survived the Blitz should perhaps have made them pause in their belief that the Germans would not be able to withstand a similar experience. In fact, the Blitz experience could easily be argued away: the Germans had been under-equipped, in comparison with what Bomber Command would be able to put into the air in a few years, and the Luftwaffe had simply not tried hard nor long enough to ensure success. Britain had been welded together, moreover, by the formation of the Churchill–Labour coalition, and by the first vague promises of a New Jerusalem after the war which began to characterise the 'People's War'.[9] Indeed, the first signs of British wartime radicalism, in 1940, could be said to have been deliberately engineered by government in order to stiffen morale for the expected onslaught from the air. Nazi Germany, on the other hand, was assumed to be politically fragile. Nazism had presented hostages to fortune, by projecting the war to the people as a series of easy victories. Bombing, on the scale intended by the RAF, would thus both cause civilian dissent and also rapidly destabilise an economy believed to be working at full tilt on the war effort.

Such assumptions were not built simply on thin air. A glance at material as different as popular newspapers and secret service estimates of the political situation in Germany shows that they shared a common understanding of the German people as a proud and independent race, many of whom might be prepared to use the pressures produced by the war to rid them of Nazism. In the case of the German economy, it was almost universally believed that the Nazis had been running a 'guns before butter' policy for years, which had left the economy brittle and vulnerable. The Air Staff had already isolated oil supply and transport as two particular bottlenecks in the German economy, though they were clearly impressed by the ability of aircraft to reach so many possible target systems that they felt unable to prioritise these particular ones. On the other hand, it was also understood that it would be years before *any* target systems in Germany could be attacked with real hope of success. Air rearmament for most of the 1930s had been based more on the diplomatic needs of appeasement than on what might be needed in wartime. The RAF had been obliged to accept expansion programmes designed primarily to keep up front-line bomber strength, to a large extent irrespective of quality, in the hope of keeping the Germans negotiating. Not until early 1938 did war preparation as such begin, and then the decision was taken to concentrate on priority for home defence and for Fighter Command.[10] This meant that it was not until 1942 that Bomber Command could even begin to test credibly the validity of it theory.

These prewar assumptions, and the delays in preparations, led to a slip into lazy thinking in the early years of the war. The defeat of France and Britain's expulsion from mainland Europe only encouraged those air power radicals who had argued that victory could come through air power alone. Internecine conflict between the British armed forces for financial aportionment in the interwar years had hardened the RAF's theoretical arteries to the point at which it had been loath to concede that the land and sea forces had any really significant role to play at all. After Dunkirk, the air power radicals were given the chance to prove their point. Once it became clear that bombers could not simply attack any target they chose at will, moreover, because of the reaction of the defence, the argument emerged that they had been attacking the wrong targets anyway. The first attempt to disrupt German oil supply, in 1941, was a case in point. It had been known in Britain before the war that Germany might be crucially short of oil reserves in a long war. Yet the first British offensive against Germany's oil was bedevilled by the bombers' inability to make the deep penetration raids necessary to reach the oil targets without potentially prohibitive losses, by their inability to hit relatively small targets accurately, and by the fact that oil targets proved very difficult to destroy with the low warloads that were all that the early bombers could carry.[11] Germany, moreover, then embarked on a war of conquest in Eastern Europe – for Romanian and Russian oil resources, among other things – which threatened to undermine entirely the argument that Germany really was critically short of oil. Experiences like these, however, only confirmed the views of those like Air Chief Marshal Harris, who believed that bombers would do a much better job hitting what they could hit, namely the centres of large cities, with the aim of generally dislocating the enemy economy and undermining the will to war. Specific target systems, such as oil or transport, were slightingly referred to by Harris as 'panaceas', and rejected by him on the grounds not only that they were extremely difficult to hit effectively, but that they would not have such a devastating effect on Germany as general area bombing.

The Butt Report of August 1941 – which showed that most British bombers were lucky to find the right city to bomb, let alone the right target within that city – would probably have led, in ideal circumstances, to a thorough re-examination of the whole principle of the bomber offensive. In context, however, at a time when Britain had no other way of attacking Germany directly, and when it could still be argued that the offensive was only going through understandable teething problems left by the inadequate preparations of the prewar years, the Report was seen as merely a temporary setback. From 1942 until the end of the war, assumptions about the effectiveness of general area attack were ground down only by the sheer weight of experience and, even then, not wholly irrefutably. Huge devastation was visited on the Ruhr and on Hamburg in 1943, and on Berlin in 1944 and 1945. It was easy to overstate, on photographic evidence especially, the import of such attacks. The continual harassment of the German population, and the impact of 'dehousing' in particular, seemed likely to lead to a progressive debilitation of the German war effort, as the attack switched from city to city, apparently laying waste the entire country.

By 1944, however, Bomber Command had run out of excuses to explain the clear failure of the general area offensive to have any quantifiable effect on Germany. The four-engined heavy bombers ordered in the 1930s began to come into the front line in 1942. Bomber Command was gradually equipped with a larger and ever larger force of heavies, and with bigger and ballistically more sophisticated bombs. By early 1945, the British could put 1,000 Lancasters into the air at the same time, each equipped with up to 20,000 lbs of bombs, including the shattering Tallboy. While the Americans had more bombers than the British in the European theatre, their total bomb-carry was smaller, so that the British continued to dominate the offensive. New technical aids to navigation, moreover, as well as increased flying skills, also meant that the Command could bomb increasingly accurately as well as heavily. The Command enjoyed a good press, too, on the whole. The British public undoubtedly yearned for news that the Germans were reaping the whirlwind, after the years of dismal news stories, and the 1,000 bomber raid on Cologne or the Hamburg fire-storm virtually wrote their own banner headlines. Yet, clear signs of a breakthrough in the air war eluded the British bombers. Certainly, the Germans had been worried: Speer remarked that six more Hamburgs would take Germany out of the war. But the almost devastating effect of the raids on Hamburg could not be repeated in the case of Berlin, a much larger target and deep into enemy territory. Indeed, in the air Battle of Berlin in 1944, and also in the raid on Nuremberg of 31 March 1944, the British bombers appeared to be on the edge of defeat.[12]

For there was another flaw in British air power reasoning, apart from the underestimate of the economic and social reserves of Nazi Germany. Demands for more and better equipment had been met and, even though Bomber Command was to complain that it never got the kind of priority that would have shown its true worth, the fact remains that the British airmen were wrong theoretically, as well as factually, in their view of the application of air power. The argument that the bomber would be the decisive weapon, because it opened the vulnerable heart of a nation to attack, had been articulated to the view that the bomber was also the offensive weapon *par excellence*. Because of the vast cubic airspace available, a defence would never be able to predict accurately an attack. The proposition that had emerged from this belief – formulated in the days before radar and the single-engined cantilever monoplane had revolutionised air defence in the early 1930s – was that the bombers should simply ignore the enemy air force and proceed straight for the vital targets. The airmen had believed that they were involved in a revolution in warfare, not simply in the sense of what was attacked, but also in the method to be employed: in short, by avoiding rather than confronting the enemy armed forces in being, they could by-pass the classical rules of warfare and produce a quicker and more efficient defeat thereby. Although those in charge of procurement before the war were already becoming worried about the new potential of air defence, it took too long for a new generation of bombers to enter the production pipeline for these fears to have any real impact on equipment during the war. The bomber-men took refuge in the belief that air defence had only stolen a march on bomber development, and that the next generation of bombers would redress the balance once more in favour of the bomber.[13] In the meantime, however, they were committed to finding a way through to the target for heavy but relatively lightly-armed bombers. A switch to night bombing, taking dog's leg routes to the targets, dropping metallised paper to white-out enemy radar, attacking in huge masses to overwhelm the defence, all failed to cope with the basic and quite simple problem. Air power was nowhere near capable of delivering a knock-out blow in one raid. Since this meant that aircraft would have to return, night after night, to achieve significant results, it also meant that these targets would become predictable and that fighters would mass to defend them. Bomber Command's dream of knocking Germany out of the war by bombing Berlin 'from end to end', as Harris put it, ended in the RAF losing 1,047 bombers between November 1943 and March 1944, roughly the number of bombers in the average daily front line. It was at this point, in effect, that Bomber Command had clearly failed in its attempt to show that independent air power could win the war virtually on its own by sidestepping the need to win command of the air.

The RAF was not alone in believing that air power was a revolutionary method of war that could only be fought by revolutionary means. It was, however, unique in its view that this involved a repudiation of the classical principle of defeat of the enemy armed forces in being.[14] The Italian General Giulio Douhet had theorised after the Great War that air power would be self-sufficient and decisive in a future war, but he was also clear that a counter-force strategy would be necessary to defeat the enemy air force, as a vital preliminary campaign.[15] The Americans lay somewhere between the two. Though they, too, proved to be misguided in their theory, the Americans' early wartime disasters set in train a sequence of events which was finally to be decisive in the war in the air. The American view was that it would be impossible to achieve command of the air in classical fashion, by aircraft-to-aircraft combat in the air. Such combat would only take place by mutual consent, which made it unlikely that an inferior air force could be brought to battle in the first place. Moreover, any losses incurred in air fighting could soon be topped up by a properly-mobilised war economy. The key to command of the air, therefore, lay in destroying the economic base of enemy air power. The rationale which underlay design concepts like that of the B17 was that bombers, heavily armed in themselves and protected by formation flying, should force their way through the enemy air force to destroy those industrial bases which were the roots of enemy air power. The Americans were also committed, by their designs and by their wish for bombing accuracy, to daylight bombing. Unfortunately, these tactics led to disaster in the first major deep-penetration raids into Germany, aimed at the ball-bearings plant at Schweinfurt.[16] In the aftermath of the very heavy losses endured by the 8th Air Force, it was decided to supplement the self-defending bomber formation with long-range escort fighters. The fact is that the long-range escort fighter had virtually been abandoned by most airmen as a technological dead end. The escort had to give up either manoeuvrability, or speed, or fire-power, or some combination of these, in order to achieve range: in comparable stages of development, therefore, it stood little chance against the fast-climbing, high-speed, heavily-armed, short-range interceptor, as the fate of the Me110 in the Battle of Britain had made clear. It was fortunate for the Allies, however, that the Germans had gambled everything on a short war, giving up their aircraft development programme in favour of the maximum production of a small number of fighter types.[17] As a result, the American long-range escorts, when they appeared, were meeting an outdated generation of interceptors and were consequently able to win mastery of the skies in aircraft-to-aircraft battles in the spring of 1944. This was at just the point when Bomber Command seemed on the verge of losing command of the air at night.

It would be too simplistic simply to dismiss pre-war theory on command of the air, whether British or American, as misguided. True, the value of radar and the potential of the new generation of fighters had not been fully taken on board. It must be remembered, however, that these developments had come very late in the day and remained unproven until 1940, by which time vital decisions on bomber procurement had been made which could not be reversed. No prewar air power would have been justified in basing its procurement policy on the apparently forlorn hope that, at some stage, escorts would be able to take on and defeat interceptors: ultimately, the winning of command of the air by the Allies relied on the Germans not producing a new generation of fighters. It is true, moreover, that the classical principle of command did need to be refined, at least, to take into account what actually happened in the air. If, in the first Schweinfurt raids, the bombers became 'committed to a race between the destruction of the German fighter force in production by the bombers and the destruction of the bombers by the German fighter force in being', as Noble Frankland succinctly put it,[18] it is also true that the American point about the significance of targetting the air force's industrial base still stood. In the series of raids in which the escorts defeated the German interceptors, there would have been no need for the interceptors to risk defeat unless the bombers were aimed at targets the Luftwaffe was bound to defend. In short, the bombers were being used as a bait, but a bait which the interceptors simply could not ignore. Technology had in fact changed things though, admittedly, not as much as the airmen believed. Nor was this uniquely a problem in the air. A similarly complicated situation arose in the Battle of the Atlantic where, in effect, the U-boats were finally defeated because the convoys were used as baited traps, like the bombers en route to Schweinfurt. The U-boats, if they were to perform any useful function at all, had no option but to attack the convoys around which the escorts had grouped in the knowledge that this was the one place where U-boats would certainly be found. What is implied by all this is that, although it may be fair to criticise the airmen for their radicalism, they also deserve some credit for realising that classical principles had been modified by technological change. The classical division of the stages of warfare into, first, winning command and, second, exploiting that military superiority – a conceptual division which had so stymied strategy in the Great War – no longer applied, as such; for it was only by aiming at the economic and/or social base that a battle for command could actually be forced. New weapons systems, such as aircraft and U-boats, did indeed make the social-industrial base vulnerable in a way that had never been true of land warfare, war in one dimension. The airmen and U-boat men both deserve credit for reinstating the principle that battle is not simply a military matter.

In a sense, then, the problem of winning command was overcome by mistake. In attempting to reinforce the defence of the bomber formations, the Americans had stumbled on a way of defeating the Luftwaffe in being. Once the Luftwaffe in being had been overborne, moreover, it was relatively easy to maintain command of the air by attacking the industrial base and the oil supply on which revitalisation of the German air force would depend. Not that winning and maintaining command necessarily made it any easier to decide what the best way to exploit that command. There were still chronic misunderstandings of how economies worked, and how they could be dislocated, to overcome. Economic historians, who have been gradually increasing their grip on Second World War studies since Professor Alan Milward's first spectacular entry into the field, have pointed out that the traditional concentration on the military side of the war does not really show how the war was won and lost. German armed forces were still fighting Russian troops through the streets of Berlin in the last days of the war, and had only been reduced to that state because the German economy had been reduced to rubble. While the economic historians may be criticised for placing strictly military factors too far in the background, they have played a major role in highlighting the significance of what went on below the surface of things, as it were, in planning and administering the capacity to wage total war. It is important to explain, after all, not only that the Allies had an enormous advantage in economic potential, but also to explain how that economic potential was brought to bear in military terms. In spite of the criticisms that have been made of the airmen for their over-reliance on general area bombing and for their misconceptions on command of the air, the economic historians have shown that strategic air power did indeed have a very significant effect on Germany's ability to continue the war. Once the wider misconceptions about air power had been ground down by experience, the way was open for a more sophisticated and telling strategy to emerge. Nevertheless, even then, there was to be a prolonged and disruptive debate on the most efficient use of the bomber.

This much is clear from Richard Overy's *The Air War*, the first book to make digestible the kind of statistics that had made *The United States Strategic Bombing Survey* a set of documents more often quoted than read, and more often read than understood. Overy's was an enormously ambitious book but, reading it, one became aware that it needed to be, simply to describe and to explain the complexity of the task that faced the airmen in their aim of shortening the war by undermining the German economy. It becomes clear, reading Overy alongside the spate of recent works on the development of the German economy under Nazism and during the war, just why the Allied air planners took so long to light on target systems that were likely to have a real effect on the German economy as a whole.[19] Industrial intelligence was a much more difficult business than military intelligence, in the sense that small snippets of information could not easily be built into the necessary overall picture nearly as reliably. The most reliable source of military intelligence, moreover, namely Ultra, did not carry a great deal of economic interest until very late in the war. It did not help matters, either, that responsibility for economic intelligence was divided not only between the Allies but between the armed forces and the Ministry of Economic Warfare. These factors made it very difficult to build up an overall picture of what was happening within the German economy, to gauge the relative importance of the various sectors, and then to judge which of these most crucial sectors were actually likely to be vulnerable to air attack. Early in the war, the intelligence community overestimated the degree of mobilisation of the German war economy, and thus overestimated the immediate effect of any disruption of war supply. In the years of the 'Blitzkrieg economy', the minor disruptions to war production caused by bombing could easily be made good from the fat of the consumer economy. Later, the planners failed to pick up the implications of Speer's organisation of the total war economy, and thus underestimated what could be achieved. Paradoxically, it was only when the German war economy was working at maximum efficiency that the system was inflexible enough to be affected by bombardment.

Another factor which had to be borne in mind in target selection was overall Allied strategy. The Casablanca Directive of January 1943 was vague and unspecific about the timing of the proposed invasion of Europe, and about the role that air power should play in the preparation. The Allied leaders proposed that the combined air forces should undertake 'the progressive destruction and dislocation of the German military, industrial and economic system, and the undermining of the morale of the German people to a point where their capacity for armed resistance is fatally weakened'.[20] Harris and Spaatz saw the Directive as carte blanche to continue a general offensive, while those arguing for a selective offensive were divided over what needed to be achieved. If the invasion was to take place sooner rather than later, then what was required was an immediate cut in German output: this would entail targetting finished products or final assembly plants to undermine the German military's short-term ability to resist the invasion. When the invasion became imminent, of course, much of the strategic bomber force would be required to interdict the beachead. If, on the other hand, the invasion was still some way off, then it would be more worthwhile to aim for a radical undermining of German capacity to continue the war after the invasion. In other words, different target systems and different results were required, depending on the date that would be set for D-Day.

The preparations for D-Day also created command problems. Both Harris and Spaatz hoped to win the war by air power alone before the invasion, and neither was willing to submit their forces to the overall direction of a Supreme Allied Commander who, as an Army man, would be likely to use air power simply as a tactical adjunct to the land forces. The appointment of Air Chief Marshal Sir Arthur Tedder as Deputy Supreme Commander was an inspired choice. He had had perhaps more experience than anyone on the Allied side of land – air co-operation, with Montgomery in the desert, yet he largely retained the confidence of the exponents of independent air power.[21] The losses that RAF Bomber Command began suffering in the months leading up to D-Day, moreover, took the wind out of Harris' sails, thus making him more pliable on the formulation of pre-invasion plans. It would be difficult to question the quite basic significance of air power to the invasion, in spite of the claims of the French Resistance to have prepared the ground more thoroughly. Overall, it has to be said that, without the almost total command of the air by daylight over France that had been achieved by the American air force, the invasion would have been quite impossible. It was a difficult enough task landing the huge land force with the minimal opposition experienced on most beaches, without the havoc which could have been caused by an undefeated Luftwaffe. D-Day could possibly have taken place without the French Resistance, but it could not possibly have taken place without command of the air. The invasion commanders could also feel confident, given the relatively simple lines of command, of a direct response from the bombers: the effectiveness of the French underground, on the other hand, was always likely to be difficult to gauge, by the very nature of their clandestine operations.

There has also been considerable debate about the relative merits of targeting oil or transport in the latter stages of the war. The Americans believed that an attack on oil would be the surest way not only of maintaining command of the air but also of breaking the back of the German economy. Given the fact that the Germans had never developed a synthetic lubricant, and that they were losing their captured natural oil resources in the East as the Red Army advanced, theirs was a seductive argument. Nevertheless, SHAEF was of the opinion that an attack on transport would have a more immediate effect on the German resistance to the invasion, and a decision was taken to concentrate attack on French transport targets for the invasion period. The way in which oil came back onto the menu is a typical example of the problems that the flexibility of air power produced. The American 15th Air Force, quietly undermining the priorities agreed, in April 1944 decided to attack transport targets in the vicinity of Ploesti, in Romania, the site of the most important German-controlled natural oil resources. The panic of the Germans at this apparent attack on their oil was picked up on Ultra and used to lay aside the decision to concentrate entirely on transport. The effects of the Oil Plan were indeed marked. Aircraft fuel in Germany was reduced from 160,000 tons in January 1944 to 54,000 by June and 25,000 by December. Synthetic production by hydrogenation was reduced as a whole from 336,000 to 56,000 tons over the year.[22]

On the other hand, the apparent effectiveness of interdiction bombing in the tactical sphere, in isolating the beachhead from German reinforcement, gave added weight to the views of those who believed that transportation bombing could also have a devastating effect on Germany on the strategic level.[23] Tedder's conviction on this point was to be crucial. Yet, given the size and diversity of the German transport system, decisions still had to be made on which part of this system was most crucial, militarily and industrially, to the German war effort. Should it be bridges, waterways or railways? If it were railways, should it be locomotives or marshalling yards? Any such decision also had to be balanced against the operational capacity of the bomber forces, huge though they now were. Harris, for one, argued that Bomber Command was not capable of the kind of pinpoint accuracy that most transport targets required. He was, however, to be proved wrong. Experience and technical innovation had made it possible for a large part of his force to bomb as accurately as only specially-trained squadrons could have done previously, such as 617 squadron in the Dams raid. Recently, Alfred Mierzejewski has argued persuasively that oil was not in fact as basic to German industry as was coal at this point in the war, that coal distribution was utterly dependent on the German railways, and that it was the assault on the railway marshalling yards in particular that brought Germany to her knees. Speer, in his monumental efforts to enlarge German industrial output, had unwittingly provided a vulnerable point in the huge interlinking mesh of production. Mierzejewski has even gone so far as to suggest that the rail/coal nexus was the real 'panacea' for strategic air power, a potentially war-winning campaign which was only narrowly superseded in eventual overall importance by the advance of the land armies. As it was, the German railways' attempt to support the Ardennes counter-offensive led to such a crushing attack by the bombers that the system was effectively destroyed, leading to the collapse of the German economy and, inescapably, the end of all organised resistance.[24]

Yet the claims of the oil offensive are not so lightly to be dismissed, if not for its effect on industry then certainly for its effect on the German Army and what was left of the Air Force, in their attempt to withstand the double-advance from East and West through the summer and autumn of 1944. Less creditable, however, is the continuation at this stage of the war of attempts to break civilian morale. Dresden had been reserved as a potential target earlier in the war, to be hit when victory seemed imminent, as a demonstration of the inexorable power available to the Allies which would, it was hoped, hasten the German collapse. There can be little question, after the Hamburg firestorm nearly two years previously, that the planners knew exactly what would happen. As in the case of the decision to drop the A-bombs on Japan, of course, such apparent cold bloodedness needs to be contextualised: it had been a long, vicious, bloody and exhausting war, and everyone wanted to finish it as quickly as possible. Nevertheless, it is still difficult to resist the suspicion that the air power radicals were anxious to have one more attempt at proving that the bomber was the decisive weapon, and that the resources used against Dresden would have had more effect if they had been aimed either at oil or at transport.[25]

The general question still remains whether the resources that were put into the strategic bomber forces could have been more usefully employed in direct support of the land and sea wars. The British airmen, in particular, were prone to fight their own corner, arguably at the expense of overall Allied war priorities. This appears to have been particularly true in the case of the sea war, after the long-standing feud between the Air Ministry and the Admiralty over the control of the Fleet Air Arm. The RAF, determined to maintain the maximum possible force of bombers, fought the Admiralty case for diverting at least some of long-range aircraft production for duty in the Atlantic. The airmen's argument was that the best way to defeat the U-boats was to target their production, which was a job for the strategic air offensive, whereas the Admiralty held the view that direct support of the convoys was more important. It was later to become clear that the use of long-range aircraft to close the 'air-gap' in the Atlantic was in fact decisive in the defeat of the U-boats. Priority for the strategic air offensive may actually have prolonged the defensive stance that the Allies had to adopt in the sea war and thus, in effect, have delayed the American build-up in Europe for D-Day. Airmen actually sank more U-boats than did the seamen: the question is not so much whether aircraft were important to the sea war, but whether the administrative separation of the Admiralty and Air Ministry had bred mutually exclusive war priorities. The wartime Ministry of Defence, and the national emergency, undoubtedly helped to break down the animosities and the mutual ignorance of the interwar years, but it was to take the much more thorough reorganisation of the post-war years to pick up on the lessons for strategic integration that such arguments exposed. There are fewer grounds for criticism in the case of the land war. Although the RAF could be criticised for attempting to play too independent a role during the Battle of France, the force did learn to integrate more effectively with the land forces, not just in the tactical role that aircraft played in the desert war, but in the combination of tactical and strategic roles that they played before, during and after the invasion of Europe.

The problem, from the very inception of air power, had always been that aircraft could hit so many targets beyond the range of land and sea forces that the argument for administrative separation was almost insuperable. Administrative separation, however, was likely to breed strategic independence. At the same time, the tactical air needs of the land and sea forces were real enough. This was especially true in the case of the land forces when faced with an enemy like Germany, where air power was primarily oriented towards co-operation with the army rather than independent action. It was understandable that the Allied armies should have felt themselves disadvantaged in the early years of the war, when faced with Blitzkrieg. Yet, such an argument ignores the advantages that the separate organisation of air power brought. In spite of the early Blitzkrieg victories, it is clear that Germany ultimately did suffer for the lack of a long-range heavy bomber force, particularly in the war against the Soviet Union.[26] The limits applied to air strategy by the Germans, moreover, gave low production priority to the Luftwaffe, allowing the Allies the numerical preponderance which eventually made command of the air possible, and which in turn produced an irreversible relative decline in industrial output. The truth is that the very categorisations 'tactical' and 'strategic' blended and became confused with the advent of air power. What was required was fewer assertions of independence and priority, and more flexibility and co-operation. It remains an unfortunate fact that at the end of the war the larger part of the heavy bomber forces, about 65 per cent of the total available bomb load, remained adamantly targeted on general area bombing while the Western Allies' land forces were struggling through France, their advance indubitably aided by the selective and specific bombing of the other 35 per cent.

Yet these were lessons that had to be learned. The Second World War was, after all, the first war in which air power had played a significant role. The experience of the thousands of years that had shaped land and sea warfare had to be telescoped into less than 30 in the case of military flight. These 30 years had been characterised by an almost incessant battle for control of the air by the surface forces, which had led the airmen to overdramatise the impact of air power in their bid to retain independence. The limited experience of the Great War had been no basis on which to build theories, yet theories had to be built to cope with the technological development of military flight thereafter. To a large extent, it was only to be expected that those theories would be conditioned by the dominant sense of crisis – in economic, social, political and cultural matters – that pervaded the interwar years.

It is fair to say, too, that without the failures of the early years of the strategic offensive, the successes of the last years would not have been possible. Combat experience not only produced the trained crews and the flying aids that made pin-point accuracy everyday practice in 1944 and 1945, it also produced the larger bombs and the refinements in target selection which were to prove so effective in the attack against the German transport system and oil industry. Those early attacks also brought to the foreground the whole question of the need for command of the air, and demanded a solution. It was, anyway, almost inconceivable that the bombers could simply have sat on their airfields while there was no other way for the Western Allies to attack Germany directly. Not only did the bombers help to ease the problem of the morale-builders in the West in the early years, they also tied down material and personnel in Germany, which consequently could not be used in the campaign in the East. When the time finally came to launch the second front, the bombers were able to play a very significant role in undermining the ability of Germany to resist. Even at this stage, it is true, no firm decisions could be reached on the most effective way of applying air power. Nevertheless, air power was very effective, even if it could have been even more effective. The bombers did not win the war on their own, as the air power radicals had assumed, but that is an unreal measure against which to judge their achievement. Neither is it the point simply that the war could not have been won without them, a sort of necessary evil, for their contribution was quite basic to the victory in the West.

NOTES

1. See, for example, Sir G. Dickens, *Bombing and Strategy* (London: Sampson Low Marston, 1946).
2. Terraine, *The Right of the Line* (London: Hodder & Stoughton, 1985).
3. Sir Arthur Harris, *Bomber Offensive* (London: Collins, 1947). See also D. Saward, *Bomber Harris: The Authorised Biography* (London: Sphere, 1984); A. Andrews, *The Air Marshals* (New York, 1970); C. Messenger *Bomber Harris and the Strategic Bombing Offensive* (London: Arms & Armour Press, 1984).
4. On the development of air power in the Great War, see N. Jones, *The Origins of Strategic Bombing* (London: Kimber 1973); M. Smith, 'The Tactical and Strategic Application of Air Power on the Western Front', in P. Liddle (ed.), *Home Fires and Foreign Fields* (London: Brassey's 1985); M. Cooper, *The Birth of Independent Air Power* (London: Allen & Unwin, 1986).
5. See T. O'Brien, *Civil Defence* (London, 1955); P. Kyba, *Covenants without Swords: Public Opinion and British Defence Policy, 1931–1935* (Waterloo, ON: Wilfrid Laurier University Press, 1985); U. Bialer, *The Shadow of the Bomber* (London: Royal Historical Society, 1980).
6. See I.F. Clarke, *Voices Prophesying War* (Oxford: Oxford University Press, 1966); P. Miles and M. Smith, *Cinema, Literature and Society: Elite and Mass Culture in Interwar Britain* (London: Croom Helm, 1987).

7. Compare T. Harrisson, *Living Through the Blitz* (London: Collins, 1976), and M. Steinert, *Hitler's War and the Germans* (Athens, OH: University of Ohio Press, 1976).

8. I.L. Janis, *Air War and Emotional Stress* (New York, 1976); F.C. Iklé, *The Social Impact of Bomb Destruction* (Norman, OK: University of Oklahoma Press, 1958).

9. A. Calder, *The People's War* (London, 1969); P. Addison, *The Road to 1945* (London: Jonathan Cape, 1975).

10. M. Smith, *British Air Strategy between the Wars* (Oxford: Oxford University Press, 1984); H. Montgomery Hyde, *British Air Policy between the Wars* (London: Heinemann, 1976); N.H. Gibbs, *Grand Strategy*, Vol. 1 (London: HMSO, 1976); N. Jones, *The Beginning of Strategic Air Power: A History of the British Bomber Force, 1923–1939* (London: Frank Cass, 1987).

11. Sir C. Webster and N. Frankland, *The Strategic Air Offensive against Germany* (London: HMSO, 1961), Vol. 1, pp.155–66.

12. The best (by far) single volume on the British offensive is still N. Frankland, *The Bombing Offensive against Germany: Outline and Perspective* (London: Faber 1965). See also N. Frankland, *Bomber Offensive* (London: Macdonald, 1970); Sir C. Webster and N. Frankland, *The Strategic Air Offensive against Germany* (London: HMSO, 1961). Following very much in Webster and Frankland's footsteps come M. Hastings, *Bomber Command* (London: Michael Joseph, 1979); R. Jackson, *Before the Storm* (London: Barker, 1972); *Storm from the Skies* London: Barker, 1974; A. Verrier, *The Bomber Offensive* (London: Batsford, 1968). See also, R.V. Jones, *Most Secret War* (London: Hamilton, 1978); Solly Zuckerman, *From Apes to Warlords* (London: Hamilton, 1978); R. Beaumont, 'The Bomber Offensive as a Second Front', *Journal of Contemporary History* (1987), 3–14.

13. Smith, Ch. 8.

14. Smith, Ch. 2. See also, B. Brodie, *Strategy in the Missile Age* (Princeton, NJ: Princeton University Press, 1959).

15. G. Douhet, *The Command of the Air* (London: Faber, 1943).

16. W.F. Craven and J.L. Cate, *The Army Air Forces in World War Two*, 7 vols. (Chicago, IL: University of Chicago Press, 1943, 1947–58); T.M. Coffey, *Decision over Schweinfurt* (New York: David McKay, 1977); R.A. Freeman, *The Mighty Eighth* (New York: Doubleday, 1970); A. Galland, *The First and the Last* (New York: Ballantine, 1968); J. Sweetman, *Disaster in the Skies* (New York: Ballantine, 1981).

17. D. Irving, *The Rise and Fall of the Luftwaffe* (London: Weidenfeld & Nicolson, 1973); I. Homze, *Arming the Luftwaffe* (Lincoln, NB: University of Nebraska Press, 1976); M. Schliephake, *The Birth of the Luftwaffe* (London: Allan, 1971).

18. Frankland, *Bombing Offensive*, p.76.

19. R. Overy, *The Air War* (London: Europa, 1980); 'Hitler's War and the German Economy', *Economic History Review* (1982), 272–91; W. Deist, *The Reichswehr and Nazi Rearmament* (London: Macmillan, 1981); A.S. Milward, *The German Economy at War* (London: Athlone Press, 1965); H. Rumpf, *The Bombing of Germany* (London: Muller, 1963); *The United States Strategic Bombing Survey*, 27 vols. (New York: Garland, 1947).

20. Reprinted in Webster and Frankland, Vol. 4, Appendix 23, p.273.

21. See Arthur William Tedder, *Air Power in War* (London: Hodder & Stoughton, 1947); *With Prejudice* (London: Cassell, 1966).

22. W.W Rostow, *Pre-Invasion Bombing Strategy* (Austin, TX: University of Texas Press, 1981); R.C. Cooke and R.C. Nesbitt, *Target Hitler's Oil* (London: Kimber, 1985).

23. H.D. Lytton, 'Bombing Policy in the Rome and Pre-Normandy Invasion Aerial Campaigns in World War Two', *Military Affairs* (1983), 53–8.

24. A.C. Mierzejewski, *The Collapse of the German War Economy* (Chapel Hill: University of North Carolina Press, 1988).

25. D. Irving, *The Destruction of Dresden* (London: Kimber, 1963).

26. M. Cooper, *The German Air Force* (London: Jane's, 1981); Air Ministry, *The Rise and Fall of the Luftwaffe* (London: HMSO, 1974); K. Bartz, *Broken Swastika* (London: Kimber, 1956); C. Bekker, *The Luftwaffe War Diaries* (London: Corgi, 1969); H. Boog, *Die Deutsche Luftwaffenfuhrung* (Stuttgart: Deutsche Verlag-Anstalt, 1982); R. Overy, 'From Uralbomber to Amerikabomber', *Journal of Strategic Studies* (1978); 'Hitler and Air Strategy', *Journal of Contemporary History* (1980).

The North African Campaign 1940–43: A Reconsideration

LUCIO CEVA

The encounter between Italian and British forces, and then between Italian, German and British troops, in the Mediterranean and in Libya resulted from early wartime strategic designs and from their subsequent adaptation following the unexpected collapse of France in June 1940. Originally the British and French wished to chase the Italians out of Africa chiefly in order to be able to pursue in safety their plans for a Balkan offensive which aimed to secure control of Rumenian petroleum supplies – the only ones which were still within the operational grasp of German land forces.[1] For the British, this aggressive design survived the defeat of France; however, they also already had considerable naval forces in this theatre. Thus at first the Middle East seemed a suitable theatre in which to win victories which would be useful not only to raise morale at home but also to dislodge the Italians from positions which, if utilised on a grander scale by the Germans, would pose a threat to major imperial interests. Later, after the German blitzkrieg had been unleashed in the East in June 1941, North Africa became the only theatre where, with growing help from the Americans, victories could be won over land forces which it was difficult for the Axis to augment.[2] What was at issue was no longer so much the need to protect the petroleum supplies at Abadan, now possibly threatened from the north, but rather that of winning welcome victories either in order to profit from the respite provided by BARBAROSSA or, so long as the war in the East continued, to give some assistance to Russia without, however, becoming involved in battles of attrition which would bleed the British armies once more just as they had been bled at the Somme and at Passchendaele.[3] There were, of course, other reasons behind the adoption of this strategy, among them that of freeing the Mediterranean from Axis control and thereby saving shipping by ending the need to sail around Africa. However, this was a debatable question since it very quickly became clear that the tonnage involved in this circumnavigation to feed the quest for victory in Libya was greater than that which would have been required on the same route for the mere defence of the Middle and Far East.[4]

For Fascist Italy the uncertainties of foreign policy at first impeded the formulation of a strategy for North Africa, although from 1937–38 the personal fancies of the governor of Libya, Italo Balbo, and of the army chief of staff, general Alberto Pariani, had been directed against Egypt. A defensive mentality prevailed in the autumn of 1939 while Italy awaited the outcome of the contest between Germany and the western democracies. On 10 June 1940 Mussolini entered the war, assuming that the collapse not merely of France but also of Great Britain was imminent. Offensive ambitions were revived – although detailed strategic plans were lacking – as Italy sought to obtain territorial pawns in Africa and the Balkans which she could use to her advantage in the political negotiations which would end the war. Instead, however, there followed the failure in Greece and a series of resounding defeats on land and at sea which swallowed up the Ethiopian empire and the whole of Cyrenaica to the point that, had the Germans not intervened, the spring of 1941 would have resembled for Fascist Italy the collapse of September 1943. However, German aid was speedily forthcoming; its purpose was to shore up Mussolini's political position by resolving the Balkan situation and avoiding the loss of North Africa. Libya might then have some value in exploiting in the Middle East the victory which Germany expected to win over the USSR. When the vision of destroying Russia in a single campaign collapsed, German strategy in the Mediterranean maintained its defensive character. There were offensive actions which were sometimes lively, such as the counter-offensives of April 1941 and of January–February 1942, the plans to attack Malta, and the advance to El Alamein, but they were chance tactical occurrences which resulted from initiatives taken by local commanders (by Rommel, but also by Cavallero and Kesselring) and which won only intermittant support from Hitler, who was firmly convinced that a decisive victory could only be won by crushing Russia.[5]

In the summer of 1940 there were considerable numbers of Italians in Libya, but they lacked mobility: 236,000 men (of whom 28,000 were native troops) formed 14 divisions which in turn made up two armies, 5th army in the west and 10th army in the east. The materiel available to meet all the defensive and offensive requirements of the vast colony amounted to some 1,500 elderly guns, 300 obsolete light tanks which were weaker even than the British bren-gun carriers,[6] 300 aeroplanes and fewer than 8,000 trucks. Against the eastern portion of this force, the British in Egypt had at their disposal some 50,000 men and 205 land-based aeroplanes. Of the 86,000 men spread across the territories under Wavell's command, which also included Palestine, Cyprus, Malta, the Sudan, Kenya, Somaliland and Aden, the best trained and most mobile was the 7th armoured division, which comprised over 300 armoured cars, light tanks and cruiser tanks, as well as numerous bren-gun carriers.[7] During the first weeks of the campaign, while nothing occurred in the west, British tanks and armoured cars carried out bold incursions into Libya to which the Italians reacted by transferring troops from the 5th to the 10th army, equipping it in all with some 2,500 motor vehicles and sending over from Italy 70 medium M-11 tanks which were all that was then available.[8]

Under direct orders from Mussolini, Graziani began his advance on 13 September 1940, with great reluctance. Seven Italian and Libyan divisions pushed forward to Sidi Barrani, 60 miles from the frontier, while the British limited themselves to spoiling actions in reply. Graziani then deployed his marching infantry divisions in strong points facing east and south and vainly requested that he be sent some motorised transport at the very least. Mussolini rejected this appeal since he wished to use what resources he had for an attack he planned on Yugoslavia. Meanwhile Wavell received significant reinforcement in the shape of 31,000 motorised troops, 120 guns, 275 tanks (among them 50 Matildas and 100 Cruisers), 60 armoured cars and 150 aeroplanes. Among the latter were a number of Hurricanes which outclassed all the Italian fighters then available. This enabled Wavell to consolidate the Western Desert Force under the command of general Richard O'Connor.

The succession of events by which Cyrenaica was overrun in 58 days (9 December 1940–6 February 1941), with the capture of 130,000 Italian troops and 845 guns and the destruction of 380 light and medium tanks, is well known. Together with the contemporaneous conquest of Ethiopia, this was the greatest land victory won by the British commonwealth during the whole of the war in the sense that other, more decisive victories such as El Alamein were not proportionally as great and were achieved with aid from the United States, which grew in volume and significance as the war continued. What then were the causes of this victory?

As far as the British are concerned, it was due above all else to the excellent training given to the Anglo-Indian and Australian infantry and to the 7th armoured division which had been formed by Percy Hobart, one of the best generals of the Royal Tank Corps. Many of its units had been in Egypt since 1935 and had acquired invaluable desert experience under the guidance of RTC officers such as Vyvyan Pope; and their aggression and enterprise, which spread to new formations such as 7th RTR, was also of very great value to infantry generals such as Wavell and O'Connor, who were among the most brilliant in the British army. No British armoured formation which reached North Africa during the years that followed, no matter how valorous, could boast a level of training equal to that of 7th armoured.

Graziani, for his part, could call on a large force of marching infantry who were of little use in this theatre, somewhat fewer than 3,000 lorries and a few ineffective tanks. However, he did have artillery in abundance and during the summer, at a time when the British Cruiser tanks were inferior in numbers (though superior in quality) to the Italian M-11s, he could have motorised one or two infantry divisions (rather than trying to move them all together on foot), supported them with artillery and tried to advance in depth. Perhaps he would not have conquered Egypt but, from the moment when he no longer dared to refuse Mussolini's orders to attack, he would at least have put up a better show. By December the means at his disposal were much too inferior to those of the British to do so. The armour plating of the British Matildas was too thick to be penetrated by most Italian guns, and the A-9 and A-13 Cruiser tanks were superior to any Italian tank. A 150-horsepower engine propelled the 12-ton A-9 at 25 miles per hour, while the 13 3/4-ton A-13 sped along at a good 30 miles per hour thanks to its 340-horsepower motor. All the British tanks, including the A-10 which was no faster than the Italian tanks, were armed with a 40-mm gun with a muzzle velocity of 2,650 feet per second firing a solid armour-piercing shot weighing 2.4 pounds; by contrast the Italian M-13 mounted an inferior 47/32 gun with a muzzle velocity of 2,060 feet per second which could penetrate only 38 mm of armour plating at 750 yards and scarcely 32 mm at 1,000 yards, compared 46 mm and 40 mm respectively by the British gun.[9] As far as the Italian tanks were concerned, the M-11, described by Ogorkiewicz as 'in fact, about the worst design of the period' was armed with a 37-mm gun in a sponson, lacked a radio, and could travel at no more than 20 mph.[10] The M-13, which appeared in significant numbers only in the last phase of the campaign, was even slower at 19 mph and was described by the British as 'slow, unhandy, uncomfortable, and unreliable' although it mounted in its turret 'a good 47 mm gun'.[11]

However, the real trump card for the British was the Matilda tank. Italian artillerymen who encountered it for the first time on 9 December 1940 at Nibeiwa fought against it with great bravery. An English combatant gave this description of the scene after the battle: 'The Italian and Libyan dead were everywhere. The guns were piled around with empty cases where men had fired to the very last. The Italians were a pushover afterwards, but they fought like hell at Nibeiwa.'[12] Thereafter this tank, which was practically invulnerable, created an inferiority complex in the Italians which still obtained at Bardia, where there were 26 Matildas, and at Tobruk, where there were only 16. At Bardia, in the only part of the field where the Matildas did not appear (the sector attacked by the 17th Australian brigade), the Italians proved in practice to be tough opposition.[13]

At Beda Fomm there were no Matildas, but by now Italian morale had collapsed. Although there were four times as many M-13s as British Cruisers, the Italian tanks 'came along in packets, instead of in a concentrated body, and kept near the road, whereas the British tanks skilfully manoeuvred to gain fire-positions where their hulls were concealed and protected by folds in the ground'.[14] However, it should be borne in mind that the M-13s, fresh from the factory, not having been run-in, almost all without radios and afflicted with teething troubles like all new machines, were in the hands of troops who had had at best one week to train on them at Bracciano.

Naturally the poor show put up by the Italian forces provided an opportunity for some colourful and exaggerated explanations for their failures, notably that their soldiers had been overfed. The journalist Alan Moorehead, who followed the British rearguard nourishing himself at the mess tables abandoned by the Italian commanders, first launched this idea, and it has been considered so amusing that even serious historians have on occasions repeated it to enliven their pages.[15] Perhaps not all of them were aware of the fact that in Latin countries wine is generally both more popular and less expensive than beer and that in Italy pasta and tomato sauce are the foods of the poor. A few good bottles, some parmesan cheese or some dried vegetables may well have been found in rear command posts, but certainly not at the front.[16]

In their turn, the Italians envied the 'spartan' diet of British generals which concluded with 'an occasional dram of whiskey', not to mention the tinned peaches, corned beef and superior cigarettes enjoyed by the English.[17] Italian infantrymen and tank units fed on tinned meat and water thick with the traces of petrol, as sometimes happened in some British units.[18] But Italian tinned meat was always bully beef, and never included either sausages or stew.[19] The economic blockade and logistic strangulation were such that the Italians had to abandon the custom followed by all armies during the 1914–18 war of encouraging the men before an attack by distributing alcohol and chocolate.[20] But when, at El Alamein and then in Tunisia, close infantry combat became common, Italians recall the strong smell of alcohol emanating from their attackers, from whom they sometimes succeeded in 'liberating'hip-flasks of rum or whisky.[21] As to chocolate, the British sometimes even gave it to prisoners.[22]

The sobriety of the Italian soldier was not a special virtue; it was a direct reflection of the centuries-old privation experienced by the working classes. It is, however, unfortunately the case that there was a great disparity in treatment between officers and ordinary soldiers in the Italian forces, not least in the matter of rations; once again, this reflected social distinctions which the Anglo-Saxons, like the Germans, had already eliminated from their armies and perhaps in part from their civil societies also.[23] But of necessity these differences tended to disappear in the most forward units, whilst they often ruled at the rear.

It is certainly true that the British official historian general Playfair attributes low Italian morale in Libya to 'poor food'.[24] But the old legend may be fated to live on because such embellishments, like the historiography of the war itself, are the prerogative of the victors.

We shall now return to the German intervention in North Africa in the spring of 1941 and to the dramatic upset by which, unexpectedly, not only Tripoli but the whole of Egypt seemed endangered. Among the many questions which surround this moment of the war – the responsibility for having neglected the threat posed by Rommel notwithstanding the information available through Ultra, the decision to assist Greece and thereby give up the chance to take Tripoli which might perhaps still have been possible, etc. – we shall consider only one.[25]

Ever since 1950 it has been claimed that a decisive German commitment to the Mediterranean theatre, which would have been better in the summer of 1940 but which could still have succeeded in the spring of 1941, would have given Hitler victory.[26] However, other scholars have dismissed this hypothesis.[27] Van Creveld, in his well-known study, has instead sought to demonstrate that the Germans never had the logistic capability adequately to reinforce the North African front and that it is therefore pointless to hypothesise about the degree of decisiveness of a non-existent alternative.[28] Even this thesis is not entirely acceptable. Van Creveld only considers the reinforcement of Rommel by way of the Libyan ports, but the real alternative, up until the moment when Operation BARBAROSSA rendered it impossible, would have been an investment in the entire Mediterranean theatre, and not merely the eastern portion of it, by crossing Spain and conquering Gibraltar. Moreover, even if we consider only the eastern Mediterranean, then up until spring 1941 the landbound advance into Libya would have been of only secondary importance if there had also been a major concentration of the Luftwaffe in that theatre accompanied by airborne operations which made good use of the Iraqi and Syrian cards which Germany held. This possibility evaporated with BARBAROSSA, but it was rightly feared by Churchill: 'These troops [German parachutists] were the very kind needed to overrun large wavering regions where no serious resistance would have been encountered.'[29]

For the rest, in war the most carefully calculated plans can fail through the unforeseen collapse of a detachment, an error by a commander, and the like: one thinks of the locally-determined consequences which could have followed if Tobruk had fallen in April 1941 or if the 1st South African division had been destroyed at Gazala on 15–16 June 1942. Nor does the belief, based on German sources, that a shift towards Turkey and the Dardanelles in 1940–41 would have resulted in Russian intervention seem wholly convincing.[30] Apart from the fact that Russia was careful not to intervene when Germany occupied Bulgaria, despite the fact that it had been openly claimed by Stalin and Molotov in diplomatic meetings a few months earlier, there is the problem of determining whether the development of a 'peripheral' war in the Mediterranean and Middle East would have allowed Germany if not to have avoided the collision with Russia, then at least to have confronted it from a stronger position thanks to possession of the Romanian petroleum supplies and the probable collaboration of Turkey.[31]

This is not the place in which to pursue such theoretical hypotheses. Instead let us turn to the African campaign as it unfolded after February 1941 when the British lost, by a matter of days or even hours, the opportunity to close it with the conquest of Tripoli.

The 23 months between 22 June 1941 and 13 May 1943 saw the mounting commitment of Britain's imperial resources, with ever-increasing support from the United States, in the attempt to defeat two or three small German divisions and Italian forces which were at that time little fewer in number than their adversaries but only modestly equipped. They also witnessed the efforts made by these same German and Italian units to turn the situation around and then latterly to defend themselves for as long as possible.

With the failure of Wavell's last counter-offensives (BREVITY and BATTLEAXE), there followed a period of preparation. For the Axis it was a matter of surviving in the expectation of being able to take the offensive once again when Hitler had eliminated the USSR and would be in a position to strike at the Middle East from the spurs of the Caucasus and Anatolia – which would be in the autumn of 1941, according to official forecasts. Meanwhile Rommel wanted to storm Tobruk, an undertaking which the Italians viewed with some pessimism in view of the progress of the 'battle of the convoys', in which Italian ships were being sent to the bottom in ever-increasing numbers first by aeroplanes and submarines and later by a division of British cruisers (K Force) based at Malta.

The throttling of Italy's sea lines of communication with North Africa was assisted by the decription, through ULTRA, of Italian radio traffic which revealed to the British the departure, nature and route of every convoy and even of every lone ship. Today everyone knows that the 'Enigma' cipher machine given to the Italian navy by the Germans guarded no secrets from the British, unlike the more humble national ciphers.[32] Naturally the stories of the deciphering of Enigma material through ULTRA could continue endlessly, and there already exists an extensive literature on this topic in addition to the multi-volume British official history. Without penetrating any more deeply into these issues, we may note that one of the consequences of ULTRA was to set Italians and Germans against one another much more strongly than had already happened spontaneously. Every time that ULTRA gave the British advance warning of Rommel's plans (at Alam el Halfa in August 1942, and again at Medenine in March 1943) the British spread rumours that the plans had been leaked by senior Italian officers. This led to considerable squabbles between the two Axis allies.[33]

The systematic attacks that were made on Italian convoys during the summer and autumn of 1941 formed part of the preparations for a great offensive promised to Churchill by Auchinleck, the new commander in the Middle East, with the aim of obtaining victory while Germany was still preoccupied with the Russian campaign. Churchill kept insisting that

Auchinleck should attack quickly, but Auchinleck delayed until the autumn in order to be sure of a crushing superiority over his opponent. In particular, he wanted numerical parity in respect of the Italian tanks and a superiority of 50 per cent (that is, an advantage of three to two) over the German tanks. By November 1941 there were 723 British tanks ready for action: so, after deducting 146 to set against the same number of Italian machines (M-13s), the remaining 577 gave Auchinleck a superiority of 3.3 to one over the 173 German tanks which were fully equipped and ready for battle. Churchill did not appreciate Auchinleck's request, remarking that 'Generals only enjoy such comforts in Heaven. And those who demand them do not always get there.'[34] In fact the degree of superiority produced by Anglo-American re-stocking applied not only to tanks but also to aeroplanes, motor vehicles and artillery. Only in numbers of men was the new British 8th army matched by the Italo-German forces.[35]

The battles of CRUSADER have been much studied. The superiority of the British tanks, both in numbers and in certain qualitative respect, was put to a stern test by virtue of the greater capacity and experience of Rommel and the Afrika Korps.[36] It was only after several severe reverses that the 8th army succeeded with some difficulty in reoccupying Cyrenaica at the end of December 1941 and chasing out an enemy who was already exhausted as a result of a supply crisis.

What is less well known is that, unpredictably, the Italians played an important part in these events. In fact, there had been some forewarning that they could pose a considerable threat in the shape of the action at Halfaya Pass on 15 May 1941. One squadron of 4 RTR (C squadron) commanded by Lieutenant – Colonel O'Carroll lost seven out of ten Matildas to the Italian 47/32 gun which, thanks to a courageous and unpublicised action, was able to defeat the large British tanks for the first time:

> The defences consisted of the typical low stone walls and sangars favoured by the Italians and, in fact, on that stony ground little else was possible. . . . The garrison was almost entirely Italian and after a short but firm resistance – chiefly by the Italian gunners, who were always stout opponents – the tanks got right on to the objectives and signalled the Scots Guards on, and the Pass was in our hands. Many of the Italian officers were still in pyjamas and many of the troops were cooking breakfast. The guns of the enemy, however, had taken a good toll of our tanks. These Matildas with their slow speed over obstacles like low walls, form an easy mark as they rear up offering their underneath to the waiting gunners.[37]

Partial successes by the only Italian armoured division – the 'Ariete' – at Bir el Gobi on 19 November, Sidi Rezegh on 23 November, El Duda on 1 December, Alam Hanza on 15 December and elsewhere caused Auchinleck to write in his official despatch in January 1948: 'The Italian M-13 tanks which, as a result of the previous campaign, we had inclined to dismiss as valueless, fought well, and had an appreciable effect on the battle.'[38]

It was very quickly apparent that the Italians were not going to repeat the worst of their performances during the previous winter, but that they were now managing to put up a worthy fight notwithstanding what Rommel later characterised as 'the sort of equipment that made one's hair stand on end'. As an English writer confirmed in 1987:

> One fact bears repetition: CRUSADER was arguably most creditable of all to the Italian forces which took part. . . . Bearing in mind the humiliating record of the Italian army in action since 10 June 1940 (with the two notable exceptions of the Keren and Amba Alagi battles in Ethiopia) CRUSADER should also be remembered as the battle in which the Italian army can claim to have recovered its self-respect.[40]

Furthermore, Italian intelligence in Rome had managed to photograph a code-book which the Americans were unwise enough not to change. It was therefore possible, up to June 1942, to read the reports which the American military attaché in Cairo, Colonel Bonner Feller, sent to Washington every evening. Logically enough, the British gave Feller the most detailed information about an offensive which was largely sustained by American materiel. These messages, which were deciphered in Rome and re-transmitted to Libya, were of the greatest importance.[41] The strong counter-offensive by means of which Rommel chased the British back to Ain el Gazala at the end of January 1942 was greatly assisted by the fruits of this exercise as well as by the efforts of the Italian navy which, after putting two British battleships out of action in the port of Alexandria by the use of human torpedoes, used all the ships and fuel it had available to transport reinforcements to Tripoli. Meanwhile the first elements of a new German air corps arrived, and in the months that followed it systematically hammered Malta and thereby helped to keep the routes to Libya open. The situation changed in Britain's favour in the summer of 1942 with the recall of many German squadrons to Russia and the arrival in the Mediterranean of ever-increasing amounts of American equipment.

The battle of Gazala–Tobruk (26 May–21 June 1942) undoubtedly marked the highest point of Rommel's professionalism and the lowest point of British generalship. Auchinleck and Ritchie succeeded neither in taking full advantage of their superiority on land and in the air nor of profiting from the moments of crisis for the Italian and German troops, and as a result the 8th army was defeated in detail. In fact, Rommel's audacity had both its high and its low points. An energetic counter-attack between 28 and 30 May, when the five Axis mechanised divisions (15th and 21st Panzer, 'Ariete', 'Trieste' and 90th German) were strung out between the minefields and the British, could have had important consequences. Instead Rommel was allowed the time to re-open his supply routes with the battles of Got el Ualeb, in which the Afrika Korps and the 'Trieste' division distinguished themselves. Another opportunity to destroy the Axis forces was squandered between 4 and 6 June 1942 (Operation ABERDEEN). According to one British authority:

> ABERDEEN [was] the code name given to the counter-attack on the Axis forces temporarily trapped east of the British minefields. This was the only attempt to use massed artillery during the period of open desert warfare, and a total fiasco. Ninety-two 25 pounders were assembled to fire a preliminary bombardment at what was thought to be the Axis outer defensive lines, but there was no reconnaissance of the target area and in fact the bombardment fell on empty desert.[42]

In fact the bombardment directed against the positions of the 'Ariete' division fell on open space and the Italian division 'signalled that the British shells were falling well short of their positions'.[43]

After this Rommel and the Afrika Korps launched a counter-attack which was disastrous for the British.[44] Neither the heroic resistance put up by the French at Bir Hacheim nor British tenacity could halt the German drive and on 17 June Rommel, with the few German tanks he had left, cut the line of retreat of the enemy infantry (50th British and 1st South African divisions). In the event these forces succeeded in extricating themselves from encirclement; and the importance of this action was revealed two weeks later when the selfsame 50th division stopped Rommel's advance-guard some 60 miles from Alexandria. According to the authoritative opinion of von Mellenthin, the failure to annihilate the British infantry at Gazala was due to an error by Rommel:

> After the defeat of the British armor on 12 June, the Afrika Korps was ordered to thrust northwards and cut the Via Balbia, while the Italian 20th Corps was given unimportant covering tasks south of Knightsbridge. Had all five German–Italian armored and motorized divisions been used in the thrust towards the Via Balbia, they would have been able to prevent the bulk of the Gazala forces slipping away. After three weeks of bitter fighting the Afrika Korps alone could not muster the necessary momentum and driving power.[45]

This judgement is important because von Mellenthin, although appreciative of the individual military conduct of the Italians, regards their performance in general as having been inferior not only to the Germans' but also to that of all the troops of the British commonwealth.[46]

The reasons why the Italian and German forces failed to conquer Egypt in the summer of 1942 are straightforward. Rommel's forces were worn down during his 600-kilometer chase at the heels of the British. For his part, Auchinleck conducted a battle in July 1942 which, although it can be criticised from certain technical viewpoints, was effective enough to halt the further advances by German and Italian units. In fact the defensive successes of the British in July 1942, although from one point of view confirming the inability of the British to attain a satisfactory level of co-operation between tanks, artillery and infantry, were such as to deny the Axis the opportunity of regaining the necessary momentum to be able to continue their offensive.

The uninterrupted series of British victories from the second Alamein to the curtain in Tunisia (October 1942–May 1943) was dominated by the personality of General Bernard Montgomery. He has been much criticised, and certain facets of his character, which he revealed in his post-war writings, are not entirely agreeable. But any military evaluation of him can only be favourable. At Alamein he made shrewd use of his enormous superiority in manpower (230,000 against 80,000, of which 53,000 were Italians), in aeroplanes (1,500 against 350), in artillery (2,311 against 1,368, of which 850 were Italian) and in tanks (1,230 plus more in reserve against 490, of which 280 were Italian).[47] It should be noted that only the German Panzer IV tank with its long-barrelled gun, of which there were a total of 30, was a match for the American Shermans and Grants, of which there were respectively 252 and 170 in the first line, with more on the way.[48] With such an advantage from the outset it would have been absurd to risk daring manoeuvres or to try for the kind of co-operation between tanks, infantry and artillery which had been so conspicuously lacking up to that time. Victory was won with methods akin to those of the First World War.

In this way Montgomery won the battle of El Alamein, followed the surviving Axis forces with great caution as far as Tunisia and there, in collaboration with the Anglo-American forces which had landed in French North Africa (Operation TORCH), he annihilated his opponents and gained the mastery of the entire coast of North Africa. It was politically as well as militarily essential that the British suffer no more set-backs, even partial ones, in this new phase of the war when the Americans were beginning to dominate the war effort in terms both of men and of equipment. For this reason Montgomery was exactly the right man in the right place. Churchill was conscious of Montgomery's boasting and of his habit of exaggerating the difficulties he had to overcome in order to magnify his own reputation: 'One of the things that Montgomery specially disliked about Enigma was that the information he read in his caravan was read also at 10 Downing Street.'[49] However, Churchill preferred not to bandy words with Montgomery as long as he served the prime minister's political purposes better than any other commander.

For the rest, it is by no means the case that the German and Italian operations necessarily constitute an ideal model, no matter how brilliant they may appear in the light of the inferiority of the Axis forces in that theatre. Soldiering is a pragmatic art, of which one important constituent is the ability to make good use of material superiority.

Nor, finally, should it be fogotten that material superiority pays its dividends only in terms of the overall outcome of the struggle. The lone British infantryman or tanker destined to sacrifice himself at the head of a column did not draw particular consolation from the knowledge that, after his death, thousands of other men and hundreds of other tanks would confer victory on the survivors.[50] With this in mind we may also note the valour of the German and Italian defenders at El Alamein, of whom Liddell Hart wrote 'It is amazing that the defence had held out so long';[51] the tenacity of the 'Ariete' division, which was such as to wring praise from Rommel, who was generally fairly hard on his Italian allies;[52] and finally the good showing of the Italians in the final battles in Tunisia, quietly but effectively recognised in Alexander's despatch on the battle of Enfidaville: 'It was noticed that the Italians fought particularly well, outdoing the Germans in line with them.'[53] Once the heat of battle had ended, there remained for more than 200,000 Italian and German survivors of the campaign – mostly personnel from the support services – only the bitter prospect of imprisonment.

In the opposing camp there was rejoicing because, as Churchill remarked, 'there is no doubt that people like winning very much'.[54] However, many British and American soldiers, staring out across the beautiful waters of the Mediterranean from the coast of Tunisia, were probably wondering how many more landings, attacks, burdens and risks still awaited them, each carrying the possibility of death or injury hitherto escaped.

Today the campaign of 1940–43 can be see to have been the largest military encounter ever to have taken place in a desert environment. Few places are so hostile to man. If appropriate clothing was available, and when the heat, the wind-borne sand and the mosquitos were not excessive, the desert could be relatively healthy. However the complete absence of water and vegetation reduced the length of time for which inadequately equipped men might expect to survive to no more than a few hours. Since for all intents and purposes no local resources existed, the logistical problems were enormous. Everything had to be carried to or with the troops: food, water, medicines, clothing, petrol, weapons and ammunition, even the sheets which were indispensable if a small area of shade was to be created – for oases, with their palm trees and springs of water, were generally hundreds of kilometers distant from one another. The limit on the numbers of troops that could be used, either in combat units or in their immediate support services, was but one of the inevitable consequences of waging war in such an environment.

In this respect the Italians showed less foresight than the British, even though they had already been occupying Libya for some 30 years when the campaign began. Graziani erred in the proportions of the different arms which comprised his army, as we have seen. Moreover Pariani had planned in 1939 to launch an offensive against Egypt which employed 13 divisions (though they were 2-brigade divisions, and were the equivalent of approximately nine 3-brigade divisions).

It is a fact that, at the end of the campaign, the British were operating with huge military forces and conducting battles of attrition in the style of the 1914–18 war, the only means by which they had a reasonable hope of destroying Rommel's forces; however, this occurred only in very favourable logistical circumstances such as at El Alamein, when the presence of supply bases close at hand allowed them to sustain more than ten large divisions, and at Mareth, where the proximity of the port of Tripoli allowed them to support seven devisions. But during the 2,500-kilometer pursuit, and despite an abundance of vehicles and petrol, no more than two or three divisions at a time carried out what were carefully calculated and prepared bounds.

Their experience during the winter of 1940–41 emphasised the same facts to the Italians. The large number of Axis divisions should not be a cause for wonder: the ten Italian and German divisions which fought during CRUSADER (three armoured, two motorised and five marching infantry divisions) amounted to only 119,000 men – exactly the same number as comprised the five divisions and four or five additional brigades of the 8th army. At El Alamein the 12 Italian and German divisions amounted to only 80,000 men, or little more than one third of the 230,000 British troops, who were divided among ten divisions. Also there was on the Axis side a difference of proportion between the numbers of troops deployed in battle and those which took part in subsequent movements. Italian divisions of marching infantry (whose numbers were continually being reduced and which, from the middle of 1941 onwards, never amounted to more than 5,000 or 6,000 men each including non-combatants) represented a force which no commander considered himself bound to save once operations had entered a phase of substantial movement. During the retreat of 1941/42 Rommel, by dint of his sheer ability, managed to save the better part of four or five Italian marching divisions, but at El Alamein the abandonment of all the Italian infantry was inevitable.

The numbers of troops involved in the campaign suggest at least two further points. At the end of the summer of 1941, when the operations in Iraq, Syria and Iran were over and only Egypt remained an active front, total British forces throughout the Middle East amounted to between 550,000 and 600,000 men (or some 16 large divisions), which then rose to approximately 750,000 men. This figure, if it does not entirely justify Churchill's powerful complaints about the paucity of numbers of those actually involved in fighting the enemy, does explain how the Allied divisions (British, Indian, South African, Australian and New Zealand) were able to rotate troops in and out of battle and allow them some months of rest in sectors far from the front and the desert conditions (in the Nile Delta, Syria and Palestine).[56] Things were very different on the Axis side, where the 80 to 100,000 men who were the most ever put in the front line represented about half of all the military forces present in the entire colony, including aviation units and those elements told off to guard the coastline and the desert, where detachments of French and British troops were in evidence. In theory the relative proximity of the European coast might have made possible a similar rotation of Axis troops, but in practice the state of communications did not permit it. The Germans, thanks to their greater wealth of resources, were able to rotate individual soldiers after 12 months' service in the desert; for the Italians, the relevant period was 30 months, but it was rarely possible to honour it. Leaving aside combat itself, therefore, the human strains of the campaign were very different for the two sides.

The other fact to be borne in mind is that the relatively small number of losses due to the war of movement can only be seen in their true light by relating them to the performance of the troops actually employed in action. There are no entirely reliable figures for the Italian and German or British losses in the North African campaign. One can however observe that the rates of loss increased as soon as the operations lost their mobile character and turned into encounters between infantry formations. This was so during the lengthy siege of Tobruk from April to December 1941, and especially somewhat later on when, at El Alamein, the logistical situation and British needs together re-created a 1914–18 style of battle, albeit for a fairly short period of time. The same phenomenon re-occurred in Tunisia, when the Anglo-American tendency to fight in this way was reinforced by the mountainous terrain and by the fact that the Axis armoured forces were by now so small as to debar them from any real manoeuvre actions.

It would be interesting, however, to compare the losses of both sides during the most mobile battles such as CRUSADER and KNIGHTSBRIDGE. It is my impression that, given the numbers of troops actually employed, they were not all that light. In fact an operation involving 100 tanks – leaving out of account infantry and artillery, which were not always present – meant the deployment of no more than 400 or 500 men, and it is these numbers one should consider in any study of this aspect of the question.

Among English-speaking peoples, the North African campaign has probably produced a larger literature than any other. As Corelli Barnett remarks: 'The desert dominated the British press and radio to the disservice of other, less glamorous and indeed more important campaigns fought in the Far East. The Desert War entered into the British folk-memory, a source of legend, endlessly re-written as both history and fiction.'[57] The reasons for this are very well known. They are also at the root of the publishing success which the same events have had in Germany: the 'Rommel myth', even though it was of British origin, could not help but produce echoes and reflections there.

One may therefore ask why the same campaign enjoys historical popularity, if such it can be called, in Italy too. There appears to be a reason for this which is specifically Italian. In contrast to the events on other fronts during the Second World War (in Greece, for example), the North African campaign provided Italians with an opportunity to redeem themselves after their poor, even humiliating, performances during the winter of 1940–41. Of course, without German intervention the North African front could not have held out at the beginning of 1941. Neverthless the German presence did not necessarily mean that there was bound to be an improvement in the Italians' technical capacities, other than whatever might be born of emulation.[58] The real change lay in the fact that the German presence and the gradual increase in the *bravura* of Italian armoured units, and above all of the 'Ariete' division, minimised the sense of fatal inevitability which had previously surrounded every set-back. In the 'Ariete', training was thorough and well thought-out – the work of a handful of fighting soldiers such as General Baldassarre, Colonel Maretti, Major Rizzo and others who were able to gain the support and collaboration of non-professional officers such as Tank Lieutenant Serra and Artillery Captain Piscicelli-Taeggi, both of whom subsequently produced war memoirs that are of considerable interest.[59]

We have already noted the improved performance of the Italian troops from November 1941 and the forerunners of this in April and May of that year. As far as the preceding winter is concerned we may concur in Michael Carver's judgement: 'The fact [is] that the Italian army had never challenged British tanks in mobile operations, and, with the exception of its artillery, had never fought hard.'[60] This was what happened after the very first encounters of 9/12 December 1940: the Italians were not mistaken in their belief that if artillery could not stop the Matildas then the infantry had no chance of doing so. The only operation in which the armoured units of the two sides might have met was at Beda Fomm but, for moral and technical reasons which we have already noted, this did not occur, even though the M13s available at that time were the same tanks which, during the following year, sometimes overcame British tanks which were even better than the A–9, A–10 and A–13.

The lengthy training during the summer of 1941, which was repeated during the following spring, bore fruit; and it is interesting to note what lieutenant Serra wrote in this regard:

> . . . we are profitting by the pause in activities to intensify the training of our units. We choose land which is variegated and irregular, and

we prepare dummies made of the shells of abandoned vehicles. I explain the lessons over and over again. Our tanks must approach the enemy at a sustained speed . . . they must pause for a moment to allow the tank commander to fire his gun and then leave as quickly as possible . . . I explain repeatedly that it is useless to fire while the tank is in motion as the rolling motion makes it impossible to aim. . . .[61]

The officers and men who manned the tanks were in no way to blame for the disastrous neglect of training in pre-war Italy, and they now had to discover for themselves concepts such as 'stationary fire' which were already part of British doctrine, having been adopted in 1931 after manoeuvres on Salisbury Plain.[62] Serra continues:

. . . success in combat rests above all on training. Once I used not to think so, but I have had to take account of all the evidence that soldiers who are under great nervous tension in battle end up by repeating automatically what they have learnt to do during their training.[63]

Curiously, the cultural and professional deficiencies of the Italians could actually be of value at times. It is a widely held view that the difficulties experienced by the British in co-ordinating their tanks, infantry and artillery along the lines suggested by the Afrika Korps were due in large measure to the lack of understanding between the men of the RTC, who were wedded to the 'all tanks' conception of the 1930s, and those of the other two arms.[64] The cultural backwardness of the Italians eliminated this obstacle with, according to MacGregor Knox's authoritative opinion, some very positive results:

The few Italian mobile units that accompanied the *Afrika Korps* in its desert peregrinations apparently learned far more quickly than the British the lesson that armor, artillery and infantry must function as a team. The German example may have helped, but Italian doctrine, precisely because it was oblivious to the work of the British all-tank theorist, was already predisposed towards integration.[65]

In other areas, however, Italian concepts such as that of centralised artillery fire, which were not adapted to the war of movement until the autumn of 1942, showed their effectiveness, notably at the battle of El Alamein and in Tunisia:

The commander of the Ariete in its final battle at El Alamein could claim with some plausibility that Italian artillery, with its emphasis on centralized direction, had in that setpiece battle cooperated with the other arms more effectively than had German artillery.[66]

Of course this does not mean that the action of the Italian artillery was always free from error, or that better training, and above all more modern guns than those left over from the war of 1915–18, would not have produced better results. The age of many of the Italian guns – something shared by the British artillery only until the winter battles of 1940–41 – was sometimes compensated for by the availability of a limited number of larger calibre guns than those possessed by the enemy.[67]

This, together with the quality of some of the positions occupied by the Italians, was important at Mareth in March 1943 and at Enfidaville on 29 April 1943, where considerable losses were inflicted on the British 56th division as soon as it reached the battlefield.[68]

It is also possible to detect an improvement in the performance of the infantry, itself the result of the belief that it would no longer be left to face the British tanks alone, as had happened in 1940–41. The official New Zealand history of the war reports the behaviour of the 9th 'Trieste' regiment of bersaglieri in its encounters with Freyberg's troops at El Duda on 26–27 November 1941 thus:

> The Bersaglieri Regt. fought with much greater determination than is usually found among the Italian troops and the numbers of their dead and the positions in which they lay showed that they had kept their guns in action to the last.[69]

The action of the 'Giovani Fascisti' battalion at Bir el Gobi has been commented upon by Michael Carver:

> Although Norrie had an overwhelming superiority in every arm in the area of Bir Gubi, the failure to concentrate them and co-ordinate the action of all arms in detail had allowed one Italian battalion group to frustrate the action of his whole corps and inflict heavy casualties on one brigade.[70]

> Thus, the remark in Alexander's final despatch to the effect that the 'Folgore' parachute division 'gave a very good account of itself' and that it was 'the best of the Italian divisions' should not be taken as simply a random observation.[71]

It has not been possible within the space of this essay to delve into all the reasons which explain why Italy's military comportment was so different in the first and second stages of the campaign in North Africa. Probably the fact that many Italians did not 'believe in the war' and regarded it as inflicted on them by Mussolini – which is true in itself – was not of much significance. Rather it appears as though the working classes were not able to generate hatred for the British for the simple reason that until the war began they were practically unaware of their existence.

Popular feelings about foreigners were focused on the Germans and the Americans. A negative attitude towards the Germans, which resulted from memories of the Great War and was also firmly embedded in the traditions of the Risorgimento, was counterbalanced by a positive attitude towards the Americans. The United States had been a dream – and sometimes even a happy reality – for millions of the Italian poor who had sought through emigration a quality of life which it was impossible for them to enjoy in their own country. In addition American films, which were very well known in Italy, had spread the idea that the United States was a great country in which anyone could make his way provided that he was honest and hard-working. Among the bourgeoisie there were certainly anti-British sentiments, but they were entirely offset by strong currents of anglophilia, especially in northern Italy.

There were also a small number (only a few tens of thousands) of active anti-Fascists, but they were generally in prison, confined to the islands or in exile. Anti-Fascists who were not constrained in this way, and those who became anti-Fascists during the war and as a consequence of it, were rarely if ever half-hearted in combat; for in war, and particularly in the relatively small units that conducted mobile operations, fighting well is a moral obligation to one's companions on whom one's own safety rests. This is the rule of the squad, so well described by Barbusse in the pages of *Feu*.[72]

Furthermore, it is notoriously difficult to draw a clear distinction between national frontiers and political and moral boundaries. This is so not just because of the primordial strength of man's links with his homeland but because it is so much a part of everyday life that even after the war it can only be perceived in small, stray minorities. It is a worthy view, but not one recognised as necessary by everyone. The British were fortunate that their fight for survival and their struggle to preserve their interests as an empire coincided with the cause of freedom in the great 'world civil war' of 1939–45. The few Britons who were especially conscious of the latter view of the war, when they had the chance to become aware of it, had no grounds of disagreement with those Italians who thought likewise. Such people, if they took part in the Second World War, were almost always among the most valorous soldiers. Ex-soldiers of the North African campaign formed a smaller proportion of the armed Italian resistance against the Germans and the Fascists between 1943 and 1945 than did the survivors of the Russian campaign, since most of them were taken prisoner in Tunisia. However, among the most dedicated fighters in the partisan war were to be found some of the best soldiers who had fought in North Africa between 1940 and 1943.

Translated by John Gooch

NOTES

1. J.M. D'Hoop, 'Les projets d'intervention des Allies en Mediterranee', in *La guerre en Mediterranee (1939–1945)* (Paris: CNRS, 1971), pp.237–255 and the bibliography cited there. Also J.R.M. Butler, *Grand Strategy* (London: HMSO, 1957), II, pp.64–70.
2. Martin van Creveld, *Supplying War-Logistics from Wallenstein to Patton* (Cambridge: Cambridge University Press 1977), pp.181–201.
3. Michael Howard, 'La Mediterranee et la strategie britannique au cours de la deuxieme guerre mondiale', in *La guerre en Mediterranee (1939–1945)*, pp.23–9. See also ibid., pp.24, 27, 33.
4. For hints that it would have been possible to defend the petroleum resources of the Middle East more economically and without seeking spectacular military victories, see Howard, op.cit., p.27; also the figures for the shipments of men and materials examined in Williamson Murray, 'British Military Effectiveness in the Second World War', in A.R. Millett and W. Murray (eds.), *Military Effectiveness* (Boston MA: Allen & Unwin, 1988), III, p.103.
5. See Lucio Ceva, *Le forze armate* (Turin: UTET, 1981), pp.249–53, 306 and also 51–2; and Ceva, *La condotta italiana della guerra* (Milan: Feltrinelli, 1975), pp.39–41.
6. R. Riccio, *Italian Tanks and Fighting Vehicles of World War 2* (Henley-on Thames: Pique Publications, 1975), pp.18–21.
7. Winston S. Churchill, *The Second World War* (London: Cassell, 1949), II, p.370.
8. For the characteristics of the M-11 see Riccio op. cit., pp.24–5. For automobiles, see Archivio dell 'Ufficio Storico dell' Esercito, C.S.-S.M.G. 10, 8.
9. B.H. Liddell Hart, *The Tanks* (London: Cassell 1959), II, pp.486–7, 496–7. I.S.O. Playfair, *The Mediterranean and the Middle East* (London: HMSO, 1960); III, pp.434–4, especially 442 and 444. S. Bidwell and D. Graham, *Fire-Power* (London: Allen & Unwin, 1982), p.182. Among the British Cruiser tanks, the A-13 was the most numerous: A.J. Smithers, *Rude Mechanicals* (London: Leo Cooper, 1987), p.68.
10. R.M. Ogorkiewicz, *Armour* (London: Stevens & Sons 1960), p.241.
11. Playfair, op. cit., I (1954), p.364; II, p.3; II (1960), p.27.
12. T.G. Needham in B. Perret, *Through Mud and Blood – Infantry Tank Operations in World War II* (London: Hale, 1975), p.59. See also A.J. Smithers, op. cit., p.69 and H. Maule, *Spearhead General – The Epic Story of General Sir Frank Messervy and his Men in Eritrea, North Africa and Burma* (London: Odhams, 1961), pp.39–41.
13. C.N. Barclay, *Against Great Odds* (Liverpool: Blake & Mackenzie, 1955), pp.48. I.S.O. Playfair, op. cit., I, p.286. G. Long, *To Benghazi* (Canberra: Australian War Memorial, 1961), pp.184–9.
14 Liddell Hart, op. cit., II, p.59.
15. Alan Moorehead, *African Trilogy* (London: Hamish Hamilton, 1944); and the same author's *The Desert War*, Milan: Garzanti, 1968 (Italian translation; originally published in English 1965).
16. Moorehead, *The Desert War*, p.35.
17. MacGregor Knox, *Mussolini Unleashed* (Cambridge: Cambridge University Press, 1982), p.156.
18 Moorehead, *The Desert War*, p.35.
19. Ibid., pp.11, 19.
20. Emilio Lussu, *Un anno sull'Altopiano* (Turin: Einaudi, 1964) (1st edition Paris, 1938), *passim.*
21. R. Migliavacca, *La 'Folgore' nella battaglia di El Alamein* (Milan: Auriga, 1983) (1st edition 1972), pp.67, 93.
22. G. Berto, *Guerra in camicia nera* (Milan: Garzanti 1969) (1st edition 1955), p.145.
23. The Piedmontese newspaper *L'Opinione* of 17 Aug. 1855, at a time when the Piedmontese army was fighting alongside the English and French in the Crimea, reported these words

from the *Times*: 'The officers of the Piedmontese army, like those of the British army, belong almost exclusively to the upper classes and it is most unusual for an officer to come from the ranks, so that the distance between officers, and men is not only disciplinary but also social.' The following remarks from the *Diario politico di Margherita Provana di Collegno 1855–1856* (Milan: Hoepli, 1926, p.308), dated 12 December 1855, are suggestive: 'General Alfonso Lamarmora [commander of the Piedmontese army in the Crimea] drinks the same wine at his table as his soldiers. The English are the worst off because the English soldier neither knows how to do anything for himself, nor wishes to do so. He waits to be served because his contract says that he will be fed, lodged and looked after; therefore he stands and waits. The English army has with it 1,700 men whose job it is to look after the soldiers: 1,700 useless mouths.'

24. Playfair, op. cit., I, p.92. On the very poor Italian rations and the differences between officers and men, see also Erwin Rommel, *Krieg Ohne Hass* (Italian translation, Milan: Garzanti, 1952), p.208.

25. The question as to whether Tripoli could have been occupied, thereby preventing the German embarkation, is extremely controversial. Michael Carver, in *Dilemmas of the Desert War* (London: Batsford, 1986, p.18), reflects the opinion of Field Marshal Lord Harding that the Italian forces would have been strong enough to check any attempt by O'Connor to take the port. However, see Long, op. cit., pp.280–81.

26. Kurt Assman, *Deutsche Schiksaljahre* (Weisbaden: Brockhaus, 1950).

27. Andreas Hillgruber, *Hitlers Strategie, Politik, Kriegfuhrung 1939/1941* (Frankfurt am Main: Bernard & Graefe, 1967), pp.201–2 and *passim*. See also L. Gruchmann, 'Les occasions strategiques manquees des puissances de l'Axe dans le bassin mediterraneen 1940/41', in *La guerre en Mediterranee*, pp.159–80; and Lucio Ceva, 'La strategia militare di Hitler, il Mediterraneo e il pensiero ipotetico', in *Storia Contemporanea*, Vol.6 (1987), pp.1513–28.

28. Van Creveld, op. cit.

29. Churchill, op. cit., II, pp.268–9.

30. Generaloberst Franz Halder, *Kriegstagebuch*. edited by H.A. Jacobsen Stuttgart 1962 (mimeographed edition, T.N. Dupuy Associates, Westview Press, Boulder, Colorado), I, entries for 4 and 24 Nov. 1940.

31. R.J. Sontag and J.S. Beddie (eds.), *Nazi–Soviet Relations 1939–1941* (Washington: Department of State, 1948), pp.233, 244, 245, 252, 259.

32. F.H. Hinsley, *British Intelligence in the Second World War* (London: HMSO), II (1981), Ch. 21 and *passim*.

33. See Lucio Ceva, 'L'"Intelligence" britannico nella seconda guerra mondiale e la sua influenza sulla strategia e sulle operazioni', in *Storia Contemporanea*, Vol.1 (1982), pp.99–122.

34. John Connell, *Auchinleck* (London: Cassell, 1955), pp.255–7.

35. Playfair, op. cit., III; J.A.I. Agar-Hamilton and L.C.F. Turner, *The Sidi Rezegh Battles 1941* (Cape Town: Oxford University Press, 1957); Michael Carver, *Tobruk* and *The Desert Dilemmas*, op. cit.; R. Humble, *Crusader* (London: Leo Cooper. 1987).

36. On the advantage of the 8th army's Cruisers over the German tanks, and the stories to the contraray current during the war, see Michael Carver, *Dilemmas of the Desert War*, p.32. The works cited at note 35 lead to the same conclusion. On the production problems associated with British and American tanks, see M.M. Postan, *British War Production* (London: HMSO, 1952); M.M. Postan, D. Hay and J.D.Scott, *Design and Development of Weapons* (London: HMSO, 1964); G.M. Ross, *The Business of Tanks* (Elms Court: Stockwell, 1976); A.J. Smithers, op. cit.

37. Liddell Hart, *The Tanks*, II, p.78.

38. C.J.E. Auchinleck, *Operations in the Middle East from 1st November 1941 to 15th August 1942*, Supplement to the *London Gazette*, 13 Jan. 1948, p.314. See also Michael Carver, *Tobruk*, p.256 and *passim*; Ronald Lewin, *The Life and Death of the Africa Korps* (London: Batsford, 1977), pp.81, 87, 119, 137, 158, 163, 164, 174.

39. Rommel, *Krieg Ohne Hass* (Italian translation), p.46.

40. R. Humble, *Crusader*, p.200. For the battle of Keren, see among others Maule, op. cit., pp.43–111.

41. See Ceva, 'L'"Intelligence" brittannico . . .', op. cit., pp.102–7.
42. S. Bidwell and D. Graham, *Fire-Power*, p.278.
43. F.W. von Mellenthin, *Panzer Battles* (London: Futura, 1977), p.132 (1st edition, Cassell, 1955).
44. Ibid., pp.132–3.
45. Ibid., p.137.
46. Ibid., pp.178–9.
47. B.H. Liddell Hart, *History of the Second World War* (London: Cassell, 1970), pp.298–9; Playfair, op. cit., II, p.30.
48. Liddell Hart, *History of the Second World War*, p.298.
49. Review by David Hunt of *British Intelligence in the Second World War*, Vol.II (London: HMSO 1981), in *The Listener*, 10 Sept. 1981, pp.279–80.
50. In 1943–44 the second generation German tanks (the Tiger, and above all the Panthers) were truly superior to the Sherman, not to mention the Churchill. Note the 'apocryphal' conversation in W. Murray, 'British Military Effectiveness', op. cit., pp.115–16.
51. Liddell Hart, *History of the Second World War*, p.304.
52. Rommel, *Krieg Ohne Hass* (Italian translation), pp.288, 340.
53. H.R.L.G. Alexander, *The African Campaign from El Alamein to Tunis from 10th August 1942 to 13th May 1943*, Supplement to the *London Gazette*, 5 Feb. 1948, p.879. See also H.Kippenberger, *Infantry Brigadier* (Oxford University Press, 1949), p.312.
54. Churchill, op. cit., IV, p.740.
55. J.M.A. Gwyer, *Grand Strategy*, Vol.III, Part I (London: HMSO, 1964), pp. 175, 202.
56. Churchill, op. cit. III, p.63 and IV, pp.810–11; Butler, op. cit., pp.380–82.
57. Corelli Barnett, *Britain and her army 1509–1970* (London: Allen Lane/Penguin Press, 1970), p.439.
58. M. Tobino, *Il deserto della Libia* (Turin: Einaudi 1955), pp.105, 107.
59. O. Piscicelli-Taeggi, *Diario di un combattente nell'Africa settentrionale* (Bari: Laterza, 1946) (published on the advice of Benedetto Croce), and E. Serra, *Carristi dell' "Ariete" (fogli di diario 1941–1942)* (Rome: privately published, 1979).
60. Michael Carver, *Dilemmas of the Desert War*, p.15.
61. Serra, *Carristi*, pp.126–7.
62. Liddell Hart, *The Tanks*, I, p.268.
63. Serra, *Carristi*, p.127.
64. G. leQ. Martel, *Our armoured forces* (London: Faber & Faber, 1945), pp.37–58; Kippenberger, op. cit., pp.159, 173–4, 180–81, 188–90; B.H. Liddell Hart, *Memoirs* (London: Cassell, 1965), I, pp.86–37, 159–82, 235–79; W.G.F. Jackson, *The North African Campaign 1940–1943* (London: Batsford, 1975), pp.252–263; Ronald Lewin, *Man of Armour: A Study of Lieut.-General Vyvyan Pope* (London: Leo Cooper, 1976), pp.71 *et seq.*; Brian Bond, *British Military Policy between the Wars* (Oxford: Clarendon Press, 1980), pp.127–90; Michael Carver, *Tobruk* p.24 and *Dilemmas*, pp.141–3. See also: John Connell, *Auchinleck and Wavell-Scholar and Soldier to June 1941* (London: Collins, 1964); K.J. Macksey, *Armoured Crusader-A Biography of Major-General Sir Percy Hobart* (London: Hutchinson, 1967; P. Warner, *Auchinleck, the Lonely Soldier* (London: Buchan & Enright, 1981); David Fraser, *Alanbrooke* (London: Collins, 1982); R.H. Larson, *The British Army and the Theory of Armoured Warfare 1918–1940* (London & Toronto: Associated University Press, 1984).
65. 'The Italian Armed Forces', in *Military Effectiveness*, op. cit., p.151.
66. Ibid., p.163 and note 97.
67. Michael Carver, *Dilemmas*, p.52.
68. Alexander, *Despatch*, p.879.
69. Michael Carver, *Tobruk*, pp.108–9.
70. Ibid., pp.130–131.
71. Alexander, *Despatch*, pp.843, 851.
72. Henri Barbusse *Le feu-journal d'une escoude (suivi du Carnet de guerre)* (Paris: Flammarion 1965) (1st edition 1916).

The Road to Defeat: The German Campaigns in Russia 1941–43*

BERND WEGNER

Compared with other theatres and campaigns of the Second World War, the war between Germany and the Soviet Union has received relatively little attention from English-speaking historians.[1] The reasons for this situation are understandable, if not convincing: in English-speaking countries, which were not directly involved in the war in the East, that war has been associated far less with those painful and glorious experiences that are evidently still the motivating force behind much historical research than have been the events of the Second World War in the Mediterranean, the Atlantic, Western Europe or South-east Asia. Moreover, the international political climate in the first decades after 1945 was not conducive to a critical historical evaluation of the war between Germany and the Soviet Union. Not the only reason for this was the fact that Soviet archives were and have remained closed to foreign scholars. In the shadow of the cold war the question of the importance of the struggle in the East possessed rather a primarily political significance. An acknowledgement of the fact, emphasised for propaganda purposes in every Soviet history book, that the Red Army had contributed more than any other army to destroying the Third Reich and liberating large parts of Europe from German occupation seemed to many people in the non-communist world to be a legitimation of the new communist order established in the states of Eastern Europe dominated by the Soviet Union.

Under these conditions Western interest in the war between Germany and the Soviet Union concentrated less on the writing of critical, scholarly history and more on the practical evaluation of military experience gained during that conflict. The most important results of this interest were the hundreds of operational studies on the war in the East produced by German generals after the end of the Second World War for the Historical Division of the United States Army.[2] A large number of these studies have been published and have strongly influenced historians in English-speaking countries and in Germany, preparing the way, in spite of the high quality of the presentation of events in some cases, for an apologetic interpretation of the German war in Russia from the point of view of the German military leaders.

This interpretation, according to which the German failure in the East was due primarily to Hitler's dilettantism, combined with unfavourable geographical and climatic conditions,[3] has been abandoned only partially in more recent works, the reason being that academic historians have concentrated their attention only on certain aspects and phases of the war in the East. Especially the 'Barbarossa' campaign of 1941 can be considered one of the most thoroughly studied and discussed subjects of the entire Second World War. There are good reasons for this: no other decision taken by Hitler had more far-reaching consequences for the course of the war and the fate of the National Socialist state than did his decision to attack the Soviet Union; no other campaign provided such numerous and clear examples of National Socialist imperial and race-ideological madness; nowhere else was the use of the German army for criminal purposes more obvious. It is thus all the more remarkable that historians (except Russian ones) have tended to neglect the course of the war in the East *after* the failure of German blitzkrieg hopes in the winter of 1941–42. Several critical studies have been published, it is true, on individual aspects such as German foreign and occupation policy, and on the war economy and operations in the years 1942–44, but a comprehensive interpretation, based on the sources and analysing the different levels of the conduct of the war in the East *after* 'Barbarossa', is still lacking.[4] As far as the writing of history in West Germany is concerned, a basic reason for this deficit is probably the widespread aversion there to military subjects in general and the consequent tendency to attribute little significance to purely military events. Proceeding from the basically correct view (which, however, dangerously simplifies the extremely complex reality of a total war lasting several years) that the battles in the East after 1941 represented only the continuation of a war which in fact had already been lost, historians have generally left the study of the prolonged death struggle of the Third Reich to memoirists, authors of picture histories and various apologists. As a result, the second German offensive, on the southern sector of the Eastern front in the summer of 1942 (as well as the enormous defensive battles of 1943 and 1944, which this study does not deal with) is still overshadowed in historical studies of the Second World War by the events of 1941[5] and thus surrounded by more legends and myths. In view of this situation and the need to limit the length of the present article, the following remarks will concentrate on the German summer offensive in 1942 ('Operation Blue'), which was decisive for Germany's final defeat.

I. 'BARBAROSSA' – THE FIRST CAMPAIGN

The theses presented by Andreas Hillgruber after the mid-1960s have dominated the discussion about the origins of the war between Germany and the Soviet Union and the genesis of the operation plan 'Barbarossa'.[6] In two respects they have withstood all attempts at refutation[7] and, with minor additions and modifications, have been essentially confirmed by more recent research. They can be summarised as follows:

(1) Hitler's decision to attack the Soviet Union was the result of a mixture of ideological and strategic considerations. The idea of a large-scale colonisation of the East, with the two main aims of annihilating Bolshevism and conquering 'living space' for the German nation[8] had been, in addition to his militant anti-Semitism, the most important element in Hitler's world view since 1924–25 at the latest. It provides the key for understanding the attack on the Soviet Union, which, from a purely strategic or operational point of view, was foolish. The emphasis on Hitler's ideology does not mean, however, that strategic considerations played no role in his decision, but rather that they can be understood only in terms of their function in his attempt to realise his overriding ideological aims.[9]

The importance of ideological aims in Hitler's strategic calculations was evident in his rejection of plans submitted by the Navy leaders and by Foreign Minister Ribbentrop in 1940 as alternatives to an offensive in the East. The plan developed by the commander-in-chief of the Navy, Raeder, to shift the main German war effort to the Mediterranean, the Near East and North-west Africa, and the concentration on the disruption of sea links between Great Britain and the United States favoured by the commander of the submarines, Dönitz, did not, in the end, receive Hitler's approval because they ignored his most important war aim, namely expansion by conquest in the East.[10] The situation was similar with regard to Ribbentrop's plan for a 'continental bloc' directed against the sea powers Great Britain and the United States and extending from 'Madrid to Yokohama' with the participation of the Soviet Union. Hitler did consider this option in the summer of 1940, but only as a means of increasing the pressure on Great Britain and not with the intention of laying the foundation for a lasting new European order.[11] In his eyes the *conditio sine qua non* for that was a war not against Britain, but against the Soviet Union.

Against this background, Hitler's decision to turn East, considered even before the end of the fighting in the West in June 1940, was obviously an attempt to correct what he regarded as a war on the wrong front: instead of waging an unwanted war against Great Britain (and thus, it was to be feared, sooner or later against the United States) with the benevolent neutrality of the Soviet Union, the real, mortal enemy, he intended to attack the latter country and force Great Britain to remain neutral. The fact that, contrary to his expectations, he was unable to achieve this last aim by defeating France reduced decisively the political value of his brilliant military victory in May and June of 1940.

(2) The war against the Soviet Union was of a fundamentally different nature from that of all other German campaigns in the Second World War. More

than a mere military operation with a clearly defined, limited aim, it was rather a 'crusade against Bolshevism' (as described quite accurately by contemporary German propaganda), a colonial war of exploitation, and a racist war of annihilation. The unprecedented brutality of the war in the East can be explained only in part as the result of the experiences of soldiers on the battlefield.[12] The decisive factor was rather that the campaign in the East was planned deliberately from the beginning with a complete disregard for internationally accepted laws of war. As early as the beginning of March 1941 Hitler ordered that 'all Bolshevik leaders and commisars' were to be 'rendered harmless immediately' (that is, killed) without the use of military courts.[13] A few weeks later, in his address to about 250 generals, he again made clear that the coming campaign would not be a normal military operation but rather a 'war between two ideologies':

> We have to free ourselves from ideas of soldierly camaraderie. A communist is not and can never be considered a fellow-soldier. This war will be a battle of annihilation. . . . It will be very different from the war in the West. In the East harshness will guarantee us a mild future. Military leaders must overcome their [humanitarian] reservations.[14]

Hitler's appeal did not fall on deaf ears. The *Wehrmacht* Operations Staff and the *Wehrmacht* legal section, as well as the Army General Staff, quickly prepared the necessary orders to take into account his wishes and at the same time the exaggerated security requirements of the officers involved. In fact, however, these orders seriously compromised the role of the *Wehrmacht* in Russia. For example, the decree on military justice of 13 May 1941 withdrew crimes committed by enemy civilians in the East from the jurisdiction of military courts, required that partisans be 'brutally eliminated' and ordered that *Wehrmacht* soldiers committing crimes against the civilian population no longer needed to be prosecuted.[15] In the so-called 'Commissar Order', issued as a supplement on 6 June, soldiers were informed that generally commissars of the Red Army, 'originators of barbaric Asiatic methods of fighting', were to be killed immediately.[16] The 'Guidelines for the Conduct of German Soldiers in Russia', issued somewhat earlier, and a number of basic orders issued by prominent field commanders (for example, Reichenau, Manstein, Hoth) during the first months after the initial German attack were similarly brutal in their aims and tone. For example, Field Marshal von Reichenau demanded in a notorious order of 10 October that German soldiers in the East should 'not only fight according to the rules of warfare' but should also 'avenge all the atrocities committed against Germans and other racially related peoples'.[17]

Such words, accompanied by a broad propaganda campaign against the slavic 'subhumans', were sharply rejected by many officers, but they opened the gates for a barbaric conduct of the war in the East much more widespread than most surviving German officers were willing to admit after the war. Not only the *Wehrmacht* High Command, but also the Army General Staff thus accepted responsibility for politically motivated annihilation measures in addition to their proper military tasks, as for example when the army worked closely with the SS in 'pacifying' conquered areas[18] (that is, the extermination of undesirable elements in the population) or in the treatment of Soviet prisoners of war. Of the 5.7 million Soviet prisoners of war captured by the Germans by February 1945, at least two to 2.5 million, more probably about 3.3 million, that is, 57 per cent, died by the end of the war, the great majority before the summer of 1942. In contrast, deaths among British and American prisoners in Germany during the Second World War amounted to only 3.5 per cent. Of the 3.15 million German soldiers captured by Soviet forces, 35 to 37 per cent died during a usually long period of captivity.[19] In this regard we must also mention Hitler's intention, accepted without contradiction by the responsible front commanders-in-chief, to raze to the ground Moscow, Leningrad and Kiev. To avoid having to feed the populations of these cities during the winter, they were to be first encircled, then cut off from all supplies, bombed and starved out.[20]

The racist view of the war in the East, typical not only of Hitler but also of many *Wehrmacht* and army generals, provided arguments for ignoring moral reservations, but its practical effects greatly contributed to making the realisation of the objectives of 'Barbarossa' difficult or impossible. Ideological prejudices repeatedly resulted in an astonishing loss of any sense of proportion and led to increasingly radical attempts to solve problems requiring pragmatic solutions. An excellent example of this was the rise of partisan groups, which began shortly after the German attack and became a significant operational factor in the second half of 1942.[21] The most important cause of this development, as even the German side eventually realised, was the inhuman character of German warfare and occupation policy. It is, however, indicative of the special quality of warfare based on National Socialist principles that this insight did not lead to any basic change in the behaviour of the conquerors. The partisan resistance remained an unsolved problem. Perhaps even more harmful was the effect of ideological preconceptions on German military intelligence, the main result in that area being constant underestimation of the enemy and an often grotesque overestimation of Germany's own possibilities.[22] As this and other examples show, the ideological view of warfare was by no means an alien idea forced upon the military 'professionals' by Hitler and fanatics of his inner circle; rather it was the natural consequence of a specific image of the enemy held by the German military elite responsible for operations in the East. In other words, the planning and execution of the German campaigns were strongly influenced by ideological factors from the beginning, a fact which has received insufficient attention, even in more recent studies, by British and American historians.[23]

Against the background presented above, how are the objectives, execution and result of the first campaign in the East to be judged? Immediately after the conclusion of the armistice with France, the Army General Staff had begun preparatory work for an offensive in the East on their own initiative and had conducted relevant map exercises in the autumn of 1940. The results were presented to Hitler at the beginning of December 1940 and led to his Directive No.21 ('Operation Barbarossa'), issued on 18 December and followed on 31 January 1941 by the deployment order of the Army High Command. These basic directives determined German objectives in the first phase of operations in the East and required the *Wehrmacht* to 'defeat Soviet Russia in a fast campaign' and advance to a line between the Volga and Archangel.[24] This would place the industrial areas of the Urals within the range of the Luftwaffe and Germany itself beyond the range of Soviet aircraft. The decisive prerequisite for the success of the German attack was, however, that the mass of the Red Army must be annihilated west of the Dvina–Dnieper line in order to open the way to the East. To achieve this objective the strongest German forces (two army groups) were to be concentrated in the area north of the great Pripet Marshes, while only one army group was to operate in the south, with the aim of conquering the industrially important Donets Basin as quickly as possible. The German army group in the middle sector of the front was, on the other hand, to advance to White Russia and then turn north with strong forces to join Army Group North, which would advance from East Prussia through the former Baltic States, in the conquest of Leningrad. Only thereafter, if Soviet resistance had not collapsed beforehand, was Moscow to be attacked.

After the offensive had begun on 22 June 1941 – with a total of almost 3.6 million German and allied soldiers (Finns, Romanians, Hungarians, Italians, Slovakians), about 600,000 vehicles, 3,600 tanks, and over 2,700 aircraft – it seemed of course for a few weeks as if the expectations of the German leaders would indeed be completely fulfilled. When the double battle of Bialystok and Minsk was over on 9 July, two Soviet armies (the Third and the Tenth) had been completely destroyed and a third (the Thirteenth) shattered. Entire divisions had deserted to the Germans. The German forces had captured more than 300,000 prisoners and destroyed or captured more than 3,000 tanks. German optimism reached its highpoint. On 3 July the chief of the Army General Staff, Colonel-General Halder, noted in his diary that it was no exaggeration to say that the campaign in Russia had been won within a fortnight.[25] The next day Hitler observed that 'the Russian' had already practically lost the war.[26] Most observers in Washington, London and other capitals completely agreed with this estimate of the situation. The final defeat of the Soviet Union seemed to be only a matter of weeks. In those July days of 1941 the war had entered a phase, seemingly like the situation in June

1940, which in the eyes of the German leaders, has correctly been described as the 'zenith' of the Second World War.[27] In that brief historical moment in which the Soviet Union seemed to have been eliminated as an international power factor, Hitler began to make plans for the time after 'Barbarossa'. In his view the world then would be dominated by the conflict between Germany and the United States, a struggle between continental empires in which Hitler hoped to have not only Japan as an Asian junior partner but also Great Britain as a European ally. He assumed that the defeat of the Soviet Union would also mean the political end of Churchill and his anti-German 'war party'. Indicative of the new orientation of German war policy in this period of expected triumph in the East was Hitler's order of 14 July 1941 for a change in armaments priorities. The main emphasis was to be shifted away from army armaments, important for a land war such as that against the Soviet Union, to the Luftwaffe and the Navy. Six months later Hitler was forced to reverse this decision.[28]

Of course reality soon caught up with Hitler's dreams about the future. At the moment of maximum German expansion the weaknesses of German operational planning became apparent. This was due in the first place to the complete underestimation of the Soviet enemy and especially of his ability to mobilise material and human resources.[29] But the German military leaders had also underestimated the Soviet soldier's endurance and ability to bear hardships. The lack of reserves for the German army in the East also made itself felt after the middle of July. In the feeling of superiority in the East such reserves as were available were often kept at home. Similarly, new tanks and tank motors were reserved for new motorised divisions planned for later operations against Britain and the British position in the Near East and were not sent to the Eastern front. Moreover, the unexpectedly high losses in the East led at this time to an even more intense struggle between the *Wehrmacht*, the armaments industry and administrative organs for available personnel.[30]

For the moment, however, another factor was more important namely the fact that Hitler and the Army General Staff had not come to any real agreement on the point of main effort of the offensive. In any case, it now became clear that Directive No.21 represented a superficial compromise between two fundamentally incompatible operational ideas. On the one hand, the Army General Staff believed that Moscow as the operational objective should have absolute priority. Its capture would mean the elimination of the political and administrative nerve centre of the Soviet Union and the fall of the most important Soviet traffic junction. On the other hand, Hitler was convinced that military successes on the flanks of the offensive were more important than capturing the Soviet capital. In the North he wanted to link up with the Finns and destroy the Soviet position in the Baltic by eliminating Leningrad; in the South he wanted to capture the all-important industrial and raw materials centres of the Donets Basin and the Caucasus and destroy Soviet air bases near the Black Sea, which posed a threat to German oil supplies from Romania.[31]

It was no accident that the conflict between Hitler and the military leaders, which had been smouldering for months, broke out into the open exactly one month after the start of the offensive when Hitler decided on 22 July that his armoured units should not advance farther to the East. With the capture of Smolensk on 16 July and the subsequent great battle of encirclement the first phase of 'Operation Barbarossa' had been concluded.[32] On the surface the victory in the battle of Smolensk appeared to be another great German success (by the beginning of August over 300,000 prisoners, over 3,000 tanks and about the same number of guns had been captured), but for the first time the German military leaders were now confronted with a number of unpleasant truths with far-reaching consequences. The duration and course of the battle had shown that the enemy's determination to stop the German advance on Moscow at any price was unbroken. Hitler observed with resignation that 'the Russian' could not be defeated by German operational successes 'because he simply refuses to recognise them'. The Red Army would therefore have to be destroyed piece by piece in small, tactical encirclements.[33] Hitler ordered Army Group 'Centre' to take up a defensive position on 30 July.[34] For him the massive resistance of the Red Army in the narrow area between the Dnieper and the Dvina and the considerable logistical problems of the German army, especially in the middle sector of the front,[35] were convincing arguments for a return to the idea, which he had favoured from the very beginning, of seeking a decision on the flanks. The fact that the successes of Army Groups 'North' and (above all) 'South' had been less impressive than those of Army Group 'Centre' probably seemed to Hitler an additional reason to transfer armoured forces from the centre to the flanks. This did not mean that Moscow had been abandoned as an operational objective, but only, as envisaged in a directive of 12 August, that its capture had been postponed until the situation on the flanks had been taken care of.[36]

While Hitler probably regarded this plan as a compromise in the dispute about the direction of further operations, the army leaders found it extremely alarming. They feared that the operation, which until then had developed considerable momentum, could run out of energy and that Moscow would not be reached in time, that is, before the beginning of winter. Moreover, the offensive now seemed in danger of failing to achieve its main objective: the destruction of the Red Army. Because the enemy expected the main German thrust to be against Moscow and had concentrated the mass of his forces in the central section of the front against Army Group 'Centre', so the Army General Staff calculated, the best chance of forcing a decisive battle would be there.[37]

However, the campaign could not be won in 'decisive battles' alone. This became clear at the end of September after the overwhelming German victory in the great battle east of Kiev, which ended with the annihilation of most of the Soviet southwest front and the capture of 650,000 prisoners. Convinced that the Red Army was now really at the end of its strength, Hitler yielded to the urging of his chief of the General Staff and ordered Army Group 'Centre' to resume its drive on Moscow ('Operation Typhoon'). Again the Germans inflicted devastating defeats on the enemy. In October they surrounded and wiped out almost eight Soviet armies under Timoshenko in the area of Vyazma and Bryansk (650,000 prisoners). The Red Army was only able to win time, but time had now become the determining factor in the campaign. The time gained made it possible for the Soviet leadership to prepare a defence of the capital and its approaches, to evacuate vital industries and to organise large numbers of new divisions or to transfer reserves from other parts of the country, including Siberia, to the West. On the other hand, the time lost because of the crisis in the German leadership and the stubborn resistance of the Red Army meant that the advancing *Wehrmacht* formations had been subjected to considerable wear and tear. On 26 September, when Army Group 'Centre' issued the order to resume the drive on Moscow, the German army in the East was already 200,000 men under strength. It was doubtful if these missing men could ever be replaced.[38] It was possible to mobilise 80 divisions with a total strength of almost two million men for 'Operation Typhoon', but this meant that, in contrast to the situation of the Red Army, the last German reserves were exhausted. From this point on the German forces used up their resources faster than they could be replaced, with the result that the *Wehrmacht's* fighting power in the East rapidly declined. Moreover, climatic conditions for a large-scale offensive worsened dramatically as winter approached. Again and again the German advance became mired down in mud, slush and snow. In addition, serious disruption of supplies for the troops made themselves felt.[39]

By the end of October at the latest the blitzkrieg against the Soviet Union had failed, although the German army in the East had not lost a single battle. Nevertheless, Hitler and the General Staff did not break off the drive on Moscow but tried to capture the city with a last effort before winter arrived. At the beginning of November they even talked of capturing Stalingrad and the oil fields in the northern Caucasus (Maikop).[40] Their intention was to reach an advantageous starting position for continuing the war in 1942, but they were also convinced that, after its long series of crushing defeats, the Red Army was in an even more desperate situation than the *Wehrmacht*. From this point of view, it still seemed possible in late autumn of 1941 to conclude 'Operation Barbarossa' successfully. Unlike the majority of the front commanders-in-chief, Hitler and the General Staff still believed[41] that the important thing was to see the battle through, stake everything on one last effort and demonstrate strong nerves. This expectation was doomed to failure, for it was based on a mistaken estimate of the possibilities open to the enemy. That became abundantly clear on 5 and 6 December when the great Soviet winter offensive began and forced the Germany army to fight a murderous defensive battle lasting several months.

II. 'OPERATION BLUE' – THE SECOND CAMPAIGN

'Operation Blue', the code name for the second German campaign in the East, planned for 1942,[42] may seem at first glance to have been merely a continuation of 'Barbarossa' with a different name and operational objectives. This impression is strengthened by the fact that the push to and over the Caucasus, the main goal in German planning for 1942, had already been envisaged and prepared by Hitler for 1941. As late as July 1941, he had assumed that German troops could reach the Volga by the beginning of October, and Baku and Batumi a month later.[43] When such hopes faded shortly thereafter, a continuation of operations in 1942 became inevitable, and petroleum production forecasts became increasingly pessimistic, Hitler quickly decided on the Caucasian oil fields as the objective of the next German summer offensive. Basic planning for the coming operations in the spring of 1942 was worked out by the responsible departments of the Army High Command as early as October 1941. In that month Hitler also informed the Italian foreign minister of his intentions.[44]

Although 'Operation Blue' was certainly an immediate consequence of the fact that the aims of the campaign against the Soviet Union in the summer of 1941 had not been achieved and the war in the East had not, therefore, been concluded, it was, on the other hand, the last German campaign in the East conducted with independent strategic aims and was fundamentally different from all earlier German offensives, including 'Operation Barbarossa'. Whereas the latter had represented the high point of an essentially European war which Hitler could still rightly consider, in terms of its origins and previous development, to be 'his' war, the situation had changed dramatically since the end of 1941. In December of that year Japan and the United States had entered the conflict. In relative terms, their weight greatly reduced the influence of the German dictator on the outcome of the worldwide struggle and consequently made a German victory in the East, even if it were achieved, less decisive. At the same time, German freedom of action had become more restricted. In 1940–41 'Barbarossa' had been only one of several conceivable options for continuing the war, but in the spring of 1942 – in view of the remaining fighting power of the Red Army – the German leadership had no choice but to resume the attack in the East. This meant, however, that such a campaign would necessarily lack the element of political and strategic surprise that had been characteristic of 'Barbarossa'. 'Operation Blue' was to be undertaken against an enemy who, after making enormous sacrifices, was now very well prepared to fight a total war. At most, surprise could be achieved with regard to the direction of the attack. Moreover, after the conclusion of the winter battles, the forces available for a second German campaign in the East were, from a personnel, material and logistical point of view, only a shadow of those which had invaded the Soviet Union the previous summer. A comparison of the fighting-value-estimates of the divisions in the East produced from time to time by the Army General Staff shows that the Army High Command was very much aware of this situation. On the eve of the German attack on the Soviet Union in 1941, 134 divisions, or 64 per cent of all participating units, were classified as completely ready for attack. Nine months later, at the end of March 1942, when Directive No.41 containing the basic instructions for the coming summer campaign was completed, the number of divisions 'suited for all tasks' had shrunk to a total of eight, that is, five per cent of all available units.[45] Even though hopes of being able to improve this depressing situation a little before the start of the new offensive were justified, it was clear to all concerned that the offensive would have to be planned on the basis of much reduced forces and restricted to the front of only one of the three army groups in the East.

Only in terms of the expected time required do the campaigns of 1941 and 1942 appear to be, at first glance, similar. The illusory belief of 1941 that the war against the Soviet Union could be ended in a matter of weeks had indeed vanished, but the campaign plan for 'Operation Blue' was in its conception and military organisation also a blitzkrieg which Hitler hoped to be able to conclude by autumn. This, however, was the only similarity. While in 1940–41 the German dictator and his military advisers had been confident of their ability to 'defeat Soviet Russia in a short, quick campaign' and eliminate that country as a military, economic and political factor, their expectations with regard to 'Operation Blue' were on the whole much more modest. There can be no doubt that the near-disaster of the winter months had taught Hitler to respect the Red Army's power and readiness to make sacrifices, although he often emphasised these qualities to excuse his own and the *Wehrmacht's* failures.[46] Although, for propaganda or tactical reasons, Hitler encouraged hopes in his relations with his allies that 1942 would bring a decision in the East, concrete German planning took as its point of orientation a goal which in retrospect was also unrealistic but at any rate less utopian: maintaining Germany's ability to continue the war. In 1942 planning for the war in the East was primarily concerned not with conquering additional land for German settlement or with smashing Bolshevism, and not even with destroying the Red Army (although the hope of achieving all these things continued to be the driving force of the German war effort), but with conquering sources of raw materials, especially oil, adequate for the middle and long term. During a visit to the front in Poltava, Hitler openly admitted: 'If I don't get the oil in Maikop and Grozny, I'll have to liquidate this war.'[47]

Indeed, since the autumn of 1941 the critical oil supply situation in connection with the failure of the German attack on Moscow, the entry of the United States into the war and the possibility of a 'second front', which Hitler feared would be opened in France or Norway in 1942 or at the latest 1943, had confronted him with the choice of either trying to end the war by negotiations (which he refused to consider) or preparing as quickly as possible for a *long* war. His decision to pursue the latter alternative[48] confronted the German war economy and military with the necessity of crossing relatively exposed a 'danger zone' between the failure of the blitzkrieg and the readjustment to a long war. 'Operation Blue' was the operational attempt to cross this 'danger zone' in time, that is, before the Western Allies could intervene on a large scale on the Continent, and thus to close as soon as possible the 'window of vulnerability' represented by the real threat of a land war on several fronts. In this situation the necessity of achieving strategic success deprived Hitler from the very beginning of the freedom to plan the coming operations in the East solely according to the principles of classical operational logic, that is, above all under consideration of the relative strength of the forces and the problems presented by the sheer distances in that theatre.

The readjustment of the German war machine to fighting a long war meant that the main task of the German army in the East was now the conquest of sources of raw materials. This new priority influenced Hitler's operational plans all the more as he also expected in this way to be able to cut the Soviet Union off from raw materials essential to her survival. In this respect his assessment agreed with that presented by the French General Staff within the framework of Allied planning for operations in the Caucasus two years earlier. In February 1940 Gamelin had also been convinced that a direct attack on the Soviet oil industry in the Caucasus could deal 'a heavy, perhaps decisive blow to the military and economic organisation of the Soviet Union'.[49] In Hitler's view there were several additional important, though not in themselves decisive political, strategic and operational reasons for choosing the conquest of the Caucasus as an operational objective: his calculation that, because of the economic and logistical importance of the region, the Red Army would not be able to avoid a decisive battle there; the expectation of being able to cut the southern Soviet supply lines to the Western Allies and establish a base for a later strike against the British position in the Middle East, and not least the hope of persuading Turkey to enter the war on the side of the Axis Powers by achieving a decisive military success so near the Turkish frontier.

The fact that German planning for the war in the East in 1942 was based largely on a strategy for securing raw materials did not mean that race-ideology had ceased to be a factor in this war of annihilation. Considerable efforts were made by political and *Wehrmacht* leaders in 1942 to indoctrinate the troops with the ideological principles on which their operations were based. Even more important was the fact that in 1942, the year of the 'Wannsee Conference' and the *Generalplan Ost*,[50] the illusory belief that the new campaign would secure German conquests in the East led to an increase in long-term *volkstumspolitische* planning. At the same time the programmes for the extermination, enslavement, deportation and resettlement of entire population groups, begun on a large scale in 1941, were continued. In a speech on 23 November 1942 (the day on which the ring around the Sixth Army in Stalingrad closed) Heinrich Himmler, the main proponent of this policy, promised that the East would be 'a colony today, an area of settlement tomorrow and part of the Reich day after tomorrow'.[51] Two months earlier, in a small group, Himmler had gone even further and had spoken enthusiastically about 'a final struggle sooner or later with Asia', of which Russia was after all only 'an outpost': 'After the Greater German Reich will come the Germanic Reich, and the Germanic-Gothic Reich all the way to the Urals, and then perhaps even the Reich of the Goths, the Franks and the Carolingians'.[52]

In contrast to such bizarre ideas, however, a striking discrepancy had begun to emerge between Germany's political ambitions and her military possibilities in the winter of 1941–42. While attempts were made to realise the former in an unspeakably murderous and barbaric fashion, as if a German total victory were still possible, strategic and operational planning was increasingly determined by the question of whether the conquests already achieved could be held or the material preconditions for that could be fulfilled. These doubts and an awareness of imponderable factors began to influence the thinking of senior German military leaders in the phase of the war between the failure to take Moscow and the defeat at Stalingrad and led to a more pragmatic conduct of the war in the East. In the area of military planning, the disillusionment with regard to the course the war had taken, which was clearly present in varying intensity at all levels of the German military leadership, forced a certain revision of imperialistic visions of conquest and a concentration on what was actually achievable. This reorientation was, however, very limited: the dogma that the war could not be lost remained officially unquestioned even under the difficult conditions of 1942. Ideological prejudices were still responsible for a continuing underestimation of the abilities of the Soviet enemy, and wherever practical solutions were actually developed, they were often frustrated by Hitler's increasingly frequent personal intervention.

In deciding to make the conquest of the Caucasus the main objective of the German summer offensive, Hitler chose an option which Germany had attempted in vain to achieve during the First World War and which he himself had already considered for 1941. It was thus not a stroke of genius resulting from sudden inspiration. Nevertheless the choice of the Caucasus was to a much greater extent than the attack on Moscow Hitler's personal decision, taken during the most serious phase of the winter crisis without any previous consultation with the commander-in-chief of the army, his chief of the General Staff, the chief of army armament programmes or even the commanders-in-chief of the army groups. In the following months their influence was limited to the practical questions of operational planning. The Army High Command and parts of the OKW, especially the War Economy and Armaments Office and the *Wehrmacht* Operations Staff, and occasionally even Keitel, had considerable doubts about the feasibility of the operation. Contrary to the impression spread by numerous post-war publications, in part under Halder's personal influence,[53] these doubts, however, never assumed the form of concrete criticism of the basic ideas of the approaching campaign. Quite the opposite: Halder himself soon adopted, at least officially, the strategic ideas of the Caucasus operation. He told the Navy liaison officer assigned to him that the conquest of the Caucasus was 'an urgent necessity' as that region had about the same importance for Germany as Silesia had once had for Prussia: only the possession of the Caucasus would enable Germany to hold the empire she had conquered during the war.[54]

The situation assessments and memoranda submitted by various departments of the OKH and OKW during the first half of 1942 on the readiness of the German and the Soviet armies and the Soviet war economy were written almost without exception in a cautiously optimistic tone.[55] They all tended to emphasise the opportunities of the planned operation more than its risks and were too often marked by extremely sketchy knowledge of the situation of the enemy and a lack of the kind of worst-case thinking generally typical of good military planning.[56] Quite obviously uncritical optimism had become a dogma in German military planning. But while in 1940–41 it had resulted from an excessive but subjectively honest feeling of superiority, the situation in the spring of 1942 was marked by a really compulsive optimism, which saved Hitler and his military advisers from having to consider the possibility and the consequences of a failure of their operation.

This fateful inclination resulted from a combination of three circumstances: the first was that there actually seemed to be no alternative to Hitler's operations plan. Neither the 'strategic defensive' perhaps considered occasionally by some members of the Army General Staff, nor a new drive towards Moscow, not to mention the global ambitions of the Navy War Staff,[57] offered a solution to the problems of the war economy, which were becoming more acute with every passing month. With regard to the 'Moscow option', the Army General Staff was, from a psychological point of view, in the most unfavourable position imaginable *vis-à-vis* Hitler: the unsuccessful operation of the previous year had, after all, been Halder's idea, and the resulting near-disaster had, so it seemed, been averted only thanks to Hitler's ruthless orders not to retreat an inch. In view of this situation, the General Staff had no choice but to either support Hitler's plan for continuing the war in the East or to argue for a negotiated peace.

The question why they did not take the latter course points to a second important circumstance: Hitler's operational thinking for 1942 assumed that the Red Army was at the end of its strength and possessed only very limited powers of regeneration. It has been generally overlooked by historians that this fundamental error was based to a considerable degree on the mistaken information which the OKH, and especially their department Foreign Armies East, had spread about the enemy during the winter crisis. When they were forced to correct this assessment in the spring of 1942,[58] the decision to conquer the Caucasus had already been taken. In a fatal reversal of rational decision-making processes, decisions were no longer determined by unpleasant but unalterable realities; rather, in discussions and analyses, these realities were presented in such a way as to make them support supposedly irrevocable decisions.

A third, and perhaps the most important explanation of the forced optimism in official German assessments of the situation in the East can be found in the communication structure of the top political and military authorities of the Third Reich. It was typical of this structure that within and outside the individual *Wehrmacht* services there were numerous staffs and departments with complementary or overlapping functions, but hardly any intermediary coordinating organs comparable to those which existed in Britain and the United States in the form of various committees and subcommittees to smooth out conflicting interests and prepare joint decisions. While 'horizontal' communication was limited largely to the small areas of personal contacts and the mutual dependence of individual departments necessitated by their specific tasks, 'vertical' communication, that is, with Hitler as the highest and in the final analysis only decision-maker, became all the more important. A real competition developed among the armed services for the favour of the 'Führer'. As Hitler was not interested in studying files or in being systematically informed about developments, winning his favour was essential to gaining his support for certain problem solutions and projects. Apart from some basic positions and unchanging ideological principles, the dictator's decisions could thus indeed be influenced by skilful and sensitive advisers. This was even more the case as the number of decisions to be taken increased, Hitler's health declined and he became increasingly selective in his perception of the realities of the war.

In this situation in the spring of 1942, in spite or perhaps even because of his doubts about Hitler's abilities as a strategist and about the operational feasibility of the Caucasus plan, the chief of the Army General Staff believed himself to be in a good position. Did the situation not offer a new chance, perhaps the last chance, for the Army High Command to display their professional superiority? As there was no promising military alternative to 'Operation Blue', did not everything depend on influencing Hitler to take the right operational decisions? In the General Staff, Halder had at his disposal the decisive instrument for planning and carrying out the operation. He probably also hoped to be able to influence Hitler more easily, as his contact with the 'Führer' had become closer since Brauchitsch's departure and he was, according to service regulations, Hitler's 'first adviser in all questions concerning the conduct of the war'. For several months, it seemed that Halder's hopes would be fulfilled. Not only did the most important parts of Directive No. 41[59] bear his imprint, but Hitler also followed Halder's advice for the most part in his operational decisions in connection with the great battles in the spring of 1942, even when, as the tank battle of Kharkov in May and the dismissal of Field Marshal Bock at the beginning of July show, they were quite incompatible with the views of the responsible field commanders.

Paradoxically the convincing operational successes of the spring battles and the rapid conquest of territory during the first phase of 'Blue' contributed to the break between Hitler and Halder shortly thereafter. Soon Hitler's optimism about operational developments in the East was again boundless, and his growing nervousness about an early landing by the Western Powers on the Continent caused him to make a fatal mistake. Trying to conquer the Caucasus oil fields as soon as possible and to bring the war in the East to at least a temporary halt before the onset of winter, Hitler divided 'Operation Blue' into two parallel offensives: against the Soviet forces west of the Volga and against the Caucasus.[60] This decision, which the Army General Staff tried in vain to prevent, again made clear the differences between Hitler's thinking and that of his first adviser. Whereas Halder based his judgement solely on conclusions derived from the operational situation in 'his' theatre, these remained for Hitler always secondary to supposedly overriding strategic necessities. Taking these as his point of orientation instead of the realities of the battlefield, Hitler rejected at a decisive point Halder's persistent attempts to bind him to the professional military thinking of the General Staff. But in contrast to his reaction half a year earlier, Halder was no longer prepared to accept the responsibility for operationally absurd decisions of his commander-in-chief. In view of the fact that the German offensive had achieved a rapid conquest of territory, but not the hoped-for annihilation of the greater part of the Red Army, Halder was well aware of the fatal consequences any reduction of the German forces moving to attack Stalingrad would have, especially as that city was obviously being turned into a fortress. In the following weeks Halder prepared to resign his commission. Not the least important reason for his decision was his realisation that it would no longer be possible to win the war against the Soviet Union, for the preparation and conduct of which he bore responsibility.

Hitler came to this realisation only at the beginning of September, after the general stagnation had set in on all sectors of the front. This led to the 'September crisis',[61] whose significance, beyond the formal break between Hitler and Halder, lies above all in the fact that, as in earlier crises in 1938 and 1941, it represented a new outbreak of the profound conflict in relations between Hitler and the traditional military elite. As in December of the previous year,[62] the inner crisis of September 1942 was triggered by an external crisis. Hitler reacted to both in the well-known fashion: he attempted to master the inner crisis by shifting the blame, removing inconvenient generals (such as List and Halder) and by concentrating additional military functions (in this case command of Army Group 'A') in his own hands; to meet the external crisis he fell back on the simple 'hold-the-line' tactic which had become basically the only acceptable form of defensive warfare for him at the latest after the experiences of the winter of 1941–42. Unlike the position Stalin had taken in his famous Order No. 227 at the end of July,[63] however, Hitler's tactic was not part of a strategy based on a realistic plan to regain the military initiative. Instead, his reaction to the dramatically worsening ratio of German to Soviet forces was nothing more than an expression of his operational incompetence and the fact that he was at a loss as to what to do. Fully aware of the second front soon to be expected in the West, he was not able to accept a second failure of his plans in the East. The ultimate price of this obstinacy was the loss of the Sixth Army at Stalingrad.

III. THE 'TURNING POINT' OF THE WAR

The imminent disaster in Stalingrad, as the SS Security Service reported, had 'aroused the deepest fears of the entire population'. Moreover, it led to a lasting change in most Germans' view of the military situation. 'Generally', the Security Service observed in another report of 4 February 1943, 'the conviction is to be found that Stalingrad represents a turning point of the war'.[64] It was hardly surprising that the morale of the population had reached 'the lowest point ever'.[65] After Stalingrad questions which had long been ignored had to be answered. Instead of anxious hope, the question was now: 'How will it all end?' The question 'How long will victory take?' was replaced by 'How long can we hold out with prospects of ending this war on favourable terms?'[66] Even the 'Führer', who had until then been largely exempt from direct criticism in spite of his increasingly tarnished image as a leader, now became a target of discontent.

The psychological effects of Stalingrad in countries allied with Germany were no less serious than those in the Reich itself. It became very clear that there, too, the morale of the population was directly dependent on the success of German arms. In this regard Finland was an especially striking example. Confidential surveys showed a dramatic decline of expectations of victory among the Finnish population,[67] which stood in sharp contrast to the repeated declarations of loyalty to Germany by the Finnish government, and to reports in the Finnish press, which were often characterised by censorship and self-censorship. The situation in other countries allied with Germany was similar, especially in those which, like Romania and Hungary, had themselves suffered the loss of a considerable portion of their armed forces in the Stalingrad debacle and which, moreover, now had to listen to serious reproaches and accusations from their German ally. It was therefore not surprising that in the weeks before and after the surrender of the Sixth Army in Stalingrad, German diplomats reported frequently 'increasing war weariness in parts of the Romanian army as well as in the population'[68] and the 'vacillation of influential [Hungarian] circles in regard to their readiness to continue the war'.[69] This change in mood, not entirely unexpected but nevertheless dramatic and only briefly stopped by the re-stabilisation of the Eastern Front in the spring of 1943, favoured the efforts undertaken with varying intensity after Stalingrad by all governments allied with Germany to persuade the German government to accept a compromise peace, or, in view of the futility of such efforts, to distance themselves from Germany's policy of continuing the war.

The fact that the German defeat at Stalingrad was almost unanimously felt to be a turning point in the war by most contemporaries[70] undoubtedly influenced to some degree the further course of the war itself. Whether or to what extent this contemporary assessment agrees with the retrospective judgement of modern historians is, of course, a different question. Indeed, more recent research in this area has been marked by a strong tendency to place the turning point in the German conduct of the war not in November 1942 (or even later),[71] but already in December 1941, or even in the summer of that year.[72] This development has been due less to the dramatic events of those months than to the growing realisation, based on a better knowledge of German sources, that Germany simply did not possess the personnel or material resources to cope with the expansion of the war, which took place in the second half of 1941, from a short, regionally limited conflict to a long, worldwide struggle.[73]

The discussion about the 'turning point' of the war has, it seems to me, pushed another, more important question into the background: the question of whether, with regard to the German conduct of the war, it is possible to speak of a 'turning point' at all. This term suggests, after all, that at some point the war took a course fundamentally different from that which it had taken until then, that is, that at some precise point a war which until then could still have been won became a war which Germany was bound to lose. This was not, however, the case. Hitler's extreme war aims, the early globalisation of the war, the completely unequal distribution of human and material resources, the American lead in the development of nuclear weapons and, last but not least, the determination of the Allied great powers not to end the war which had been forced upon them before they had defeated Germany – all of these factors taken together clearly show, at least in retrospect, that the thesis that Germany at some point had a real chance of winning the war as a whole is untenable.[74] It is therefore misleading to speak of Moscow, Stalingrad or Kursk generally and without qualification as a 'turning point' of the war.

It is, however, another matter to ask whether the loss of the Sixth Army on the Volga marked a turning point of the war *in the East*. There the *Wehrmacht* had in fact twice been close to achieving a strategically important victory. In the autumn of 1941 before Moscow and in the following summer on the southern section of the front a collapse of organised Soviet resistance, or even of Stalin's regime itself, had been within the realm of possibility. In any case, in both instances the outcome was determined by a constellation of relatively few factors and not by some kind of 'historical necessity'.[75] With its defeat on the Volga the German army in the East also lost irrevocably the ability to force such potentially decisive battles. The strategic initiative in the East (and elsewhere) now passed to the other side. In this sense Stalingrad did indeed represent a 'point of no return'. More precisely, it marked the culmination of a process of shrinking options to achieve victory in the East. The most important stages in this process had been the battle of Smolensk in July 1941 and the resulting halt of the German advance, the failure of the drive to take Moscow in December 1941, the transfer of much of Soviet industry farther east, which has been correctly described as an 'economic Stalingrad',[76] and Hitler's decision to divide the forces used in 'Operation Blue' in July 1942. After each of these events the foundation on which any German victory in the East would have to be built became weaker and the number of options smaller. The German defeat at Stalingrad represented the final military consequence of this development. After Stalingrad there was no longer any basis for hope of victory in the East. The realisation of this fact could have led to a change in German war policy. That it did not, but rather resulted in a further radicalisation of the German conduct of the war was perhaps the most noteworthy result of the battle on the Volga.

NOTES

*This article was translated from German into English by Dean S. McMurry. It is dedicated to Klaus-Jürgen Müller (Hamburg) on the occasion of his 60th birthday.

1. The few really important exceptions prove the rule. See, above all, John Erickson, *Stalin's War with Germany. Vol.1: The Road to Stalingrad; Vol.2: The Road to Berlin* (London: Weidenfeld & Nicolson, 1975 and 1983 respectively); Earl F. Ziemke, *Stalingrad to Berlin: The German Defeat in the East* and ibid. (together with Magna E. Bauer), *Moscow to*

Stalingrad: Decision in the East (Washington, DC: Government Printing Office, 1968 and 1987 respectively). In addition, in spite of its considerable shortcomings, Albert Seaton, *The Russo-German War 1941–45* (London: Arthur Baker, 1971) should be mentioned; see also the older but still important work by Alexander Dallin, *German Rule in Russia 1941–1945* (London: Macmillan, 1957).

2. On the circumstances under which these studies were written, see Charles B. Burdick, 'Vom Schwert zur Feder. Deutsche Kriegsgefangene im Dienst der Vorbereitung der amerikanischen Kriegsgeschichtsschreibung über den Zweiten Weltkrieg', *Militärgeschichtliche Mitteilungen* 2/1971, 69–80.

3. This type of explanation is prominent in almost all accounts written by former German generals; see *pars pro toto* Alfred Philippi and Ferdinand Heim, *Der Feldzug gegen Sowjetrußland 1941–1945* (Stuttgart: Kohlhammer, 1962).

4. See also the author's research report 'Kriegsgeschichte – Politikgeschichte – Gesellschaftsgeschichte. Der Zweite Weltkrieg in der westdeutschen Historiographie der siebziger und achtziger Jahre', in Jürgen Rohwer (ed.), *Neue Forschungen zum Zweiten Weltkrieg: Literaturberichte und Bibliographien* (Koblenz: Bernard & Graefe, in print).

5. The most important exception is the Battle of Stalingrad itself, most aspects of which have been thoroughly examined. See in this regard, above all, Manfred Kehrig, *Stalingrad: Analyse und Dokumentation einer Schlacht* (Stuttgart: Deutsche Verlagsanstalt, 1974); Jürgen Förster, *Stalingrad: Risse im Bündnis 1942/43* (Freiburg: Rombach, 1975) and Geoffrey Jukes, *Hitler's Stalingrad Decisions* (Berkely, CA: University of California Press,1985).

6. See especially Andreas Hillgruber, *Hitlers Strategie: Politik und Kriegführung 1940–1941* (Munich: Bernard & Graefe, 2nd ed. 1982).

7. For example, most recently in Hartmut Schustereit, *Vabanque: Hitlers Angriff auf die Sowjetunion 1941 als Versuch, durch den Sieg im Osten den Westen zu bezwingen* (Herford and Bonn: Mittler & Sohn, 1988).

8. Historians still disagree on the question as to whether these aims were limited to a German hegemony in Europe or rather extended to global domination. See in this regard the extensive literature references in Gerhard Schreiber, *Hitler: Interpretationen 1923–1983* (Darmstadt: Wissenschaftliche Buchgesellschaft, 2nd ed. 1988), pp.280 ff., 362 ff.

9. It is not necessary to discuss here the debate begun recently by Viktor Suworow about Stalin's alleged intention to attack Germany in 1941, for even if Suworow's thesis should prove to be true (which does not seem very probable), that would make no difference as far as Hitler's own motives are concerned. It is certain that the fear of an imminent attack by the Soviet Union was not one of those motives. See Viktor Suworow, *Der Eisbrecher* (Stuttgart: Klett-Cotta, 1989), and also Bianka Pietrow, 'Deutschland im Juni 1941 – ein Opfer sowjetischer Aggression?', *Geschichte und Gesellschaft* 14 (1988), 116–35.

10. See Michael Salewski, *Die deutsche Seekriegsleitung 1935–1945*, Vol.I (Munich: Bernard & Graefe, 1970), pp.287 ff.; Karl Dönitz, 'Die Schlacht im Atlantik in der deutschen Strategie', in Andreas Hillgruber (ed.), *Probleme des Zweiten Weltkriegs* (Cologne and Berlin: Kiepenheuer, 1967), pp.159 ff.

11. See Wolfgang Michalka, *Ribbentrop und die deutsche Weltpolitik 1933–1940* (Munich: Fink, 1980), pp.287 ff.

12. See the interesting methodological approach in the study by Omer Bartov, *The Eastern Front, 1941–1945: German Troops and the Barbarisation of Warfare* (London: Macmillan, 1985).

13. Percy E. Schramm (ed.), *Kriegstagebuch des Oberkommandos der Wehrmacht (Wehrmachtführungsstab) 1940–1945*, Vol.I (Munich: Bernard & Graefe, 1965), p.341 (3 March 1941).

14. Colonel General Halder, *Kriegstagebuch: Tägliche Aufzeichnungen des Chefs des Generalstabes des Heeres 1939–1942* (Stuttgart: Kohlhammer, 1962–64). Vol.2, pp.336 ff. (30 March 1941).

15. See here the exhaustive account by Jürgen Förster in *Das Deutsche Reich und der Zweite Weltkrieg*, edited by the *Militärgeschichtliches Forschungsamt*, Vol.4 (Stuttgart: Deutsche Verlagsanstalt 1983), pp.426 ff.; see also Jürgen Förster, 'New Wine in Old Skins? The Wehrmacht and the War of Weltanschauungen, 1941', in Wilhelm Deist (ed.), *The German*

Military in the Age of Total War (Leamington Spa: Berg, 1985), pp.304–22.

16. Gerd R. Ueberschär and Wolfram Wette (eds.), *'Unternehmen Barbarossa': Der deutsche Überfall auf die Sowjetunion 1941: Berichte, Analysen, Dokumente* (Paderborn: Schöningh, 1984), p.314 (doc. 8).

17. Ibid., p.339 (doc. 20); see also *Das Deutsche Reich und der Zweite Weltkrieg*, Vol. 4, pp.1049 ff.

18. See the thorough study by Helmut Krausnick and Hans-Heinrich Wilhelm, *Die Truppe des Weltanschauungskrieges: Die Einsatzgruppen der Sicherheitspolizei und des SD 1938–1942* (Stuttgart: Deutsche Verlagsanstalt, 1981).

19. Christian Streit, *Keine Kameraden. Die Wehrmacht und die sowjetischen Kriegsgefangenen 1941–1945* (Stuttgart: Deutsche Verlagsanstalt, 1978); Alfred Streim, *Die Behandlung sowjetischer Kriegsgefangener im 'Fall Barbarossa'. Eine Dokumentation* (Heidelberg: C.F. Müller, 1981).

20. *Kriegstagebuch des OKW*, Vol.I, p.1021 (doc. 69); *Adolf Hitler: Monologe im Führer-hauptquartier 1941–1944: Die Aufzeichnungen Heinrich Heims*, edited by Werner Jochmann (Hamburg: Knaus, 1980), pp.39, 93; Halder, *Kriegstagebuch*, Vol.3, p.53.

21. For a new general account, see Matthew Cooper, *The Phantom War: The German Struggle against Soviet Partisans 1941–1944* (London: Macdonald and Jane's, 1979); see also the important contribution by Bernd Bonwetsch, 'Sowjetische Partisanen 1941–1944', in Gerhard Schulz (ed.), *Partisanen und Volkskrieg: Zur Revolutionierung des Kriegs im 20: Jahrhundert* (Göttingen: Vandenhoeck & Reprecht, 1985), pp.92–124.

22. In addition to the somewhat older works by Hans-Heinrich Wilhelm and David Kahn there are several new studies of the German intelligence service on the Eastern front; see Michael Geyer, 'National Socialist Germany: The Politics of Information', in Ernest R. May (ed.), *Knowing One's Enemies: Intelligence Assessment before the Two World Wars* (Princeton, NJ: Princeton University Press, 1984), pp.310–46; David Thomas, 'Foreign Armies East and German Military Intelligence in Russia 1941–45', *Journal of Contemporary History* 22 (April 1987), 261–301; Bernd Wegner, 'The Tottering Giant: German Perceptions of Soviet Military and Economic Strength in Preparation for Operation Blau, 1942', in Christopher Andrew and Jeremy Noakes (eds.), *Intelligence and International Relations 1900–1945* (Exeter: University of Exeter 1987), pp.293–311.

23. For example, in the otherwise excellent works of Earl F. Ziemke (see note 1 above).

24. Walther Hubatsch (ed.), *Hitlers Weisungen für die Kriegführung 1939–1945* (Koblenz: Bernard & Graefe, second edition, 1983), pp.84 ff. By far the most thorough analysis of the military preparations for 'Barbarossa' is to be found in *Das Deutsche Reich und der Zweite Weltkrieg*, Vol.4, pp.190–326. See also the concise analysis by Jürgen Förster, 'The Dynamics of Volksgemeinschaft: The Effectiveness of the German Military Establishment in the Second World War', in Allan R. Millett and Williamson Murray, *Military Effectiveness* (Boston, MA: Allen & Unwin 1988), Vol.III, especially pp.199 ff.

25. Halder, *Kriegstagebuch*, Vol.3, p.38 (3 July 1941).

26. *Kriegstagebuch OKW*, Vol.I, p.1020 (doc. 67).

27. See Andreas Hillgruber, *Der Zenit des Zweiten Weltkrieges, Juli 1941* (Wiesbaden: Steiner, 1977).

28. *Hitlers Weisungen für die Kriegführung*, pp.136 ff. (doc. 32 b). Thorough analyses of the reorientation of armaments production in the summer of 1941 can be found in Dietrich Eichholtz, *Geschichte der deutschen Kriegswirtschaft 1939–1945*, Vol.II (Berlin, GDR: Akademie-Verlag, 1985), pp.11 ff., and in Rolf-Dieter Müller in *Das Deutsche Reich und der Zweite Weltkrieg*, Vol.5/I, pp.567 ff.

29. Two recent studies give an idea of the gigantic organisational problems and achievements of the Soviet leadership in those first critical months of the war: Mark Harrison, *Soviet Planning in Peace and War 1938–1945* (Cambridge: Cambridge University Press, 1985); Klaus Segbers, *Die Sowjetunion im Zweiten Weltkrieg. Die Mobilisierung von Verwaltung, Wirtschaft und Gesellschaft im 'Großen Vaterländischen Krieg' 1941–1943* (Munich: Oldenbourg, 1987).

30. The first to describe this conflict in detail was Bernhard R. Kroener in *Das Deutsche Reich und der Zweite Weltkrieg*, Vol.5/I, pp.871 ff.; for a summary see ibid., 'Squaring

the Circle. Blitzkrieg Strategy and Manpower Shortage 1939–1942', in Deist (ed.), *The German Military*, pp.282–303.

31. See the account by Ernst Klink in *Das Deutsche Reich und der Zweite Weltkrieg*, Vol.4, pp.496 ff.

32. On the political and strategic significance of the battle of Smolensk, see Andreas Hillgruber, 'Die Bedeutung der Schlacht von Smolensk in der zweiten Juli–Hälfte 1941 für den Ausgang des Ostkriegs', in ibid., *Die Zerstörung Europas: Beiträge zur Weltkriegsepoche 1914 bis 1945* (Frankfurt a.M. and Berlin: Propyläen, 1988), pp.296–312.

33. Halder, *Kriegstagebuch*, Vol.3, p.123 (26 July 1941).

34. Directive No.34 of 30 July 1941, printed in *Hitlers Weisungen für die Kriegführung*, pp.145 ff.

35. See the new study by Klaus A. Friedrich Schüler, *Logistik im Rußlandfeldzug* (Frankfurt a.M. and Bern: Peter Lang, 1987), pp.308 ff.

36. See 'Ergänzung der Weisung 34' of 12 Aug. 1941, in *Hitlers Weisungen für die Kriegführung*, pp.148 ff.

37. See the memorandum of the army leadership of 18 Aug. 1941: 'Vorschlag für die Fortführung der Operation der Heeresgruppe Mitte im Zusammenhang mit den Operationen der Heeresgruppen Süd und Nord', printed in *Kriegstagebuch OKW*, Vol.I. pp.1055 ff.

38. Halder, *Kriegstagebuch*, Vol.3, p.254 (26 Sept. 1941).

39. Klaus Reinhardt, *Die Wende vor Moskau: Das Scheitern der Strategie Hitlers im Winter 1941/42* (Stuttgart: Deutsche Verlagsanstalt, 1972), pp.146 ff.; Schüler, *Logistik*, pp.410 ff.

40. See Memorandum of the chief of the Army General Staff of 7 Nov. 1941 (Bundesarchiv-Militärarchiv: RH 20–4/279).

41. This conflict was very evident at a General Staff conference in Orsha on 13 Nov. 1941. See Reinhardt, *Wende vor Moskau*, pp.135 ff., 139 ff., and *Das Deutsche Reich und der Zweite Weltkrieg*, Vol.4, pp.589 ff.

42. A detailed account of the objectives and course of 'Operation Blue' will be available in the near future in my contribution to *Das Deutsche Reich und der Zweite Weltkrieg*, Vol.6.

43. Halder, *Kriegstagebuch*, Vol.3, p.107 (23 July 1941).

44. *Kriegstagebuch OKW*, Vol.1, pp.1072–3 (doc. 105); Andreas Hillgruber (ed.), *Staatsmänner und Diplomaten bei Hitler*, Vol.1 (Frankfurt a.M.: Bernard & Graefe, 1967), p.629.

45. Bundesarchiv–Militärichiv: RH 2/427 and RH 2/429.

46. For example, in his conversation with Marshal Mannerheim on 4 June 1942; see Carl G. Mannerheim, *Erinnerungen* (Zurich: Atlantis, 1952), pp.482 ff.

47. Testimony of General Field Marshal Paulus, quoted in *Der Prozeß gegen die Hauptkriegsverbrecher vor dem Internationalen Militärgerichtshof* (Nuremberg: International Military Tribunal, 1947), Vol.VII, p.290.

48. Various measures were connected with this decision: a new shift of priorities in armaments, a reorganisation of armaments production (under Albert Speer), more intensive exploitation of occupied areas, increased mobilisation of the military and economic potential of Germany's allies, etc.

49. Gamelin's memorandum of 22 Feb. 1940, in: Auswärtiges Amt, *Weißbuch Nr. 6: Die Geheimakten des französischen Generalstabs* (Berlin: Zentralverlag der NSDAP, 1941), p.50 (doc. 22).

50. On the origins and content of this planning, see Helmut Heiber (ed.), 'Generalplan Ost', *Verteljahreshfte für Zeitgeschichte* 6 (1958), 281–325.

51. Quoted in Bernd Wegner, *Hitler's Politische Soldaten: die Waffen-SS 1933–1945* (Paderborn: Schöningh, third edition, 1988), p.48 (English edition: *The Waffen–SS*, Oxford: Blackwell, 1990), p.23).

52. Quoted in ibid.

53. See Halder's own book *Hitler als Feldherr* (Munich: Dom-Verlag, 1949), pp.48–9; the book by Adolf Heusinger, *Befehl im Widerstreit* (Tübingen: Wunderlich, 2nd ed. 1957), pp.176 ff. is another good example of this tendency.

54. Letter of the Naval Liaison Officer attached to the Army General Staff of 4 April 1942

(Bundesarchiv–Militärarchiv: RM7/259).

55. See, above all, the memoranda of the department Foreign Armies East (*Fremde Heere Ost*): 'Die personelle Wehrleistungsfähigkeit der UdSSR' of 23 March 1942; the War Economy and Armament Office (*Wehrwirtschafts- und Rüstungsamt*): 'Die wehrwirtschaftliche Lage der UdSSR Anfang des Jahres 1942' of 31 March 1942, and the *Wehrmacht* Operations Staff (*Wehrmachtführungsstab*): 'Wehrkraft der Wehrmacht im Frühjahr 1942' of 6 June 1942 (Bundesarchiv–Militärarchiv: RH 2/1924, Wi/ID 138 and RM 7/395.

56. In more detail, see author's article 'The Tottering Giant' (note 22 above).

57. See Salewski, *Seekriegsleitung*, Vol.II, pp.72 ff.

58. See especially the memorandum submitted by the department Foreign Armies East, 'Gedanken über die vermutete Kampfkraft der sowjetischen Armee bei Winterbeginn 1942', of 28 June 1942 (Bundesarchiv-Militärarchiv: RH 2/932).

59. Hitlers Weisungen für die Kriegführung, pp.183 ff.

60. Directive No.45 of 23 July 1942, printed in ibid., pp.196 ff.

61. For a critical analysis of this crisis, see *Das Deutsche Reich und der Zweite Weltkrieg*, Vol.6, soon to be published.

62. On the 'December crisis', see ibid., Vol.4, pp.605 ff.; on the function of crises in Hitler's system of rule, see also Reinhard Stumpf, *Die Wehrmacht-Elite. Rang- und Herkunftsstruktur der deutschen Generale und Admirale 1933–1945* (Boppard a.RH.: Boldt, 1982), pp.303 ff.

63. Printed in *Voenno Istoricheskii Zhurnal* 1988, No.8, pp.73 ff.

64. Heinz Boberach (ed.), *Meldungen aus dem Reich 1938–1945: Die geheimen Lageberichte des Sicherheitsdiensts der SS* (Herrsching: Pawlak, 1984), Vol.12, pp.4720 (28 Jan. 1943) and 4751 (4 Feb. 1943).

65. Quoted in Ian Kershaw, *Der Hitler-Mythos: Volksmeinung und Propaganda im Dritten Reich* (Stuttgart: Deutsche Verlagsanstalt, 1980), p.168.

66. Meldungen aus dem Reich, Vol.12, pp.4784 (11 Feb. 1943) and 4761 (8 Feb. 1943).

67. See Eino Jutikkala, 'Mielialojen Kirjo jatkosodan aikana', in Eero Kuparinen (ed.), *Studia Historica in Honorem Vilho Niitemaa* (Ekenäs, Finland: Turun Historiallinen Yhdistys, 1987), pp.131 ff., 145 ff.

68. Report of the German general attached to the High Command of the Romanian armed forces (5 March 1943), quoted in Förster, *Stalingrad*, p.138 (Annex 1).

69. Report of 17 Feb. 1943 from the German minister in Budapest to the Foreign Ministry, *Akten zur deutschen auswärtigen Politik 1918–1945*, series E, Vol.v (Göttingen: Vandenhoeck & Ruprecht, 1978), p.237 (doc.136).

70. Halder's successor as chief of the Army General Staff, General Zeitzler, also gave his unpublished account of the battle of Stalingrad the subtitle 'Der Wendepunkt des Krieges' (Bundesarchiv–Militärarchiv: N 220/126).

71. Walter Hubatsch, for example, saw the year 1943 as 'the culminating year of the war'. See his thoughts in this regard in *Kriegstagebuch OKW*, Vol.III, pp.1487 ff.

72. See also Jürgen Rohwer and Eberhard Jäckel (eds.), *Kriegswende Dezember 1941* (Koblenz: Bernard & Graefe, 1984).

73. This is also the conclusion reached in the most recent studies, based on an enormous wealth of material, by Hans Umbreit, Bernhard R. Kroener and Rolf-Dieter Müller in *Das Deutsche Reich und der Zweite Weltkrieg*, Vol.5/I, pp.1003–16.

74. For a summary of the main arguments, see Alan J. Levine, 'Was World War II a Near-run Thing?', *Journal of Strategic Studies* 8 (March 1985), 38–63.

75. See Jakushevsky's account in *Voenno Istoricheskii Zhurnal*, 1982, No.12, pp.41 ff.

76. A.M. Belikov, 'Transfert de l'industrie Soviétique vers l'Est (juin 1941–1942)', *Revue d'Histoire de la Deuxième Guerre Mondiale* 11 (1961), No.43, p.48.

The Italian Campaign, 1943–45:
A Reappraisal of Allied Generalship

BRIAN HOLDEN REID

The progress of the Italian Campaign resembles the career of its greatest architect, Winston Churchill. The initial promise, impulsive moves and glittering opportunities were followed by disappointments and set-backs; but these were overcome by resolution; triumph came at the end – though of a rather empty and incomplete kind – just as Churchill was brushed aside by Roosevelt and Stalin at Yalta, and then rejected by the British electorate in 1945. Consequently, it has never failed to excite extreme judgements. Some contemporaries (especially American) were highly critical of the Italian Campaign, regarding it as an expensive diversion from the decisive theatre which should have been opened in France. Its defenders stress how important it was to open up the Mediterranean Sea to Allied shipping and tie down German divisions in Italy before 'Overlord'. Winston Churchill himself declared that 'There can be no doubt at all that Italy was the greatest prize open to us at this stage, and that a more generous provision for it could have been made without causing any delay to the main cross-Channel plan of 1944'. The Italian Campaign is a vessel which holds endless disappointment: opportunities are squandered, blunders committed. From which ever position it is scrutinised, this negative attitude is encountered. Either the campaign should not have been launched; or it was conducted ineptly; or it would have been conducted less ineptly if more resources had been found to sustain it. Critics of Churchillian strategy, notably General Fuller and Captain Liddell Hart, offer a harsh indictment of its conduct. Fuller claimed that it squandered the initiative won in North Africa, and regarded it as 'a campaign which for lack of strategic sense and tactical imagination is unique in military history'. Liddell Hart is hardly less scathing.[1]

Given the sense of anti-climax which surrounds the campaign, what was its aim? Was it fulfilled? The Italian Campaign was the result of an opportunistic effort to seize and hold the initiative after the Axis collapse in Tunisia. 'We had now arrived in the orchard', wrote Alan Brooke, the Chief of Imperial General Staff, 'and our next step should be to shake the fruit trees and gather the apples'. In 1942 Churchill had foretold that

If . . . we move northward into Europe, a new situation must be surveyed. The flank attack may become the main attack, and the main attack a holding operation in the early stages. Our second front will, in fact, comprise both the Atlantic and Mediterranean coasts of Europe, and we can push either right-handed, left-handed, or both-handed as our resources and circumstances permit.

By December 1942 Churchill was thinking increasingly in terms of knocking Italy out of the war; that the Mediterranean should be made an important theatre of war. Brigadier Jacob, Assistant Secretary to the War Cabinet wrote that Churchill 'Made no secret of the fact that he was out to get agreement on a programme of operations for 1943 which the military people will think beyond our powers, but which he felt was the least that could be thought worthy of two great powers'. This consideration would bear heavily on Allied deliberations. They had to be seen to be doing *something*. The Germans had now been forced back on the defensive. But how was the pressure to be kept up? All the options available involved prodigious difficulties; and the initiative could only be kept if time was not wasted. Attacking in the Mediterranean had the advantage of striking at the enemy immediately, of removing Italy from the Allies' list of enemies, offering bases for attacks on the Balkans, providing access to the Soviet Union through the Black Sea, and the British had hopes, too, of tempting Turkey to enter the war on the Allied side. 'Success breeds success in these cases', Brooke predicted, 'and the ball was at our feet. . . . What was wanted was to knock the props from under the Germans in the defence of the Mediterranean, let them alone bear the full burden . . .'.

These arguments had varying degrees of persuasiveness. The most convincing was that it would take less time to attack in a theatre where large forces were already stationed than to ship these back to Britain and then prepare a Channel crossing. Thirteen British and nine American divisions could attack on a wide front and keep the enemy dispersed. But one other factor weighed more heavily than any other on the scale of these preliminary thoughts: that no successful large-scale amphibious operation had yet been launched against German forces. The Dieppe Raid of August 1942 was still a bitter and haunting memory; a fiasco that would not bear repeating on a larger scale. Operation 'Torch', the North African Landings, the following November, had been a complete success; but then the Allies had only faced the Vichy French whom it was assumed (quite wrongly as it turned out) were not disposed to open fire on the Americans.[2]

The United States Chief of Staff, General George C. Marshall, was inclined to consider operations in the Mediterranean as 'periphery picking'. So the British Chiefs of Staff had undergone an intricate mind-clearing operation, not only to anticipate his opposition, but to clarify and develop their own views. Operations in the Mediterranean were an inevitable consequence of President Roosevelt's decision to overrule Marshall's advice and permit American troops to take part in Operation 'Torch' in November 1942. All other schemes grew out of this initial step which once made was difficult to unmake. At the Casablanca Conference in January 1943 the Allies had agreed to assault Sicily, but a decision on carrying the war over on to the Italian mainland had been postponed. A decision was eventually reached in May 1943 to invade Italy once victory was clear in Sicily. This series of strategic compromises had profound influence on the character of operational planning: amphibious operations were hurriedly improvised with little time for considering all aspects of the problem. There were three basic alternatives. That Italy could be eliminated from the war by a full-blooded invasion; that a limited attack could be mounted to seize airfields in south east Italy as a base to launch aerial strikes at southern Germany; and that Italy could be ignored all together and help offered instead to Tito's partisans. But there was another possibility. Corsica and Sardina offered air bases which could neutralise Italy without the necessity of an invasion. This had the added bonus of threatening Southern France without entering into costly military commitments. Indeed, Churchill conceded in a telegram to President Roosevelt that a sudden occupation of Italy by German troops would render a full-scale invasion futile. If Italy suddenly collapsed then Allied forces could be dispatched at great speed to the Brenner Pass and the French Riviera. Should she stay in the war, propped up by German support, then a limited invasion would appear preferable, so that aid could reach Tito in Yugoslavia. Once more the theme underlying these reflections was *speed*. Time could not be wasted.

When it was clear by the spring of 1943 that Germany would not collapse dramatically now that the tide of war had turned against her, then the Chiefs of Staff declared that the aim of operations in the Mediterranean basin 'was to assist Russia in knocking out Germany by diverting German forces from the Russian front; and it was with this view that it had been decided to knock Italy out of the war'.[3] The Chiefs of Staff still thought in terms of gaining a base to strike at Italian cities from the air; and of gaining a bridgehead for future moves across the Adriatic. But it was the help that could be offered to the Soviet Union which was the criterion by which the value of these future operations should be judged.

It soon became obvious that a limited invasion would be a costly exercise for little discernible gain. It would not only be costly in lives but in time. The same amount of time was needed to plan for a small invasion as for a large one, and once committed surprise would be forfeited. Ground forces, furthermore, would be required to consolidate any hold over the airfields seized in the Italian 'toe'. As Brooke pointed out, an invading force however limited its initial liability, would require reinforcement to guarantee its security.

The Joint Planning Staff calculated that Germany would require a further 24 divisions to protect its southern flank from an invasion. Transferring these to Italy could lead to strategic disaster elsewhere. They concluded that a small force could bring about large results:

> it would not be in our interests to try and drive the Germans north west from the Ravenna–Pisa line if they decided to hold North Italy. Any forces we have to spare would be better employed in exploiting the very unfavourable situation likely to obtain in the Balkans.

This whole line of reasoning was what the Prime Minister liked to hear. But the Chiefs of Staff deferred a decision, and with this recommendation ringing in their ears, set out on the five day sea voyage to the Washington Conference. Such trips provided just about the only periods during the war when they could escape the pressure of the day-to-day running of the war, and have leisure to think.[4]

At the Second Washington Conference in May 1943 ('Trident') perhaps the most important point laid before the US Joint Chiefs of Staff by the British Chiefs on their arrival, in an *aide memoire* drawn up by Churchill's Chief of Staff, General Ismay, was the paramount need to sustain the momentum of operations against the Germans between the successful conclusion of the Sicilian campaign and Operation 'Overlord'. Though further amphibious operations would undoubtedly stretch shipping capacity to the uttermost, this would be counter-balanced 'by the fact that successful Mediterranean operations, and still more the elimination of Italy, will ease the task confronting an army landing in Europe from the United Kingdom'. Marshall disliked this argument. He perceived at once that such operations could only be sustained by forces drawn from the build-up of Allied forces in England for 'Overlord', Operation 'Bolero'. Alternative American suggestions, which tried to avoid this unwelcome development, notably Bedell Smith's advocacy of an invasion of Sardinia by five infantry and one armoured division, thus providing a base from which aerial attacks on Southern France and Italy could be mounted, greatly overestimated the capacity of air power to 'pin down' German forces. An invasion of Sardinia, in itself an object of the utmost insignificance, was an approach so indirect as to be invisible.[5]

The British Chiefs of Staff returned to the attack. 'We do not believe that Germany can hold both North Italy and the Balkans without risking a collapse on the Russian front.' It led logically to the conclusion that the 'Mediterranean offers us opportunities for action in the coming autumn which may be decisive. . . . If we take these opportunities, we shall have every chance of breaking the Axis and of bringing the war to a successful conclusion in 1944'. They may have over-egged the pudding in this paper.

But the time factor once more returned to push events forward. Armies were already in place in the Mediterranean. To prepare an offensive in this region would take far less time than anywhere else. The troops were experienced, and furthermore, would gain more experience, especially in amphibious operations, if they were used in this theatre. The logic underlying arguments for the immediate use of armies already stationed in the Mediterranean theatre appeared overwhelming, even to sceptics like Marshall. There simply was not time to return all these troops from the Mediterranean to Britain, train them for 'Overlord', and then launch the Normandy invasion in 1943. This simple fact undercuts the clever reconstructions of John Grigg, who is highly critical of the Mediterranean strategy.[6]

To sum up the results of this hectic planning process. It was dominated by haste: to maintain the initiative and seize as much advantage as could be gained from the triumphs of North Africa. But in view of the scepticism of the American Chiefs of Staff, great claims had to be made on behalf of any campaign in Italy. As this was fundamentally a strategic indirect approach towards the enemy's heartland, the argument that Italy would be knocked out of the war carried little weight. By 1943 she was obviously a liability to Germany, and a perverse argument could have been advanced suggesting that it was in the Allies' interests to keep Italy in the war rather than knock her out. Thus two other arguments were advanced to justify the operation which had an appropriately indirect connection with Italy. First, that the campaign would be a contribution to taking the strain off Soviet Russia; and second, that it would draw away enemy reserves from France before the Normandy landings.

These arguments influenced conduct at all three levels of the art of war. Strategically, the aim was rather negative. It was an important contribution to other campaigns, whether real or merely projected. But what it was actually *for* was rather less unambiguously defined. And on agreeing at 'Trident' that Italy should be invaded, the American Chiefs sought an unequivocal British commitment to 'Bolero' – the build up of American divisions in Britain as a prelude to landings in Normandy. Two months later at the first Quebec Conference ('Quadrant'), President Roosevelt made a decisive contribution to securing a commitment by pressing Churchill on this issue. The US Secretary of War, Henry L. Stimson, recorded that 'The President went the whole hog on the subject of ROUNDHAMMER [that is, 'Bolero']. He was more clear and definite than I have ever seen him since we have been in this war and he took the policy that the American staff have been fighting for fully.'[7] Thus the decision to invade was hedged about with strategic qualifications that would detract from the operational aim which always remained obscure. Yet all agreed that speed would be the soul of the forthcoming operation. But this was to be realised by an operational means – amphibious operations – that all textbooks on strategy agreed were the most complex, intricate and hazardous in the military canon. At the tactical level, too, speed was stressed. Yet adequate tactics had to be developed in a theatre of war quite unsuited to mobile warfare. Under the pressure of events these contradictions could not be resolved. General Fuller's verdict is a harsh one, but it cannot be disregarded. The Italian Campaign was 'A campaign with inadequate means, with no strategic goal and with no political bottom'.[8]

More than a glimpse of the difficulties caused by these problems could be discerned in the conduct of the Sicilian Campaign in July 1943. This was the first fully-fledged exercise in Allied 'jointery' – when the British and American armies, navies and air forces fought side by side. The campaign began with a superbly executed intelligence operation, Operation 'Mincemeat'. This involved the landing of the corpse of 'Major Martin' on a Spanish beach carrying documents suggesting that Allied landings could be expected in Sardinia (which was under discussion) and in Greece (which was not). As Ralph Bennett has argued, this ingenious scheme fitted in well with existing lines of German thought (perhaps the guarantee of any successful intelligence operation). The Germans expected an attack on Sardinia as the prelude to an invasion of northern Italy, thus driving them back to the Alps. Ultra intelligence, furthermore, had informed the Supreme Commander Mediterranean, General Eisenhower, that there were no more than two German divisions in Sicily; but it warned also of the arrival of several other formations, including XIV Panzer Corps, LXXVI Panzer Corps and 26th Panzer Division – ominous signs of a build-up in Italy and comforting confirmation that a campaign in the Mediterranean would act as a diversion from the two more important theatres.[9]

An emerging pattern began to take shape. The intelligence work was excellent, the operational opportunities appeared glittering, but they were never fully exploited. The planning for Operation 'Husky' did not go smoothly. The Army Group Commander (designate), General Sir Harold Alexander, was preoccupied until May with the successful termination of the North African Campaign. As Alexander complained to Brooke, 'It was quite impossible for me to give the necessary attention to Husky planning – I was hundreds of miles away at the front and far too busy to come back to Algiers or to really give the required thought to such a complicated affair'.[10] This lack of attention was rather unfortunate because of the dissension that broke out among the operational commanders of all three services as to the structure of the plan. Montgomery had been so impressed by enemy – especially Italian – tenacity before Enfidaville in the Tunisian Campaign, that he thought Sicily would be a tough nut to crack. He believed, therefore, that any invading force should be *concentrated*. But the Royal Navy and the Royal Air Force needed ports and airfields to sustain the naval and air campaign, and under their influence a plan emerged from the planning staff, Force 141 based in Algiers, envisaging widely separated thrusts at either end of the island, one towards

Palermo, the other towards Scoglitti and Gela on the south east coast. 'As far as I can make out the trouble with Husky', wrote Montgomery with breezy self-confidence, 'has been that no experienced fighting commander ever read the proposed plan made out by the planning staff in London. And yet Algiers accepted it almost in toto.' Montgomery, in what Carlo D'Este calls 'an act of calculated insubordination', then attempted to have the whole planning process overturned: it 'breaks every common-sense rule of practical battle fighting and is completely theoretical'.[11]

Montgomery did not make himself popular with either Tedder, AOC Mediterranean or the CinC Allied naval forces, Admiral Cunningham (who afterwards exclaimed that Montgomery's name was not to be mentioned in his presence). 'I understand that Cunningham and Tedder have expressed to you their complete disagreement of my proposed plan as forwarded to you', Montgomery signalled in that cock-sure tone which infuriated so many. 'I cannot repeat not emphasise too strongly that if we carry out the existing plan it will fail. I am prepared to state on whatever reputation I may possess as a fighting man that the plan put forward by me will succeed.' Montgomery's critics complained that he was being vainglorious. Yet there was another issue at stake. Montgomery objected in principle to a planning process whereby the planners were instructed to plan without bearing operational responsibility for the outcome. They then presented a series of 'options' to those entrusted with the ultimate responsibility. 'It is like an orchestra trying to play without a conductor.' He continued:

> The plan for all battle ventures or operations of war must be made by the commander who is to carry it out; he must make the original outline plan on which detailed planning will begin . . . to think that a planning staff can work out a plan without a commander, is merely to ask for trouble.[12]

Montgomery's revised plan called for the landing of Eighth Army and the US Seventh Army side by side on the south east coast of Sicily. They could seize the neighbouring air fields and then mount a strong blow towards Catania and Messina. 'We must get the initial stage-management right before we go on to details', Montgomery had concluded in his methodical way. 'I consider that we shall require all our resources to capture Sicily, and that the further exploitation on to the mainland – with a view to knocking Italy out of the war – is definitely unlikely to be possible' – at least in one bound. Montgomery's prudence is praiseworthy here – as it shows an awareness of the limits of Allied resources, the implications of which were so often overlooked. But Montgomery was convinced that we 'must use experienced troops to utmost extent'. This was a code word for Eighth Army. Montgomery attempted to have himself appointed as Ground Forces Commander, with the US contribution placed directly under Eighth Army command. 'With the new plan it is a nice tidy command for one Army HQ and Eighth Army should run the whole thing.'[13]

Thus far American troops and their commanders had not made a good impression on British generals. Whispers were heard that they were 'our Italians'. This low opinion dates from the American defeat at Kasserine Pass which contrasted so unhappily with Montgomery's triumph at Medenine. Alexander visited II US Corps after Kasserine and was shocked by what he saw. 'It is serious, very serious indeed, but not gloomy', Alexander consoled himself. 'I myself believe that the Americans have the human material for a first class army.' But he was convinced that 'they are going to play a very poor part in Husky and in that they shoulder a responsibility as great as our own'. But once impressions had made their mark on Alexander's brain, they were shifted with difficulty. From this point Alexander nursed a profound distrust of American fighting capacity, although he was rather more successful in concealing his views than Montgomery. The latter appears to have been temperamentally incapable of understanding that operational requirements (no matter how correct on their own terms) would have to be subordinated to the paramount need of holding the Grand Alliance together. Montgomery's staff, reflecting the arrogance of their master, spoke of 'irrelevances' when referring to Alliance relations. This was symptomatic of a failing to understand that no factor was more relevant to securing victory than the contribution of American armies. British commanders got off to a poor start in the Sicilian campaign which foreshadowed the greater tensions that would follow in Italy.[14]

Despite Montgomery's forebodings, the amphibious landings in south eastern Sicily went well (except for the parachute landings, as many landed in the sea – a lesson well worth learning for Overlord). It was the 'prolonged dogfight', at which Montgomery was usually so proficient, that proved troublesome. The Germans had made effective use of the mountainous terrain north of Catania. Montgomery's concept, as usual, was simple. 'If they [US Seventh Army] can press inland and secure Caltagirone and Canicatti and hold firm against every action from the West I could then swing hard with my right with an easier mind. If they draw enemy attacks on them my swing north will cut off enemy completely.' This role as Eighth Army's flank guard was not one calculated to please Seventh Army's commander, Lt. General George S. Patton, Jr. Furthermore, despite Montgomery's preference for concentration, his advance towards Messina had become somewhat dispersed. It had virtually broken up into three separate thrusts; a 'left hook' through the mountains; a central thrust; and a coastal drive. Montgomery had not directed operations with the same control as at Mareth and his plan was not only over-ambitious but his forces were over-extended.[15]

What Eighth Army really needed was the support of US Seventh Army on its left flank in accordance with Montgomery's basic concept. An attack here through the mountains west of Catania would have enabled Eighth Army to regroup and strike a really powerful blow towards Messina. But Montgomery's initial arrogance had left Seventh Army's commander disinclined to cooperate with him. Patton wrote home to his wife, 'Monty is trying to steal the show and with the assistance of Devine Destiny [a sarcastic reference to Eisenhower] may do so but to date we have captured three times as many men as our cousins'. Patton began to cast his eyes in a westward direction, and as a first step towards advancing on Palermo captured Agrigento. Then he flew to Tunis. Taking Alexander off-guard, he secured permission to advance on Palermo. The plain fact of the matter was that Alexander had been hoist by his own petard. He had not discouraged Montgomery from his headstrong schemes, and was in a weak position to deny Patton his pet scheme. Letting him have his way seemed a lesser evil than admitting to the distrust he felt for American military competence. But the resulting campaign in pursuit of geographical objectives was a distraction from the main effort. Patton began his advance towards Palermo at about the time the Germans began their evacuation of the western part of the island; once this region was occupied, US Seventh Army then had to find garrisons to hold it. When Montgomery suggested that Patton should organise a four division assault on Messina from Palermo, he had to scour his reserves to find two divisions. But operational issues were secondary. 'This was a horse race', Patton declared, 'in which the prestige of the US Army is at stake. We must take Messina before the British.'16

It was symptomatic of American generalship in the Italian Campaign that it appeared hypnotised by place names. These assumed immense importance in operational matters in Sicily just when Ultra intelligence revealed that the threat from the west was as solid as vapour blowing on a breeze. The striking power concentrated on the all-important north-eastern sector of the island was insufficient to secure a decisive victory; Allied strength was too dispersed – factors that would recur frequently. Before 17 August, when the conquest of the island was complete, 60,000 Germans and 70,000 Italians escaped to the mainland carrying, moreover, much of their heavy equipment. There can be little doubt that by permitting Patton's diversion to Palermo, and in their failure to grasp as late as 14 August that an evacuation was underway, Eisenhower and Alexander blundered. Ralph Bennett rightly concludes that 'a widespread failure to make proper use of available intelligence was a major contributory cause of the Axis armies' escape'. Instead of intelligence nourishing operational opportunity, its importance appears to have been lost sight of in competing and rather petty national rivalries. These more than any other factor shaped the operational conduct of the campaign.17

Thus, wails Nigel Hamilton, the Sicilian Campaign 'now ushered into Allied operations a political principle that committed the Allies to failure upon failure', as no single commander combined either the tact or the military talent to command *and* reconcile national differences. It is clear that Hamilton believes that Montgomery had the skill. But he was more guilty than most of falling victim to chauvinism and in failing to see the need for an institutional mechanism that could weld the Allied armies together operationally and make more effective use of the one resource that could compensate for numerical weakness – intelligence. The Italian Campaign would be won by a modest series of victories. A shattering decisive victory always eluded the Allies. Given the intense rivalries between the British and American armies this was no bad thing if one side had been perceived to have made the crucial contribution to victory. But these modest victories were a reflection of the modest operational skills of the Allied armies.[18]

Montgomery's generosity in calling for an advance by US Seventh Army towards Messina was prompted less by operational necessity or foresight than the expectation that Eighth Army would make the landings in the Bay of Naples in September, Operation 'Avalanche'. In this he was to be disappointed. His sulking would be a not inconsiderable factor in the developing crisis at Salerno. But so much of this was the result of the tension in the Allied conduct of the war stemming from an intersection of the strategic and operational levels. For much of the campaign, political consequences flowed from the operational stalemate; but at the outset operational exploitation was determined by political deadlock. For the first time since the announcement of the doctrine of Unconditional Surrender at the Casablanca Conference, this formula had to be worked out in practice on the eve of a great and hazardous campaign. Considering the advantages on the Allied side: that the Italians actually wanted to surrender; that they were keen for the Allies to invade their country and occupy as much of it as possible before the Germans could move in strength; that Mussolini had fallen; it is staggering how pusillanimously the Allies behaved in the face of these opportunities. It confirmed a common post-war criticism that whatever its advantages from a grand strategical point of view, Unconditional Surrender proved an excessively restricting declaration in that area of military activity between grand strategy and the operational level. General Fuller observed in 1943 that 'though our aims must be fixed, as they are in the Atlantic Charter, our means of attaining them must be as flexible as possible'. But this whole question was complicated by the insistence of the Americans that General Eisenhower should carry the great weight of political responsibility on his shoulders as Supreme Commander. This Eisenhower was well equipped to handle, but the constant recourse to consultation with his political masters had the inevitable result that the negotiations proceeded slowly.[19]

Indeed these tortuous negotiations almost came to a halt in the face of a conundrum well put by Michael Howard: 'the Italians felt they could not surrender until the Allies landed in strength near Rome; but the Allies considered that such a landing was out of the question ... unless the

Italians surrendered first'. This raised a further issue. It was probable that this dilemma could be resolved if the Allies could fall back confidently on careful planning and prudent calculation of resources. But these were conspicuous by their absence. And such faltering and hesitant moves as were made contrasted starkly with the speed and assurance of German counter-moves: in these weeks OKW moved 16 divisions into Italy.[20]

Planning for the invasion of Italy had continued hastily and rather scrappily after the conquest of Sicily – a victim of the sheer pace of events. No staff officer, for example, could state with any degree of certainty the number of landing craft that could be used in an amphibious landing at Salerno. Many had been despatched to the Pacific theatre. Those that were available in the Mediterranean were either being refitted after Sicily or were en route to England. A good number were arriving brand new from California. This was only one of many muddles which staffs were frantically attempting to sort out before the invasion. All plans had to be submitted to Alexander by 30 August, that is within two weeks of the fall of Sicily. He, in turn, had to give his assent some ten days before the landings. A need for hurry led to carelessness and a lack of thought. On the day of the landings Churchill warned Alexander of the dangers ahead with an historical allusion to Gallipoli which would have amused sceptics in Washington who were convinced that the follies of that campaign were being repeated.

> I hope you are watching AVALANCHE which dominates everything. None of the commanders engaged have fought a large-scale battle before. The Battle of Suvla Bay was lost because Ian Hamilton was advised by his CGS to remain at a remote central point where he could know everything. Had he been on the spot he could have saved the show.

Alexander would need to take heed of Churchill's advice.[21]

The senior American commanders in the forthcoming battles were woefully inexperienced. The Army commander, Mark Clark, had not seen a shot fired in anger. A protégé of General Marshall, he was a staff officer of considerable energy and ability. He was self-confident and vain – his enemies (which were not few) whispered that he spent more time examining photographs of himself than maps of enemy positions. He was disliked by his American colleagues, mainly because of his rapid promotion. Indeed this had occurred so rapidly that Clark found himself placed in command over two major generals, Dawley of US VI Corps, and Fred Walker of US 36 Infantry Division, both of whom had taught him as a student at various points in his career. Despite Clark's determination to make cooperation with the British work, underneath his handsome, charming and affable exterior lurked a rampant anglophobia – though no British officer guessed this at the time. And then there was Montgomery

– appalled that his Eighth Army had not been given the plum job at Salerno.

The main reason why US Fifth Army had been given this task was to ensure that American troops were given a prominent role in an Italian Campaign. Eisenhower advocated a landing at Salerno not only for political reasons but because an assault across the Straits of Messina was too predictable and could be bottled up in the 'toe' of Italy without too much effort (as the Allies had been at Salonika in 1915). A landing at Salerno offered the chance for decisive operational success. It could build on the experience gained in the Sicilian landings and capitalise on the Allies' great naval and aerial superiority (indeed the Luftwaffe had been driven virtually from the Mediterranean). As Eisenhower observed in 1948, the Salerno operation was 'undertaken because of our faith in the ability of the [Allied] air forces, by concentrating their striking power, to give air cover and emergency assistance to the beachhead during the build-up period, and in the power of the Navy to render close and continuous gunfire support to the landing troops until they were capable of taking care of themselves'.[22]

But, as before, the pattern of the Italian Campaign re-asserted itself. Deliberations at the highest level, which were characterised by indecision and compromise, stifled operational opportunity. It was a grim lesson of Salerno that no matter what degree of flexibility was conferred by command of the sea and in the air, there was no compensation for a sound plan of operations on the ground. At Salerno this, too, was lacking. The available force was spread over an excessively wide area; it was not concentrated. The errors of Sicily were repeated within two months – the consequence of bringing in new and untried staffs to consider old problems. The Salerno landings amounted to two separate beachheads ten miles apart, separated by the River Salo. In the opinion of Dominick Graham and Shelford Bidwell: 'The whole plan was an example of the Fifth Army staff's propensity to make plans on the map without any study of the ground or possible enemy reaction.' This inexperience was compounded by complacency. It was assumed, quite wrongly, that the only forces to be encountered in the Bay of Naples would be Italian. Sunbathing aboard ship as the convoys steered towards Salerno, the troops believed that it would be a 'walk-over'; they cheered loudly after news of the Italian surrender was announced. The men, like their commanders, were inexperienced and poorly trained. Yet so complex were amphibious operations that a naval navigating error of only half a degree would result in troops being landed on the wrong beach, in panic, confusion and chaos. Determined to attain complete surprise, Clark ruled that there would be no preliminary naval bombardment – a great error. The British X Corps insisted on one in accordance with Eighth Army practice, so Clark was not even consistent in error. As security surrounding this operation was lax, any hope of gaining a surprisal was forlorn. So strategic fumbling and tactical error combined to snuff out such operational opportunity as existed.[23]

The German response was decisive: the Allies were almost driven back into the sea. The earlier complacency was shattered. On 7 September Alexander signalled the CIGS, 'the Germans were becoming highly suspicious of the Italians, but will lack the rapidity of our intended moves [which] will forestall any Axis coup d'etat'. This was delusion. The Allies learnt the hard way that in mechanised wars, armoured forces on land could move faster to strike at amphibious landings than these could build up defences. Alexander visited the scene to see things for himself. He was appalled by Dawley, who was elderly, uninspiring and out of his depth. He turned to Clark and said quietly, 'I do not want to interfere with your business, but I have some ten years' experience in this game of sizing up commanders. I can tell you definitely that you have a broken reed on your hands and I suggest you replace him immediately.' This indirect reference to his inexperience may have wounded Clark's vanity but its wisdom could not be gainsaid and Dawley was sacked. The beachhead was reorganised, saved by the weakness of the initial German counter-attacks rather than by Allied efforts. None the less areas held were consolidated; new defensive positions were reorganised, and gradually it became clear that the Allies would stay at Salerno.[24]

The true significance of Salerno was, as Graham and Bidwell point out, that it was decisive in its indecisiveness. Its results shaped the Italian Campaign. They stress what an odd battle it was with a small ratio of troops to space with great gaps between formations at all levels. If Clark had been given stronger forces, had they landed with a concentrated punch, crushing the weak German divisions that opposed them, then the strategic arguments that were being conducted around the Fuhrer's person in the autumn of 1943 would have taken a quite different turn. Kesselring, the CinC South, argued that as Italy was ideal defensive country, the southern flank of the Reich should be defended as far away from the Alps as possible. Rommel, the commander of Army Group B sent to occupy northern Italy, perhaps over-sensitive to the overwhelming might of the Allies in the air, believed that such a defence was impossible and that resources should be mustered in the north. Had Salerno been a disaster and Rommel's gloomy warnings confirmed, then Kesselring's arguments would have been discredited. German Army Group C, as it was now designated, would have been withdrawn, and the great battles fought south of Rome around Cassino would never have been fought. The other result of Salerno was that Kesselring formed a very poor opinion of Anglo-American soldiers. They were flabby, whining amateurs; one German, he thought, would see off three Anglo-Americans. Even before the Battle of Salerno was over he had issued orders for the construction of a great defensive line stretching from the River Sangro to the mouth of the Rapido-Garigliano (called by

Allied intelligence the 'Hitler Line'), an outer bastion for an even stronger fortification – the Gustav Line. So though the ratio of troops to space did not rise over much in future operations, the gaps disappeared. Each battle fought henceforth aimed to break gaps in the enemy's defensive lines; each battle became a battle of attrition.[25]

Fifth Army was not the only formation that drew Kesselring's scorn. Ultra intelligence had made it very plain indeed that the Luftwaffe was not flying reconnaissance missions, that Montgomery's preparations were going forward unobserved, and that German formations were being withdrawn from southern Italy. Still, Montgomery insisted on drenching the northern shore of the Straits of Messina with artillery fire, an act of 'absurd over-insurance', in Michael Howard's opinion. The ponderous advance northward was similarly uninspired. Montgomery seemed to be wilfully fulfilling the worst caricature of his generalship drawn by American critics. Nor did the crisis at Salerno spur him on. He took the view that Fifth Army had got themselves into this mess and they could get themselves out of it. Such mean-spiritedness would resurface again in this campaign.[26]

A foretaste of what was to come was revealed in operations that developed after the fall of Naples. The advance to the Sangro and Garigliano was a frustrating experience for both Fifth and Eighth Armies. It revealed a major difference in British and American operational procedures. In Sicily, Patton boasted, 'Our method of attacking all the time is better than the British system of stop, build up and start, but we must judge by the enemy reaction'. But in Sicily the enemy was virtually non-existent on Patton's front. In Italy against Clark he made his mark felt. Montgomery visited Fifth Army in November and found it 'whacked'. He wrote to Brooke that night a letter revealing not only grave doubts about the American way of doing things but a measure of profound condescension that must have infuriated Clark privately.

> So long as you fight an army in combat teams and the big idea is that every combat team should 'combat' somebody all the time, then you don't get very far. . . . Clark would be only too delighted to be given quiet advice as to how to fight his army; I think he is a very decent chap and most co-operative. If he received good and clear guidance he would do very well.

Here was a resurrection under quite different conditions of Montgomery's proposal that US II Corps be brought under Eighth Army command. But Montgomery's own plans were not going well. He was entering an anti-climactic period; perhaps his thoughts were focusing more on the problems of Overlord; perhaps he was just plain 'tired out' as Brooke thought when visiting Italy in December 1943. The appalling weather and difficult terrain rendered forward movement sluggish.

I don't think we can get any spectacular results [Montgomery reported] so long as it goes on raining; the whole country becomes a sea of mud and nothing on wheels or tracks can move off the roads. Given fine dry weather we could really get a move on.

On the same day, he wrote to his friend 'Simbo' Simpson in the War Office. 'If you make mistakes in war it is not easy to recover.' This was a fitting curtain-raiser to the Battles of Cassino that would open within six weeks.[27]

The four battles of Cassino, 12 January–5 June 1944 brought to a head all the contradictions and muddles in the Allied conduct of operations in Italy. When Brooke visited Italy in the previous December he talked with Clark. He confided to his diary certain worries. 'He seems to be planning nothing but penny-packet attacks and nothing sufficiently substantial.' Once the Battle of Cassino began his worst fears seemed confirmed. 'I am not happy about our relative success in Italy. We have not got a sufficient margin to be able to guarantee making a success of our attacks.' But the fundamental problem was that these attacks were not linked to an agreed strategy. In consequence, there was no operational aim with an acknowledged timetable for fulfilling it. The only objective that Alexander had been given by Eisenhower was the capture of Rome and the need to maintain pressure on the enemy. But given the optimistic even heady expectations in London that the Germans would withdraw northwards and that the Allied armies would soon reach the line Pisa–Rimini, this was less than helpful. It is not surprising that the Allies were forced to improvise hurried and rather poorly co-ordinated attacks in order to break through the Hitler Line. But what is less understandable is the poor level of technique exhibited after some four years of war. Throughout the Battles of Cassino the Allies consistently underestimated the defensive skill of the Germans.[28]

The first and foremost factor influencing these great battles – the most sizeable operations yet undertake by Allied forces – was the topography. As Alexander had observed in November 1943, 'They are really large mountains and very steep and mostly covered in trees and shrub . . . the attack is made difficult by the exhaustion of the climb and the number of men required for porterage.' Moreover, as the Allies were so dependent on road transport they were tied to roads. Thus advances by divisions along narrow mountain passes and tiny tracks were often reduced to the widths of battalions and even companies. The full weight of Allied fighting power could not be brought to bear on the immensely strong German defences. Central Italy was ideal defensive country. The Germans enjoyed the advantage of being on the heights, of observing Allied movements behind lateral river lines; their lines were strengthened by concrete and steel casements and bunkers, anti-tank guns, machine guns, mortars and booby traps, all supported by artillery fire.

The Allies were attacking in winter weather, and because of the hard rock, the infantry could not 'dig in'; they remained exposed to the weather. It was under such uncomfortable conditions that the lack of an Allied overall numerical superiority had very serious results. The rapid movement of a single German division could frustrate the advance of two Allied divisions. The Germans showed tremendous skill at husbanding their reserves at the operational level. Never was the dictum popularised by Liddell Hart, that an attacker requires a 3:1 superiority, more relevant than in the mountains around Cassino. Instead Allied thinking was dominated by two other considerations: that weight of metal, whether delivered by artillery or by aircraft, could compensate for a numerical deficiency of troops on the ground; and secondly, that the 'fighting spirit' of certain contingents of fighting troops, whether they be American or British Commonwealth, would be sufficient to break through – an attitude fostered by fierce nationalistic pride which seems to have been stimulated by working closely along side so many different nationalities (a total of 21 in 15th Army Group). This aggravated a basic tendency in both the British and American armies to think in terms of corps-sized operations because national contingents were grouped in corps. As General Juin of the French Expeditionary Corps (FEC), a body not respected in Fifth Army until they broke through the Gustav Line, because they carried the sins of the French collapse in 1940, wrote, 'As far as the British are concerned there is . . . a congenital inability to think in terms of large-scale manoeuvres with an Army Group or even an Army.' In Italy this criticism was just as valid of the Americans.[29]

The paradox underlying these factors was at Cassino the Allies were drawn into a battle of attrition under the most disadvantageous circumstances on ground not of their choosing, which they were not prepared to fight either mentally or physically, and for which they lacked the resources. Lack of progress threw the whole *raison d'être* of the campaign into doubt. It was German forces that were supposed to be diverted and mangled. In Washington it appeared rather that Allied forces were being worn down for no discernible benefit. This perspective reinforces an argument advanced persuasively by General Strawson. Throughout the Italian Campaign, though they remained on the defensive, the Germans retained the strategic initiative leaving the Allies floundering to organise sufficient strength to hit them hard. One may go further and argue that in the Italian Campaign no consistent strategic aim was being fulfilled. What was accepted and agreed in London was not necessarily the view prevailing in Washington. In a coalition war this was to prove a handicap of no small significance.[30]

The First Battle of Cassino opened inauspiciously on 12 January 1944 with an attempt by X Corps, the FEC and US II Corps of Fifth Army to strike at the 'back door' of the Cassino defences. The British and French Corps were to provide diversionary attacks on the flanks in support of

US II Corps' main attack in the Liri Valley. As Clark wrote, a bridgehead across the Rapido River was vital 'in order to permit the debouchement of our tank forces into the Liri valley'. Given the strength at his disposal, Clark's plan was over-ambitious and ill-coordinated. General Juin observed accurately that 'The plan drawn up by the Anglo-Saxon high command was at fault in that it lacked any logical and clearly defined conception of manoeuvre involving the whole army'. The French offensive on the right made good progress. The British secured some shallow bridgeheads across the Garigliano but were reluctant to press further attacks – an attitude which earned Clark's scorn. But the US II Corps failed to get across the Rapido in strength and thus the armour could play no part in the battle. Not a single soldier from US 34 Infantry Division got nearer than a thousand yards to the German defences. Despite the great weight of the supporting Allied artillery bombardment, the strength of Allied infantry on the ground was too weak. Clark insisted that attacks on US II Corps front continue across the Rapido north of Cassino town long after there was any remote possibility that he could make worthwhile gains. The co-ordination of these operations left a great deal to be desired, and some of the worst blunders were worthy of those committed on 1 July 1916. None the less, although it is difficult to resist the conclusion that the American 'combat team' style of operations accentuated the breakdown at Cassino into weak piecemeal blows, something other than personal pride compelled Clark to continue his offensive – the fate of the Allied beachhead at Anzio.[31]

On Christmas Day 1943 Alexander accepted rather reluctantly plans for yet another amphibious operation, Operation 'Shingle'. At this formative stage it consisted of little more than a raid with one division that should dash behind the Gustav Line and link up with a triumphant Fifth Army moving down the Liri Valley. Although one of the scheme's most voluble champions was Churchill, the object of this operation, like so many in the Italian Campaign, was never clarified. It grew in a very short time into an ambitious amphibious landing involving US VI Corps of 110,000 men, and it seems to have taken on a logic and function of its own. After seizing the ports of Anzio and Nettuno, Alexander expected US VI Corps to advance on the Alban Hills; the seizure of these would cut enemy communications south of Rome and threaten his rear. This would lead to a substantial German diversion northwards to deal with this threat and permit Fifth Army to break into the Liri Valley. But no directives were issued embodying this view. Indeed, Clark held the view that such a design was beyond the capability of two divisions. After the Salerno experience, he would be satisfied with a successful landing and US VI Corps commander, Lucas, received orders to this effect.

The landing – unlike Salerno – prefaced by a fierce bombardment which damaged Anzio and Nettuno severely, was a complete surprise. Lucas had received some bland suggestions from both Alexander and Clark which proved less than helpful; at least his written orders were unequivocal: 'Advance on the Alban Hills' only after he had secured the beachhead. The tortuously slow progress at Cassino depressed Lucas. If Fifth Army could not break through, his Corps would be isolated and destroyed, strung out along the roads south of Rome. He took counsel of his fears and strengthened his defences. It was at this point that the ambiguity in the operational design for Anzio almost proved fatal. Which was the chicken and which the egg? Was Lucas to advance in order to facilitate Clark's breakthrough, or was he to remain behind his defences until Clark broke through? Alexander urged the former; Clark veered towards the latter. In the event the double negative prevailed: Clark did not break the Gustav Line and Lucas did not advance to the Alban Hills. German recuperative powers were such that not only were forces detached from the Gustav Line without endangering its defence, but reserves were mustered and a strong counter attack launched against Anzio. The beachhead was beleaguered, its destruction feared. Thus the strategic design was virtually reversed. Clark was forced to renew his offensive in order to take the strain off troops whose landing had been calculated to relieve the burden facing the Fifth Army; and he was forced to do this at a time when the fighting power of his divisions had been severely eroded by four weeks of ferocious fighting.[32]

Anzio was yet another in a series of hurried operations in the Mediterranean theatre planned in a scramble. 'We have had a hard time since I last saw you', Alexander wrote to Brooke, 'we were a bit rushed into the Anzio Landing – it was put on in 3 weeks, no time to get out a good Corps Commander and Staff, like Dick McCreery. I had to be content with Lucas . . . – he proved to be an old woman.' This was rather hard on Lucas. He had concerned himself more with preserving his force from defeat rather than defeating the enemy, hardly the mark of a great general. But the beachhead did survive the German onslaught. In war opportunities are offered fleetingly. An advance on the Alban Hills may well have surprised the Germans and given the morale of Fifth Army a welcome boost; perhaps it would have ended in catastrophe; no firm prediction can be hazarded. Certainly Ultra intelligence reveals that Allied generals (at least down to Army level) were aware that these opportunities existed. But the operation would only have succeeded decisively if it had been envisaged as a whole at the Army Group and Army level. Clark only interested himself in it because it involved American troops; Alexander might have made his intentions clearer if he had not to deal so circumspectly with Allied sensitivities. At any rate, during the Anzio battles, Maitland Wilson, the new Supreme Commander Mediterranean, visited Clark to discuss the possibility that he might be transferred to Seventh Army and take over planning for Operation 'Anvil/Dragoon'. Clark made his views clear on another matter that would affect strategic opportunity in the future.

> I told him I wanted to speak frankly, that the Fifth Army had landed at Salerno, taken Naples, and battled its way to the north through hellish terrain and with bloody losses and that it was entitled under my command to take Rome.

He would not permit the unscrupulous British the chance of manoeuvring him out of the way so that they could have all the glory to themselves.[33]

Operations in support of the Anzio bridgehead were a costly burden to an overstretched army. In the First Battle of Cassino, the Fifth Army had advanced seven miles, lost 16,000 casualties and exhausted eight divisions, all for a number of bridgeheads that were too shallow to act as bases for an armoured thrust down the Liri valley. 'How is Clark playing up now?', enquired the CIGS of Alexander, voicing doubts about Clark's ability which Alexander certainly shared. 'I do hope you are getting his full and loyal support? At any rate, in Oliver Leese you should have a tower of support.' Leese had taken over command of Eighth Army from Montgomery who had returned to England (with seven of Alexander's divisions) to prepare for 'Overlord'. Alexander had never been very confident in Clark's ability, and for the Second Battle of Cassino he turned to the Eighth Army and brought over into Fifth Army's line the freshly organised New Zealand Corps under Freyberg. This was an ad hoc force with no experienced staff or properly organised headquarters. Once 'British' troops were brought into the Fifth Army sector Clark lost interest, and he played a marginal role in the succeeding drama. The command structure was unwieldy and Freyberg tended to deal directly with Alexander, a short circuiting of the Army commander which Clark resented.[34]

The essence of Freyberg's plan was a direct approach towards the massif dominated by the monastery at Monte Cassino. General Tuker, commanding 4 Indian Division, thought this would merely repeat the errors of Clark's failed offensive. 'To go direct for the Monastery Hill now without softening it up properly is only to hit one's head against the hardest part of the whole enemy position and to risk the failure of the whole operation.' Tuker was also flabbergasted to discover that the only way he could find out precise details of the monastery's specifications was by rummaging in the bookshops of Naples; in this mission, at least, he was successful.

Tuker's complaints led logically to supplementing the advance with additional firepower – aerial bombing. As Tuker observed, 'If we intend to put infantry through we have only one means to do it and that is by the surprising weight of our fire. . . . Artillery weapons will not give this effect. The only effect left to us is the weight of our airpower and that must be used in its fullest weight and concentrated and co-ordinated with artillery and ground small arms.' The last point was perhaps the most important. Alexander and Freyberg gained the support of General Ira A. Eaker, commanding the Mediterranean Allied Air Force who, smarting under criticism that it was playing a poor part in the campaign, sought to make the bombing of Cassino a model of ground–air co-operation. To his credit, Clark opposed the bombing – mainly on the grounds that the destruction of buildings would actually aid the defenders in creating strong points where they had previously not existed. This was another example of the way in which he was cut out of the command system. Certainly the troops wanted to see the monastery bombed for all kinds of irrational reasons and Alexander reflected their feelings accurately. But this was not a firm basis on which to found tactics. In the words of John Ellis, 'it is difficult not to accuse Alexander and Freyberg of wishful thinking if they really thought that just one bombing raid would somehow completely obliterate an edifice whose main walls were 150 feet high and 10 feet thick'.

But the real issue arising from the battle was not so much *whether* the monastery should have been bombed, but rather why the experiment in ground–air co-operation was so incompetently executed. In part this was due to hurried improvisation resulting from organising bombing raids when the weather was so bad. But the failure to inform the attacking troops that the bombing was about to begin was inexcusable; the first they heard of it was when the bombers flew over. The damage inflicted on the monastery was not really sufficient to help the advancing troops. But none were there to follow up. No attack was launched that day. Thus any advantage accruing from the raid was frittered away. By the time attacks were thrown in the defenders were manning their weapons behind strengthened defences, and by then they had occupied the monastery itself. The appalling conditions on the ground whittled away the New Zealand Corps's fighting strength to such a degree that attacks were being organised on a battalion-wide frontage.

General Juin grasped that the offensive should have been co-ordinated by 'a general attack . . . along the whole Fifth Army front'; but Alexander and Clark were in such a hurry to achieve a breakthrough that they did not spend their time organising such an effort. They indulged in wishful thinking and did not give the massive problems involved in organising such an operation the attention they deserved. Their efforts were slapdash and counter-productive. General Fuller's verdict delivered more than 40 years ago has stood the test of time remarkably well: 'the bombing of the Abbey was not so much a piece of vandalism as an act of sheer tactical stupidity'. '[I]n the face of all the evidence, the dogma that weight of metal could so stun the defenders that all the ground forces would have to do was merely occupy the paralysed target held the field.' But these same errors were replicated in the Third Battle.[35]

The Third Battle was indeed a repeat performance of the Second. Massive firepower was unleashed on ground already well churned over. This firepower was deployed to minimise casualties – or so it was hoped: 1060 guns plus medium and heavy bombers. The town of Cassino was a prime target. As before, the strength of the infantry was reduced by the ground; it was held back from the town behind bomb safety lines. Several hundred yards would have to be traversed before the enemy's defences could be assaulted, giving him time to man his weapons after the bombing had ceased. Armour would accompany the attacking infantry into the town. Actually it slowed the advance down as even tanks could not move easily over that rubble-strewn ground. Added to the catalogue of blunders committed during the earlier battles was the extraordinary oversight of omitting the monastery from the list of targets. Thus it was bombed when unmanned and not bombed when it was fully manned. Freyberg admitted at one point that given the levels of destruction resulting from the bombardment, tanks would face difficulties breaking through. Yet the whole *raison d'être* of this offensive was to create conditions under which the armour would force a breakthrough into the Liri Valley. Such is the tangled knot of contradictions that Fuller's astringent views ring true: 'Our own bombing was piling up obstacles in the way of the advance of our ground forces . . . in these battles of obliteration all that took place was the transference of the psychology of strategic bombing from the enemy's cities to the battlefields.' The 'colossal crack' became a 'fixed convention, and, as in the years 1915–17, tactical imagination was petrified.'

The offensive followed the same gruesomely predictable pattern of the first two. The courage, endurance and sacrifice of the troops was not compensated for by any meaningful advance. Clark's interest in the offensive was restricted to how much pressure it took off the Anzio beachhead. Isolated attacks could have no more strategic dividend than this. Yet it continued, a ceaseless pounding on the lines of the winter battles of 1916–17, as Fuller pointed out shrewdly. At Cassino the destruction was on an even greater scale. One eye witness observed of the town that 'There was no vestige of a road or track, only vast heaps of rubble out of which peered the jagged edges of walls. The whole of this mess was covered by huge, deep craters that needed hand and foot climbing to get in and out of.' Under these conditions a breakthrough, let alone an exploitation was hopeless. Yet hope persisted: the enemy would break first. He might have done if greater weight had worn him down. But Allied attacks were fitful and scattered and, furthermore, the framework of the plan, by relying so excessively on blasting a way through, increased rather than reduced the problems of topography that counted so heavily against the Allies. On 23 March to the relief of all, the Third Battle was brought to an end.[36]

The Fourth (and final) Battle of Cassino was embodied in Operation 'Diadem' which would culminate in the fall of Rome. At last 15th Army Group, rechristened since 11 January 1944 Allied Armies in Italy (AAI), would actually conduct itself like an army group and not a miscellaneous string of corps. This was in part due to the influence of Major General A.F. 'John' Harding, Alexander's new chief of staff. A man of fine intellect and great industry, he provided the necessary 'grip' which was lacking occasionally in Alexander's somewhat lackadaisical, though certainly very diplomatic style of command. The course of events after 'Diadem' would show that diplomacy was often more important than grip. Alexander resorted to his favourite device of a two handed punch. He was convinced that the longer the German armies remained south of Rome, the greater would be their ultimate defeat, so long as their defences could be ruptured and a turning movement organised. US VI Corps at Anzio was a vital element here. Two corps were brought over from Eighth Army and alloted to the Cassino front. This was not the least important part of a thorough revitalisation of the strategic concept. Alexander wrote home to Brooke:

> I am regrouping the whole of our forces. The main reason is I want Oliver [Leese] to lay on, stage, mount and run the break into and I hope – through Minouri in the Liri Valley. Between ourselves Clark and his Army HQ are not up to it, its too big for them.

At last the problem of scale was being properly addressed – after three months of bitter and incessant fighting. Alexander himself was capable of designing a plan on an ambitious scale, but he had doubts whether Clark could carry it out. These doubts were not unjustified.

Alexander's intention was 'To destroy the right wing of the German Tenth Army: to drive what remained of it and the German Fourteenth Army North of Rome' and rein in his forces on the Rimini–Pisa line – his objective eight months before. The operational aim was at last spelt out – the destruction of the German Army south of Rome. This would be effected by 'an attack from the Anzio Bridgehead on the general axis Cori-Valmontone to cut Highway 6 in the Valmontone area, and thereby prevent the supply and withdrawal of the troops opposing the advance of Eighth Army and Fifth Armies'. The Gustav Line would be breached by a two fisted punch mounted by both armies. Eighth Army would deploy two corps, Polish and XIII, with 1 Canadian Corps in reserve to exploit down the Liri Valley. Leese preferred this direct approach because Eighth Army could not exploit across the Cassino massif without a mountain corps which he lacked. Each operation was given a corps – virtually a doubling of the force available for the previous battles. This serves to underline a previous weakness of British generalship in the Second World War. It was too frequently assumed that economy of force meant being forced to use (sometimes by the exigencies of the moment admittedly) understrength forces at once without any careful husbanding or forethought. On the contrary, a true economy of force in *the attack* actually implies *overwhelming* force at the decisive point. All of the units deployed in the Fourth Battle had been available for the earlier battles notwithstanding the fact that the army group did not enjoy a great material advantage over Army Group C. But they had not been husbanded correctly, allowing the Germans to withstand attacks with even smaller forces.

Clark on the Fifth Army front had to co-ordinate widely scattered forces. The opinion of General Juin, on the strength of his earlier achievements, now at last counted for something, and he persuaded Clark of the value of an indirect approach through the Aurunci mountains. The result was an audacious plan which combined movement along the whole of his front, a methodical step-by-step progression through the mountain ranges, with an out-flanking move. Some 600 guns were mustered to support Fifth Army's advance. But on one matter Clark was determined. 'I fear the same results from Eighth Army', he wrote suspiciously. 'It will not put in its full effort, for it never has.' It would let Fifth Army do all the fighting and then march into Rome. Clark seems to have given more thought as to how to block Eighth Army's routes towards Rome than he did to sealing off the German retreat.[37]

Alexander, at least, was confident who his main enemy was. 'Everything is now ready', he assured Brooke, 'all plans and preparations are complete. Our object is the destruction of the enemy South of Rome'. A skilful deception scheme had convinced Kesselring that further amphibious landings would be made behind the Gustav Line. Ultra revealed, too, that Kesselring was unaware of the movement of Eighth Army from the Adriatic to the Cassino front. The success of 'Diadem' depended above all on two factors: skilful and integrated planning and surprise. The German supply position was being closely monitored; Kesselring's tanks were being counted twice a week; his weakness in the air was checked. Considering that the Allies enjoyed almost total air superiority the comparative failure of the air campaign was rather disappointing. In part it was a function of terrain. Tactical bombing in mountainous country was much less effective than it would be on the plains of northern Europe; indeed it had acted as a brake on mobility. The Germans had withdrawn twice – from Sicily and from Salerno – in face of air superiority and demonstrated a certain immunity to it. Operation 'Strangle', the over-ambitious plan to force the Germans to withdraw from the Gustav Line by destroying their lines of communication on road, rail and at sea, was doomed to failure – although it was not the first or last air plan which would set itself unattainable objectives. The Germans revealed considerable organisational prowess – which was again underestimated – in repairing routes and by-passing damage.[38]

Intelligence played an immensely important part in laying the ground work of the Allied plan; but only the generals could garner victory from operational opportunity; here the record was much more chequered. A massive bombardment opened up at 2300 on 11 May. The fighting was still stubborn, and the Germans resisted with their customary defensive skill. The attack fell behind schedule. But Leese committed his reserves intact, and not worn down by premature assaults. XIII Corps, supported by 400 guns and the tanks of 26th Armoured Brigade, in a closely co-ordinated attack and despite heavy casualities, ruptured the Gustav Line. Once the low ground had been occupied, the high ground could no longer be held. General Anders of the Polish Corps grasped his opportunity. 'The critical moment had indeed arrived', he wrote, 'when both sides faced each other in complete exhaustion apparently incapable of making any further effort, and when the one with the stronger will, who is able to deliver the final blow, wins'. The fighting was brutal, but on 18 May the Monastery, symbol of German omniscience and resolve, at last fell.[39]

The startling progress of the FEC on the Fifth Army front completed the dislocation of Kesselring's defensive line. It was broken in four places and some 30–40 per cent casualties had been inflicted on the Germans. Kesselring had three panzer divisions in reserve but he refused to commit these because of the danger represented to his flank by Anzio. This momentary weakness permitted the FEC to press on and overrun the Hitler 'switch line' which ran from Piedimento, west of Cassino, to Pontecorvo, a feat rightly described by two leading historians of the campaign as 'one of the most remarkable feats of a war more remarkable for bloody attrition than skill'. This operation was significant also in that it allowed US II Corps to break through the steadily thinning coastal sector of the Gustav Line. A complete disaster stared Kesselring in the face. His line was stretched to breaking point. He was forced to commit his reserves and did so in the direction of the Liri Valley – the decisive point. Monitoring these orders through Ultra, on 23 May Alexander issued the order for the Anzio breakout. By 25 May the two fronts had linked up.[40]

Military theorists have always impressed on their pupils the importance of the pursuit. Clausewitz averred that 'pursuit is now one of the victor's main concerns, and the trophies are thus substantially increased'. J.F.C. Fuller agreed. It was the decisive area of military activity; from it flowed decisive results. The pursuit should be viewed as a new and separate battle, he argued, and its problems anticipated beforehand. Alexander had given considerable thought to his concept. He had, however, communicated it indifferently. Orders directing American forces to Valmontone had not been issued. Intelligence does not illuminate the controversy as to why Clark issued orders to *change direction* before his troops arrived at Valmontone. The whole problem was one of concept. All of Clark's thoughts were concentrated on the glory of seizing Rome – in itself a military object of trifling importance – and denying that glory to others. As Graham and Bidwell suggest, the significance of Valmontone was that it 'was simply the centre of gravity of a potentially critical area. It was not, as Clark seemed to argue, a spot where the VI Corps would stand on the Via Casilina like so many traffic policemen ordering the stream of German refugees pouring up it to a halt'. That all of Clark's later justifications were tactical – that there were too many roads in the Valmontone area, that US VI Corps was too weak to mount an envelopment – quite missed the point. What was significant about such a move was its *operational* direction: by mounting a thrust into the enemy's rear, which in *cooperation* with all the other units, could psychologically paralyse Army Group C and secure its disintegration. 'The fighting is severe now, but . . . I pray for decisive results soon', wrote Clark. That Clark still thought of these 'decisive results' as corps-sized operations in pursuit of geographical objectives, confirmed Alexander's fears that 'Diadem' was 'too big' for him.[41]

This argument should not be construed as an attempt to single out General Clark as the sole culpable party upon whom all the blame should be loaded for the failures of 'Diadem'. What may be contended is that American arguments used in justification for inaction – at Anzio – or the wrong action – as at Valmontone – invariable veered on the side of caution. American generalship demonstrated the kind of caution at the operational level which it was prone to accuse the British of at the tactical level. Clark gained his prize before the British and before 'Overlord' – a propaganda coup which lasted a little more than 24 hours. But the comparative failure of 'Diadem' to destroy the enemy and mount a devastating pursuit – even after the fall of Rome – cannot be put down solely to American failures. The blame was equally Alexander's. His armies appeared incapable of carrying through a deep, mobile penetration at which both the German and Soviet armies had proved themselves such masters. The pursuit mounted after 7 June was rigid and unimaginative. The CCS required that the Germans be defeated north of Rome but south of a new formidable defensive line which Ultra had first indicated was being built in April – the Gothic Line. The rather fumbling efforts to fulfil this directive gave the impression that Alexander was more concerned to gain positions as a preliminary to a new set-piece battle rather than destroy the enemy before he could seek shelter behind his fortifications. As General Jackson has observed, 'it was one of the weaknesses of British Army command and staff training that so much emphasis was placed on the foresight needed to be ready for the major set-piece offensive like Diadem that shorter term opportunities for decisive action in the mobile phases of a campaign were lost'. 'Diadem', like the Second Battle of El Alamein and Mareth fitted a consistent pattern of incomplete victories: like them, an unfinished masterpiece.[42]

The Fourth Battle of Cassino was also the last time in which a complete victory could be achieved in Italy. Since January 1944 plans for 'Anvil/Dragoon' had been moving forward steadily. The Americans were using it as a lever to scale down operations in Italy to which they were never fully committed. Against British protests that the theatres in France and Italy were interdependent, the CCS had conceded that no troops would be withdrawn while it seemed possible that Army Group C could be defeated before it retired to the Gothic Line. Once that opportunity, too, slipped away, they acted with ruthless despatch. The US VI Corps and the FEC, a total of six divisions were withdrawn, plus valuable logistic support. On 1 July Harding estimated that Army Group C comprised 18–21 divisions, and AAI 18 (14 infantry and four armoured). Withdrawals on this scale rendered the theatre secondary; it could not be envisaged as a right fist co-operating closely with the left fist in France. Thereafter operations in Italy had an anti-climactic air. The CCS issued a new directive four days later. Alexander was ordered to seize the line of the Po. 'Should the situation permit you should bear in mind the importance of denying to the enemy the important road centre of Piacenza.' The directive continued in a tone which confirmed the subsidiary status of the Italian Campaign:

> It is appreciated that these manoeuvres, coupled with the advance of 'Anvil' formations up the Rhone Valley, will almost certainly result in the clearance of North-West Italy of all German formations without the necessity of undertaking an offensive in that direction.

Arguing, rather disingenuously, that 'I have two highly organised and skilful Armies capable of carrying out large-scale attacks and mobile operations in the closest cooperation. Neither the Appenines nor even the Alps should prove a serious obstacle to their enthusiasm and skill', Alexander instructed Harding to develop plans for operations in three phases: first, to advance and secure bridgeheads over the Po; second, gain the line Padua–Vicenza–Verona; and third, 'force the crossing of the Piave and exploit to secure the Llubljana Gap'.[43]

There was an academic air about this planning exercise, but at least Alexander had the forces to realise the first stage. The German withdrawal had been slow and measured. Night withdrawals were made from one defensive position to another behind a shield of booby traps and demolitions which prevented Allied mobile troops from getting around their flanks, or even making contact. The original plan formulated through these summer months had envisaged a thrust in central Italy from Florence to Bologna which would entrap the Tenth Army against the south bank of the Po. But this intricate process was suddenly interrupted on 4 August 1944 when General Leese prevailed upon Alexander and Harding to meet him at Orvieto airfield. At this hurried meeting he persuaded them to concentrate on an Adriatic offensive rather than a central thrust. As a careful deception operation had already been operating to persuade Kesselring that an offensive could be expected in this sector, and not in the centre, the immense administrative and planning burden, and no little ingenuity, that would be required to reverse this would consume scarce resources and sacrifice military time.

Leese made a superficially persuasive case for the change. He assumed that the 'going' for armour north of Pesaro was better than the steep mountains of the Northern Appenines. Harding recalled in 1946 that Eighth Army disliked mountain warfare. 'They had no mountain trained troops; further their traditions were more of armoured trained battles and rapid movements on flat ground, supported by heavy artillery fire on fixed programmes.' But there was another factor. The Adriatic coast was distant from Fifth Army. Harding concluded:

> Gen Leese was still very jealous of Gen Clark over the capture of Rome when the two armies had fought more or less on the same axis. He . . . wanted to make quite certain that credit for the next Allied success . . . should go to him alone. This would be ensured if 8 Army fought its battle well away on one flank where there could be no question of 5 Army having had any effect on the result.

As Tacitus observes in *The Histories*, 'malice gives the false impression of being independent'. The withdrawal of two corps had increased the British predominance in the Mediterranean theatre, and Clark's suspicion of all things British had correspondingly increased. Both the British-dominated character of the autumn offensive, Operation 'Olive', and the increasingly ambitious plans emanating from HQ AAI calling for a drive to Vienna, are the result of an increased British dominance in a theatre which fails to reflect the overall American dominance of the Alliance and is, in part, a reaction against that striking dominance. Certainly, by emphasising the virtues of an all-British operation, and playing on Alexander's grave doubts about Clark and his staff (so amply confirmed during 'Diadem'), Leese made the mistake of repeating earlier failures which had neglected to use AAI as an army *group*. Indeed he resisted attempts to transfer XIII Corps to Clark: 'I was struggling in my own mind to think of some way to maintain 8 Army intact', and suggested that McCreery be appointed as Fifth Army's Deputy Commander who would deal with Kirkman, GOC XIII Corps, directly. This was too blatant an effort to by-pass Clark; Clark objected, and Leese was forced to acquiesce in the transfer of XIII Corps to Fifth Army.

Despite Leese's transcendent faith in the skill of Eighth Army, he was mistaken in his thinking. He was wrong in assuming that the area north of Pesaro was better for armour. He was wrong in arguing that the obstinancy of the German defence during the Battle of Florence had indicated that the German reserves had been committed in the centre. The only way he could have secured the great victory he hankered after was by organising yet another improvised amphibious landing, this time on the Adriatic coast.

But given the time constraints and the reluctance of the Americans, this was out of the question. Although it is true that the mountain barrier had been replaced by steep rolling hills, Leese had now to confront an entirely new barrier – the innumerable rivers flowing west-east into the Adriatic. Mountains do not move up and down; the water level of rivers does.[44]

The three corps of Eighth Army mustered three armoured divisions and seven infantry divisions for Operation 'Olive'. They faced three infantry divisions of LXXVI Panzer Corps. The margin of superiority in armour was even greater: 1,376 against 237. This handsome margin reinforced a widespread feeling that left in the hands of the veteran Eighth Army the war in Italy would grind soon to a close. Leese toured the Army addressing senior officers; he let it be known that this would be their last great battle. Initial progress more than matched his buoyant mood. Under the weight of a massive aerial bombardment, the Germans complained that the outer ramparts of the Gothic Line, called Green I, had been 'simply lifted from the air', and 'plastered by bomb carpets'. Leese then moved to the second stage of his plan – the attempt to 'gatecrash' the Gothic Line. By 1 September I Canadian Corps moved to strike towards Montecluro amid great clouds of dust in the summer weather. Progress was satisfactory, the mood still optimistic. Then on 3 September the weather broke and Eighth Army struggled forward in thunder storms. 1st Armoured Division failed to break out at Coriano. Air support slackened. As the Official Historian observes, 'The billowing white dust . . . turned quickly to a slippery slime; hard fields became glutinous mud; and sapper-made diversions and bulldozed tracks sank into quagmires whenever they lay through undrained hollows, across streams or at approaches to river crossings'. Leese halted on 6 September to regroup. Green II and the new Rimini Line still had to be overrun.

Von Vietinghoff pointed out to Kesselring that it was not 'the number of men which was decisive, but artillery fire. When he [the British] has chosen his point of assault he concentrates his artillery and shells everything to pieces'. During the second phase of 'Olive', MAAF flew 1,145 bomber sorties to support the artillery. But the margin of superiority in either firepower or men was not sufficient to break the German defensive lines entirely, and secure the degree of mobility which would guarantee his destruction. Leese's offensive was concentrated on too narrow a sector of the front. Fifth Army supported in the centre in an attempt to hold Tenth Army's reserves. But a successful offensive had to employ the full fighting power of the Army Group. This 'Olive' failed to do and was closed down to await better weather. It was not without its tactical successes. On 18–20 September Eighth Army breached the Rimini Line and broke out, at last, into the Romagna. This turned out to be a mixed blessing. Leese's whole plan had assumed that once Eighth Army's armour got through the Gothic Line Army Group C would be destroyed. He was wrong here too. Eighth

Army had indeed made its reputation in a rapid war of manoeuvre, but its recent fighting had been exclusively in mountainous terrain, and most of its veteran Desert units had been withdrawn for 'Overlord'; those remaining had been forced back to learning first principles. 'It is extraordinary how difficult it is', Leese informed the ACIGS, 'to make new troops realise the interdependence of tanks and infantry until they have gained the knowledge by bitter experience in battle'. Yet 'Olive' was drawn up as if Eighth Army had nothing to learn about mobile warfare.

The campaign cannot be written off as a failure. Eleven German divisions had been defeated; the Gothic Line had been breached – though not broken; it was a tactical success not a strategic triumph – the operational level cementing the two had been neglected. But when set against the material superiority enjoyed by Eighth Army, and the massive hopes (and pride) invested in the offensive, it enjoyed a small dividend. Leese had been determined to fight the kind of battle he wanted to fight; he had gambled and failed. General Jackson concludes harshly but not unfairly of Leese's generalship, that 'Leese was essentially an emulator rather than an innovator. He tried to copy Montgomery in personal style and military technique without the professional qualities which made Montgomery so successful'.[45]

On the overall conduct of the war, 'Olive' had no impact – except in the negative sense. It confirmed General Marshall in his view that the Mediterranean theatre was a sideshow. The failure of 'Olive' showed conclusively that the level of resources available in the autumn of 1944 was not sufficient to secure decisive results. This consideration is an important factor in understanding Alexander's ambitious plans for an attack through the Llubljana Gap and a drive for Vienna laid before the CIGS earlier that autumn. A revised version was resuscitated in December 1944. Its object was to stretch the German defensive cordon, thin out its density by extending the front line, reduce the defensive factors operating in his favour while increasing mobility on the Allied side. This grandiose operation did not please Brooke; its ambitious aims only served to increase American suspicions and made attempts to influence American strategy in North-West Europe that much more difficult. As Brooke had been the great champion of the Mediterranean strategy in 1943, this was a striking indication of how relative a backwater it had become.[46]

Indeed when Brooke visited the Italian front in December 1944 he was depressed by what he saw, and even doubtful that Alexander could break out after February 1945, as he appeared stuck in the mountains. But a number of factors which had earlier failed to make an impact now operated in the Allies' favour. The interdiction campaign at last caused severe shortages and communications blockages in Army Group C. The Brenner pass, for instance, remained closed permanently after 22 March 1945. Petrol was so scarce that the rapid reinforcement of threatened points by armoured forces was now out of the question. Ultra intelligence was closely geared to planning; this had occurred during 'Diadem' but with indecisive results. Ultra revealed that four German divisions, including two panzer, had been withdrawn to deal with the gathering crisis in Hungary, as the Soviets advanced unremittingly on Vienna. After the Yalta Conference, Alexander, now Supreme Commander Mediterranean, was instructed to exert pressure on the enemy but seize any opportunities that might present themselves to destroy the enemy. This was the final and fittingly vague directive issued for the Italian Campaign. His mission, at least, was clear – to pin down the maximum number of German divisions in Italy whilst the German collapse in the West continued apace.[47]

Alexander decided that the best way to fulfil the CCS's directive was to prevent the Germans from withdrawing to the Alps (which both he and Clark dreaded because it would deprive them of a decisive battle) by a battle of annihilation, a two-handed punch along the lines of 'Diadem'. Clark, now commander of the rechristened 15th Army Group, was responsible for the operational planning. As usual, geographical objectives dominated his thoughts. Bologna was his objective. But as an army group commander he discovered that he had to defer to his new Army commanders, Truscott and McCreery. They were responsible for much of the operational design that emerged. Their plans for sweeping strokes towards the Alps were imaginatively conceived and well executed. For the longer the Germans attempted to resist the inevitable and delayed withdrawal to the Alps, the more inevitable their destruction became.

The plan was initiated by a deception scheme which persuaded von Vietinghoff, now commanding Army Group C after Kesselring was transferred to the West, to move such reserves as he deployed to the Adriatic coast to throw back into the sea an amphibious operation that Alexander lacked the resources to launch. By thinning the westerly end of the line, Fifth Army would strike west and wheel north east, while Eighth Army smashed its way through the Argenta Gap. In Operation 'Grapeshot', both strategic and tactical surprise was attained. The offensive was supported by powerful artillery barrages and tactical bombing. But German resistance was tough; many units made a 'last stand'. Eighth Army attacked first (Fifth Army was delayed by bad weather), and to Clark's dismay gained rapid victories – getting across the River Senio before the Germans could organise its defence, and then crossing Lake Comacchio to outflank Argenta, which fell on 17 April. Fifth Army's offensive, too, was successful, US II Corps swinging around behind Bologna. On 25 April this corps and British V Corps joined hands around Finale Emilia to entrap Army Group C south of the Po; its disintegration was complete. An armistice was signed at Caserta on 25 April; the guns ceased fire on 2 May. It is significant – as at Salonika in 1918 – that the German defeat in Italy followed rather than prefaced catastrophe in the West.[48]

Thus ended the Italian Campaign. It had been hard fought. Allied casualties were 188,746 for Fifth Army, 123,254 for Eighth Army. German casualties were probably in the order of 434,646 (including 214,048 'missing'). The process of attrition, therefore, was far from self-defeating – though the number of Allied casualties was certainly greater than expected. But had the campaign fulfilled the strategic objectives laid down for it? These were, at bottom, threefold. First, to draw off German forces from the Eastern Front. Second, create a diversion that would aid the establishment of a lodgement in Normandy. Third, the destruction of German forces in Italy when the opportunity presented itself. As General Strawson reminds us repeatedly, it is the degree of help that the Italian Campaign afforded to other more important campaigns that serves as the measure of its success. It may be doubted surely whether the Italian Campaign had any influence on the course of events in Soviet Russia. Operation 'Citadel' was launched, thrown back and finally crushed without reference to the faltering Allied moves in July-September 1943. Some German units, it is true, were withdrawn from the Eastern Front. But the disastrous collapse predicted by the British was not even a distant hope; perhaps an indication of the comparatively small-scale conceptions in which they indulged themselves; the vast scale of the Eastern Front seemed beyond the ken of Churchill and Brooke, let alone Alexander and Clark. Expectations that a small force could attain great results seem absurdly sanguine.

As a contribution to 'Overlord', the case seems more convincing. Army Group C was a well commanded, seasoned force of veterans, whom it was preferable to keep bottled up in Italy. But it is as well to remember that Hitler managed to find 26 divisions for the Ardennes counter offensive in December 1944 without recourse to using troops from Italy. Indeed, as Strawson also points out, the Italian Campaign 'was essentially a *defensive* strategy waged by offensive means . . . to hold the Germans on the southern flank in order that advances could be made on the main fronts, and as such turned out to be a major distraction for the Allies too'. This was particularly true for the British, who concentrated so much of their fighting power in a secondary theatre of war, reducing significantly their power to influence strategy in North West Europe in 1944–45. Furthermore, the German cordon strategy of keeping the Allies as far away from the Alps as far as possible for the longest possible time, did succeed. This was due to operational failures.

The Italian Campaign was an object lesson in the constraints imposed by scarce resources. These constraints were imposed largely for political reasons. The Allies may not have had the strength to advance right-handed, then left-handed, or even both-handed, as Churchill envisaged in Western Europe and Italy and secure decisive results. Certainly the somewhat slap-dash attitude towards preparation for and organisation of the Italian Campaign resulted in either repulses or lost opportunities.

Perhaps indifferent operational technique – especially the failure to utilise the full power of an army group – may account for the Allied failure to grasp the fruits of the opportunistic strategy upheld by Churchill and Brooke. Both were of the view that 'great prizes' could be seized in Italy. It is difficult to underestimate the effect on Nazi Germany of a simultaneous collapse of the German armies in both France and Italy as seemed likely in the summer of 1944. The root cause of the failure to achieve this can be put down 'to treating the two theatres as rivals when they should have been treated as a single whole'. This accounted for the lack of clarity in operational aims during the course of the campaign. Montgomery complained in September 1943 that 'Before we embark on major operations on the mainland of Europe we must have a master plan and know how we propose to develop these operations. I have not been told of any master plan and I must assume that there was none.' He was, of course, quite correct. There was no master plan because to have worked one out would have exposed all of the rivalries and jealousies that lurked beneath the surface of superficial Allied amity. Montgomery and his fellow commanders were forced to unravel the tangled skein of operational problems bequeathed to them, and this they achieved, not without difficulty, but ultimately not without success.[49]

NOTES

1. Winston S. Churchill, *The Second World War* (London: Cassell, 1952), V, p.137; J.F.C. Fuller, *The Second World War* (London: Eyre & Spottiswoode, 1948), p.261; B.H. Liddell Hart, *History of the Second World War* (London: Cassell, 1970), pp.447–50, 526–27.
2. Quoted in Michael Howard, *The Mediterranean Strategy in the Second World War* (London: Weidenfeld & Nicolson, 1968), p.34; much of this and the following paragraphs is drawn from Michael Howard, *Grand Strategy*, IV, Aug. 1942–Sept. 1943 (London: HMSO, 1972), pp.241, 245, 276. Arthur Bryant, *The Turn of the Tide* (London: Collins, 1957), pp.683–4.
3. Howard, *Grand Strategy*, IV, pp.412–13.
4. Ibid., pp.412–14.
5. Ibid., pp.415–17.
6. John Grigg, *1943: The Victory That Never Was* (London: Eyre Methuen, 1985 paperback edition), especially pp.95–115.
7. Quoted in William R. Emerson, 'F.D.R., 1941–45', in Ernest R. May (ed.), *The Ultimate Decision: The President as Commander in Chief* (New York: Brazilier 1960), p.164; Forrest C. Pogue, *George C. Marshall: Organizer of Victory* (New York: Viking, 1973), pp.199–205.
8. Fuller, *The Second World War*, p.325.
9. Ralph Bennett, *Ultra and Mediterranean Strategy, 1941–1945* (London: Hamish Hamilton, 1989), pp.226–8.
10. Alexander to CIGS, 19 May 1943, Alanbrooke Papers 14/63, quoted in Brian Holden Reid, 'Alexander', in John Keegan (ed.), *Churchill's Generals* (London: Weidenfeld & Nicolson, forthcoming).
11. Mongomery to Alexander, 13 March 1943, Alexander Papers PRO WO214/20; Carlo D'Este, *Bitter Victory: The Battle for Sicily, 1943* (London: Collins, 1988), pp.112–14.
12. Montgomery to Alexander, 25 April 1943, Alexander Papers PRO WO214/20; Nigel

Hamilton, *Monty: Master of the Battlefield, 1942–1944* (London: Hamish Hamilton, 1983), p.271.

13. Hamilton, *Master of the Battlefield*, pp.246, 267–77, 296; Montgomery to Alexander, 13 March 1943, Alexander Papers PRO WO214/20; D'Este, *Bitter Victory*, p.124.

14. Brian Holden Reid, 'Tensions in the Supreme Command: Anti-Americanism in the British Army, 1939–1945', in Brian Holden Reid and John White (eds.), *American Studies: Essays in Honour of Marcus Cunliffe* (London: Macmillan, forthcoming); Alexander to CIGS, 3 April 1943, Alanbrooke Papers 14/63.

15. Hamilton, *Master of the Battlefield*, pp.300, 317.

16. Ibid., pp.325–6, 334; D'Este, *Bitter Victory*, pp.412–18; Reid, 'Alexander'.

17. Bennett, *Ultra and Mediterranean Strategy*, pp.234–5.

18. These points are covered in more detail in Brian Holden Reid, 'Alexander'; Hamilton, *Master of the Battlefield*, p.270.

19. David W. Ellwood, *Italy, 1943–1945* (Leicester: Leicester University Press, 1985), pp.4–5, 23–43; Brian Holden Reid, *J.F.C. Fuller: Military Thinker* (London: Macmillan, 1987), p.201.

20. Howard, *Grand Strategy*, IV, pp.528–9; John Strawson, *The Italian Campaign* (London: Secker & Warburg, 1987), pp.115–16.

21. Churchill to Alexander, 14 Sept. 1943, Alexander Papers PRO WO214/13; Eric Morris, *Salerno* (London: Hutchinson, 1983), p.32.

22. Ibid., pp.30–31; Martin Blumenson, *Mark Clark* (London: Jonathan Cape, 1985), pp.59–60, 116–17, 120–21; Dwight D. Eisenhower, *Crusade in Europe* (New York: De Capo Press edition, 1977), p.187.

23. Dominick Graham and Shelford Bidwell, *Tug of War: The Battle for Italy, 1943–1945* (London: Hodder & Stoughton, 1986), pp.53–4; Morris, *Salerno*, pp.40–43.

24. Alexander to CIGS, 7 Sept. 1943, Alexander Papers PRO WO214/13; Reid, 'Alexander'; Graham and Bidwell, *Tug of War*, pp.91–2.

25. Graham and Bidwell, p.91; Shelford Bidwell, 'Kesselring', in Correlli Barnett (ed.), *Hitler's Generals* (London: Weidenfeld & Nicolson, 1989), pp.280–81; *The Rommel Papers* (ed.), Capt. B.H. Liddell Hart (London: Collins, 1953), pp.439–40.

26. Bennett, *Ultra and Mediterranean Strategy*, pp.241–2; Michael Howard, *The Causes of Wars* (London: Temple Smith, 1983), p.219; Hamilton, *Master of the Battlefield*, pp.401–2.

27. D'Este, *Bitter Victory*, p.417; Hamilton, *Master of the Battlefield*, pp.446–7, 451–2.

28. Arthur Bryant, *Triumph in the West* (London: Collins, 1959), pp.122, 139; CIGS to Alexander, 29 Sept. 1943, Alexander Papers, PRO WO214/13; Bennett, *Ultra and Mediterranean Strategy*, p.252.

29. Alexander to CIGS, 25 Nov. 1943, ibid., PRO WO214/13; John Ellis, *Cassino: The Hollow Victory* (London: Andre Deutsch, 1984), pp.16–17, 52, 63–5, 90, 201.

30. Ellis, *Cassino*, pp.160–61; Strawson, *Italian Campaign*, p.102

31. Blumenson, *Clark*, pp.170–71; Ellis, *Cassino*, pp.51–2, 60–1, 66–9, 85, 96–108, 110; Graham and Bidwell, *Tug of War*, pp.160, 178.

32. Blumenson, *Clark*, pp.170–71; Ellis, *Cassino*, pp.112–13; Graham and Bidwell, *Tug of War*, pp.129–30.

33. Alexander to CIGS, 22 March 1944, Alanbrooke Papers 14/65, quoted in Reid, 'Alexander'; Blumenson, *Clark*, p.174; Bennett, *Ultra and Mediterranean Strategy*, p.264.

34. Strawson, *Italian Campaign*, p.140; CIGS to Alexander, 10 March 1944, Alexander Papers PRO WO214/15; Ellis, *Cassino*, p.165

35. These paragraphs are based on CIGS to Alexander, 10 March 1944, Alexander Papers PRO WO214/15; Ellis, *Cassino*, pp.165–7, 170, 183–5; Graham and Bidwell, *Tug of War*, pp.198–202; Fuller, *Second World War*, p.272.

36. Ellis, *Cassino*, pp.199–203, 208–12, 225–6, 228; Fuller, *Second World War*, p.266; Graham and Bidwell, pp.219–22

37. See Reid, 'Alexander', and the sources cited there; Brigadier C.J.C. Molony, *The Mediterranean and the Middle East*, VI, Pt. 1 (London: HMSO, 1973), pp.57–8, 60–64; Blumenson, *Clark*, pp.211–12; Michael Carver, *Harding of Petherton* (London:

Weidenfeld & Nicolson, 1978), pp.121–3, 133.

38. Molony, *Mediterranean and Middle East*, VI, Pt. 1, pp.38–42; Bennett, *Ultra and Mediterranean Strategy*, p.282.

39. Ellis, *Cassino*, pp.311–12; Graham and Bidwell, *Tug of War*, pp.282–7.

40. Graham and Bidwell, *Tug of War*, pp.315–18; Molony, *Mediterranean and Middle East*, VI, Pt.1 pp.170–73; W.G.F. Jackson, *Alexander as Military Commander* (London: Batsford, 1971), pp.287–92; Bennett, *Ultra and Mediterranean Strategy*, p.284; Carver, *Harding*, pp.135–6.

41. Clausewitz, *On War* (eds.), Michael Howard and Peter Paret (Princeton, NJ: Princeton University Press, 1976), IV, 12, p.266; J.F.C. Fuller, *Lectures on FSR II* (London: Sifton Praed, 1931), p.36; Bennett, *Ultra and Mediterranean Strategy*, pp.284–5, 339; Graham and Bidwell, *Tug of War*, p.248; Blumenson, *Clark*, p.212; Alexander's biographer, in a chapter based heavily on interviews with General Clark, tends to give him the benefit of the doubt, see Nigel Nicolson, *Alex* (London: Weidenfeld & Nicolson, 1973), pp.248–54.

42. Bennett, *Ultra and Mediterranean Strategy*, p.282; General Sir William Jackson, *The Mediterranean and Middle East*, VI, Pt.2 (London: HMSO, 1986), pp.18–19.

43. Jackson, *Mediterranean and Middle East*, VI, Pt.2, pp.51–3; Alexander to Wilson, 13 June 1944, Alexander Papers PRO WO214/15; Reid, 'Alexander'.

44. Jackson, *Mediterranean and Middle East*, VI, Pt.2, pp.84, 119–26; Tacitus, *The Histories* (Harmondsworth, Penguin, 1972 edition), I, i, p.21; also see the interesting Canadian perspective on Olive planning in William J. McAndrew, 'Eighth Army at the Gothic Line: Commanders and Plans', *RUSI Journal*, 131 (March 1986), pp.50–57.

45. Jackson, *Mediterranean and Middle East*, VI, Pt.2, pp.225–32, 241–306, 360–63; Graham and Bidwell, *Tug of War*, pp.347–66; Strawson, *Italian Campaign*, pp.173–9; William J. McAndrew, 'Eighth Army at the Gothic Line: The Dog-Fight', *RUSI Journal*, 131 (June 1986), pp.55–62.

46. Memorandum on the Command and Staff Organisation in the Mediterranean Theatre of Operations, 1 December 1944, Alanbrooke Papers 14/66; David Fraser, *Alanbrooke* (London: Collins, 1982), p.434.

47. Bennett, *Ultra and Mediterranean Strategy*, pp.311–13; Graham and Bidwell, *Tug of War*, pp.386–7.

48. Bennett, *Ultra and Mediterranean Strategy*, p.321; General Sir William Jackson, *The Mediterranean and Middle East*, VI, Pt. 3 (London: HMSO, 1988), pp.204–6, 215–16, 258, 261–94; Graham and Bidwell, *Tug of War*, pp.386–95.

49. Strawson, *Italian Campaign*, pp.5, 23, 27–8, 210–11; Jackson, *Mediterranean and Middle East*, VI, Pt.1, p.30; Graham and Bidwell, *Tug of War*, p.404; Ellis, *Cassino*, p.xix.

The Campaigns in Asia and the Pacific[1]

LOUIS ALLEN

The most celebrated Japanese marching song of the 1939–45 period was not a spontaneous creation but the result of an official competition. Many of the songs inspired by Japan's war in China were felt to be not quite punchy enough; they tended to be sentimental and melancholy, in a minor key. So *Aikoku Kōshinkyoku* (Patriotic March) was written deliberately to inspire military ardour. Yet in spite of its insistent marching rhythm, its content is not aggressive. It is not sexually reminiscent like *Lili Marlene* or *Shanghai no hanauri musume* (The flower selling girls of Shanghai), nor tawdry and braggart like *We'll hang out our washing on the Siegfried Line*. Its theme is much more like the mood of 1914 in young Japanese writers, giving vent at last to a sense of glory, of Japan's beauty and greatness, not of her hostility to anyone else:

Miyo tōkai no sora akete	See, the sky is opening, over the Eastern sea
Kyokujitsu takaku kagayakeba	When the rising sun lights up the heavens
Tenchi no seiki hatsuratsu to	Our hope dances on the Eight Great Islands
Kibō wa odoru oyashima	Filled with the life and vigour of the world
O seiro no asakumo ni	Oh, in the fine bright clouds of morning
Sobiyuru Fuji no sugata koso	The shape of Fuji towers on high
Kinō muketsu yurugi naki	Firm as a rock, perfect like a vase of gold,
Waga Nippon no hokori nare.	The pride of our Japan.

Japan's experience of the Second World War finds an echo not in the forces opposing her, but in the young men of Europe going to battle in 1914 and, as surely, after the Somme and Passchendaele, seeing warfare with new eyes. 'My nature was utterly changed', wrote the novelist Dazai Osamu after the news of Peal Harbor, 'There was a feeling of being utterly transparent, as if shot through by a strong ray of light. Or receiving the breath of the Holy Spirit – a feeling as if a single cold petal had melted in my breast. From that morning on, Japan had become a different country.' The socialist writer, and later translator of *Lady Chatterley's Lover*, Itō Sei, exclaimed 'In the midst of turbulent emotions, I felt a curious inner tranquillity: this is good, it's terrific. I remember the feeling of relief bubbling up inside me. The joy of having been given a direction clearly, a lightness of the whole being. It was wonderful.' 'I thought it was splendid', wrote the novelist Agawa Hiroyuki, then a student at Tokyo Imperial University. 'Then came the announcement of the great victories, about noon. No question of moaning that if there is war some of us must die. No lamentations, that was our mood.'[2] 'Thanks be to God who has matched us with his hour'?

There are, I think, no British songs for the Far East. And the mood of our literature is reflective, gloomy, if not despairing. The reason is not far to seek. The Japanese exaltation in the first weeks of war is that of a nation fighting for its very *being*. When the verb is 'to be', then every effort is permissible, every sacrifice willingly undertaken. When the verb is 'to have', there is reluctance to go to the limit of sacrifice. This is the difference between Dunkirk and Singapore. Both were crushing defeats. Both knocked the British temporarily out of the ring. But Dunkirk became a watchword, a tocsin; Singapore a reminder of shame and ineptitude. One was fought on behalf of *being*, the other of behalf of *having*; and the difference marked the entire war.

It will seem paradoxical to refer to the war in the Pacific as one between Japan and Great Britain. The USA defeated Japan. Massive as it was, the British effort was more localised – chiefly in South-East – and the Russian invasion of Manchuria and North China in August 1945 was a gambler's political calculation, made when the war was as good as over. It is also true that the British government, obsessed by Europe in 1940 and 1941, allowed the Americans to take the lead in the 1941 diplomatic negotiations with Japan which ultimately led to war. The terms of the Hull Note, delivered to the Japanese envoys on 26 November 1941, made the Japanese realise that the Americans were not prepared to rescind their economic embargo unless Japan promised to withdraw all her forces from China and Indo-China, and that was a concession the Japanese Army would not allow its government to make. Those terms were not even known to the British ambassador in Tokyo, Sir Robert Craigie, and when he was told of them after war broke out he declared to a Japanese diplomat that he would have advised against their use.[3]

So it was the USA, endlessly provoked by a ruthless Japanese campaign to subjugate China, which forced Japan to the point of no return, and drew the British in their wake, just as it was the USA which provided the vast naval fleets and air fleets which bombed and sank Japan out of the war. But the nature of the American state was not altered by the war in the same way as the British. However weakened economically Britain might have emerged from an ultimate victory over Germany, it was the war against Japan which robbed her of her Far Eastern possessions and put into motion the decolonisation process which in the space of a quarter of a century put paid to the British Empire, and radically altered the relations between being and having, in the British perspective. This is true, whether we view Japan's claim to be the liberator of Asia from the West as a sincere assumption of a historical mission or as a machiavellian hoax (both views are tenable, depending which side you are on).

NARRATIVE OF EVENTS

The years provide adequate segments. Wishing to cut the supply lines which kept alive Chiang Kai-shek's Nationalist government in the Chinese interior long after the Japanese were sure they controlled 'useful' China (the mouths of the major rivers, and the seacoast), the Japanese insisted on cutting the rail supply lines through French Indo-China into Yunnan, after the fall of France in 1940. A year later they established themselves, again with the unwilling consent of the Vichy French, in Southern French Indo-China. This put them within 600 miles of the coast of Malaya. In order to prise them loose, Roosevelt ordered an economic embargo of Japan, depriving them of the means of acquiring oil. When they saw this would bring their navy and industries to a standstill, the Japanese decided to use force to obtain from the Dutch in East Indies what they had not been able to obtain through diplomatic pressure. But to seize the oil of the Netherlands East Indies, they needed to hold the Philippines and Malaya to keep open the sea lanes between the Indies and Japan. So they attacked the Philippines and Malaya in December 1941, and, in a rash sideways move to keep the US fleet from interfering, Pearl Harbor and the fleet at anchor (less its aircraft carriers, an omission which was to be crucial) were bombed on 7 December 1941. For the first six months of 1942, as the commander-in-chief of the Combined Fleet, Admiral Yamamoto Isoroku, had predicted, the Japanese were triumphant everywhere. Mistress of the seas from Hawaii to Ceylon, Japan occupied most of South-East Asia by the summer of 1942.

From the second half, with her defeat in the battle of Midway, her fortunes went slowly into reverse.[4] In 1943, the Allies sketched out a counter-strategy, and prepared to assault the Japanese perimeter in Asia and the Pacific Ocean. The occupied Aleutian Islands in the far north, and Guadalcanal in the south, were abandoned, and the Allies began to re-enter Burma. In 1944 the Japanese Navy was defeated in the Philippines (Leyte Gulf); the Japanese Army was thrown back from its invasion of India (three starving divisions retreated to the Chindwin at the end of that campaign); Myitkyina in North Burma was taken by a mixed Sino-American force under Stilwell; the back door to China was re-opened; and island by island the US Navy under Admiral Chester Nimitz crept back across the Pacific, while MacArthur's American and Australian forces hopped along the coast of New Guinea, leaving the cut-off Japanese garrisons to wither, and stretched out to re-take the Philippines. By the end of 1944, Nimitz had taken bases from which it would be possible to bomb the Japanese mainland with the heavy B-29s which flew too high (30,000 feet) for interception by Japanese fighters.

1945 saw Japan crumble. The island keep was assaulted, Iwojima and Okinawa were occupied after ferocious fighting, and Tokyo was bombed with a devastating fire raid in March, with casualties higher than those from the atomic bomb. The British–Indian forces re-took Burma (Rangoon was captured in May) and were poised to attack Malaya and Siam. The fortress surrendered in August, when Russian forces invaded Manchuria in the last nine days of the war (Stalin taking a belated revenge for the humiliation of Tsar Nicholas II in 1905) and US planes dropped atomic bombs on Hiroshima on 6 August and Nagasaki on 9 August. The Japanese surrendered unconditionally, withdrew their forces and civilian settlers and administrators from China and other parts of Asia, and submitted to a joint Allied occupation under General MacArthur which lasted until 1952.

So much for chronological sequence. How should we define these events? The Second World War in Asia was essentially a siege on a continental scale, across a moat of unparalleled dimensions, in which, after a preliminary successful sortie by the castle forces, the attackers were brought from a great distance by modern transport (ships and aircraft) and with superior siege weapons (bombs and fire). The castle was laid waste, and on the spot in the final moments there was little intervention in terms of infantry combat (that was for episodes on the periphery), so that the queen of battles counted for little in the upshot. In common with other areas of the Second World War, the most conspicuous slaughter was that of civilians.

Strategically, the one crucial factor is *distance*. Hence the prominent role of air-power, to deliver food, guns, fuel, troops. And not just in supply but in assault: witness the landings in Malaya, the Wingate expeditions in Burma, the USAAF assault on the Japanese mainland.

WEAPONS AND INSTRUMENTS OF WAR

In the end, only one campaign counted: Nimitz's thrust of the US Navy across the Central Pacific to bomb Japan. Every other campaign, however bitter, however desperate, was either ancillary to this or sideshow. What mattered was the line that led direct from Hawaii to Saipan, Tinlian, Iwojima, Okinawa, the core offensive to the heart of Japan, which, if Japan had not surrendered, would have culminated in landings on Kyushu and Honshu in 1945 and 1946. It was a justification, of a sort, of Bomber Harris's conviction of the efficiency of saturation bombing; and also, in theatres of war where everyone thought the solution lay in looping round everyone else, and coming in from the rear and the sides (a favourite Japanese manoeuvre), it was a justification of a Clausewitzian view in which you encounter the enemy's main strength with your main strength and reap victory from that confrontation.

Japan's most interesting contribution, tactically and psychologically, was the use of *shinpū (kamikaze*, 'Divine wind') pilots and submariners. On an assumption that the Allies would be compelled to invade Japan with their ground troops, since Japan would not surrender merely to the bombing campaign, the use of suicide pilots might have made Operations *Olympic* (Kyushu) and *Coronet* (Honshu) unspeakably costly to the Allies, already tired after their massive offensives against Germany and using troops who were by this time eager to be home. The *kamikaze* weapon was not simply a *samurai* 'noble failure'. It was a perfectly feasible calculation. If one life, or two, and a piece of expendable machinery could incapacitate or sink a ship, then the invasion might fail or be halted, and the Allies be persuaded to a negotiated peace instead of unconditional surrender.[5]

Less suicidal allied tactics (though demanding no less courage) lay in the use of long-range penetration groups like Orde Wingate's (Burma 1943 and 1944) in which thousands of men were supplied with food and weapons from the air, freeing them from dependence on roads.[6] Similar to these were the use of stay-behind parties (in the Philippines, the Pacific Islands, Burma, Malaya) and the occasional gallant piratical adventure like the combined British and Australian raids into Singapore harbour in 1943 and 1944 (Ivan Lyon's Operation Rimau).[7]

The impact of these expeditions was more often on morale than anything else. In terms of manpower, Wingate's first expedition, in which his men walked into Burma, was a costly failure: he lost a third of his force. But the gain in morale was quite real. The constant fear of British generals in the East was that their men had gone soft, that they were, not to put too fine a point on it, cowards. The correspondence between Wavell, then C-in-C India, in command of the forces facing the Japanese in Burma for 1942 and the first half of 1943, and General Irwin, demonstrates this point without a doubt, and it is against a background of weakness and inertia that Wingate's results must be judged. His second campaign was planned to assist Stilwell and his Sino-American force, not Slim's XIVth Army, and it might have done great things if it had remained under Wingate's command. But he died just as his forces had planted themselves in the heart of Northern Burma, in March 1944, behind the Japanese lines and astride their communications. His command was taken over by one of his column commanders who loathed him and his ideas, and his force was whittled away and villainously misused by Stilwell.

Wingate had strategic dreams far beyond Burma. He saw Long-Range Penetration Groups re-taking Indo-China and ultimately bases on the South China coast. If he had survived, it might well have happened. The Japanese have mixed feelings about him. General Mutaguchi, who was about to lead his offensive into India when Wingate's forces flew over his head and landed behind him, was not unduly concerned. He pointed out that if his offensive against India succeeded, he would soon have Wingate's bases in his hands anyway, and the airborne forces would be strangled.[8]

But the commander of the Japanese airforces in northern Burma, Major-General Tazoe, was thunderstruck. In the second Wingate expedition, he saw the possibility of the Allies sending supplies from India to China in far greater quantities than could be flown over the Hump from Assam to Kunming, and hence a direct threat from USAAF bases in China to the Japanese mainland. He begged Mutaguchi to break off his offensive and deal with Wingate, he pleaded with the higher command in Rangoon to call it off, but in vain. He was refused everywhere, and the final dispersion of Wingate's efforts after his death supported Mutaguchi's view of the force's capacities. Had Wingate lived the story might have been very different, and the debate is still alive.

We should not be too deceived about dates, nor about modernity – or otherwise – of equipment. The war saw the most primitive hand-to-hand combat and the most lethal destruction of the modern age. At Kohima, during the attempted invasion of India in 1944, enemies hurled hand grenades at each other across the length of a tennis-court. A year later, the most advanced and hideous explosive known to mankind was dropped on Hiroshima from a height of 30,000 feet. The British seemed, on occasion, to be re-fighting Rorke's Drift, the Japanese were experiencing their equivalent of the Somme and Passchendaele four decades on, and the Americans, in the end, took the war into the age of science fiction. Hence the difficulty of assuming that the war in Europe and the war in Asia were the same world war. Of course there were links (German submarines, for instance, occasionally made the hazardous journey from the Baltic to Singapore and Tokyo) and Germany's defeat of Holland, France and Britain in 1940 changed the course of Asian history by its impact on Japan's desires for the colonial empires of South-East Asia. But the wars were not just in different locations, they were different wars.

The British lost at Singapore their great Far Eastern commercial capital. It was this much more than a 'fortress', which it obviously never was. That loss provided the Japanese with a propaganda victory that echoed throughout Asia precisely as the news of the Russian defeat at Tsushima had, 36 years before. To retrieve their prized possessions, the British fought at first an old-style colonial war, mostly with raw Indian recruits and topeed British garrison troops in Burma, and in Malaya more Indian recruits, leathery and experienced Australian First World War veterans and complete rookies, and, in the last few hectic minutes, bewildered farm boys from East Anglia's 18 Division who, after the surrender, endured hideous imprisonment for three-and-a-half terrible years. The British learned, very quickly, that a colonial war with a mildly despised coloured enemy had suddenly turned into the loss of empire and the air age.

The Americans need never have been in the war at all, if the Japanese could have been sure they would not come to the help of the beleaguered Dutch and British. The British themselves were not sure of American help till almost the last few days of peace, but the Japanese were not to know this. So they crushed the battleships of the US Pacific Fleet at Pearl Harbor, thus gaining for themselves a quick victory which, in the end, inexorably, ensured they would lose the war. And as an act of prime folly their Axis partner in the Tripartite Pact, Adolf Hitler, declared war on the United States and thus ensured that he would lose *his* war.

Of all the powers in the conflict, the Americans, with their enormous and rapidly expanding industrial base, were best able to summon up the aircraft that annulled distance. The war became not a struggle for the recovery of lost territory in the Pacific, but rather an attempt to create air-bases, coral reef after coral reef, from which the B29 bomber could eat out not merely the industrial heart of Japan but every one – bar one – of her major cities.

It may seem almost prosaic to refer to the tank in the same breath as those vast aircraft which flew the thousands of miles separating their base from their target in Japan. And what have tanks to do with warfare on tropical islands and in impassable jungles? In fact, the lack of tanks in Malaya in 1941 was a major cause of the British defeat: the Japanese victory was won not in the steaming jungles but on the very good roads of the Malay peninsula, and one engagement, the advance of Major Shimada's tanks through 19 miles of British-held territory at Slim River, can arguably be regarded as one of the crucial defeats on the road to Singapore. At Kohima, too, in almost impossible terrain, the use of tanks was crucial in knocking out Japanese bunkers. Massed tanks in the battle of the 'Admin Box' (Sinzweya, Arakan, February 1944) were vital in defeating the encirclement of 7 Indian Division by the Japanese 55 Division, thus ensuring that the Japanese would not penetrate into Bengal through Chittagong, and freeing both 7 and 5 Indian divisions for action at Imphal and Kohima (whither they were transported by air, just as they had been supplied by air in the Box). The tank dash to Meiktila by 17 Indian Division and 255 Armoured Brigade was done with such speed and dash that the Japanese were already defeated before they began to react to it (March 1945). Meiktila was Slim's greatest strategic triumph of the campaign, and placed his hand firmly on the jugular of the Japanese. They fought hard to retake Meiktila, but failed; and that failure meant the road to Rangoon was open, and the final re-conquest of Burma within Slim's grasp. But it was tanks which guaranteed he would win.[9]

Both sides planned horrific weapons; some were used, some not. For the individual victim the distinction between horrors may not have mattered all that much: the Japanese infantryman, smoked out of a cave on Okinawa and washed over by a jet of flame from a flame-thrower, died no less horribly than the civilians in Hiroshima and Nagasaki. But worse might have been on the way, particularly if the peace overtures of the summer of 1945 had gone wrong, and the Allies had been compelled to invade the Japanese mainland. Chemical warfare and bacteriological warfare weapons had been prepared by both sides, though only the Japanese side has been fully revealed. Recent revelations about the ghastly experiments of Unit 731 with Chinese and other prisoners have reminded a forgetful public that the facts were made known to the world nearly 40 years ago in an English-language version of a Soviet war crimes trial.[10]

The death of the Nobel Prize winning physicist Yukawa Hideki revived accounts of Japan's own fumbling attempts to build a nuclear bomb.[11] On a very minor, tactical, scale, the Japanese use of poison gas in Burma was sporadic and seems to have made no impact at all, on either side, not even as hostile propaganda, though one imagines it would have been a gift to British Political Warfare. (The weapon used – a frangible glass grenade – was actually logged in US intelligence manuals at the time.)

The military instrument which inflicted upon the Japanese their greatest defeat on the continent of Asia in their entire history was, of course, that old and long-tested mercenary force, the Indian Army. Its loyalty had been sorely tried by racial discrimination in Malaya, and after the fall of Singapore some of its raw recruits had fallen easy prey to Japanese propaganda, by the tens of thousand (fewer, though, than those who did not). But by and large that army served its British masters splendidly in the last days before Partition put an end to it for ever. Partition, of course, endows the narratives of the last days of the united Indian Army with a sad air of swansong. There is a passionate valedictory in John Master's description of the Indian divisions advancing on Rangoon down the Mandalay road, in the pre-monsoon days of 1945, slicing through Burma faster than von Rundstedt through France in 1940:

> . . . past the ruins of the empire the Japanese had tried to build there, it took possession of the Empire *we* had built, in its towering rising dust clouds India traced the shape of her own future. Twenty races, a dozen religions, a score of languages passed in those trucks and tanks . . . The dust thickened under the trees lining the road until the column was motoring into a thunderous yellow tunnel, first the tanks, infantry all over them, then trucks filled with men, then more tanks, going fast, nose to tail, guns, more guns . . . This was the old Indian Army going down to the attack, for the last time in history, exactly two hundred and fifty years after the Honourable East India Company had enlisted its first ten sepoys on the Coromandel Coast. . . .[12]

There is a magnificence in it. But it is paternal, and that was the seed of its end. For John Masters, the Army and its Empire were *his* creation, his and his fathers'. The historians of that Army, on the other hand, among its own people, while recording its achievements with pride in 1958, had nevertheless to note that although 'the fighting in these early stages (i.e. of the Burma campaign) was mainly done by Indian troops on the Assam Front and the India Command was able to mobilise the resources of the country, even to a breaking point, to bring back to life the British Empire in the East', that Indian Army was not serving its own people, nor the interests of the people across whose territory the war was fought: 'Indian interests were nowhere considered and Burma's aspirations were not taken account of'.[13]

What was coming to an end was not just an empire but a symbiosis, one of those strange moments in history when the geniuses of two peoples lock together in hatred and love.

COMMAND

Distance, and the fact that more than one Allied nation was involved, raised at once problems of command on the Allied side. More important on the Japanese side were the by now familiar conflict between Army interests and Navy interests, and the *gekokujō* ('lower overcomes higher') phenomenon in which lower ranks – usually field rank officers – took the initiative from higher commanders. Hence the entrusting – at any rate at first – of the important political task of recruiting native armies against the British to Suzuki Keiji, a colonel, raising the student-led Burma National Army, and Fujiwara Iwaichi, a major, raising the Azad Hind Fauj.

On the Allied side, unified command was proposed once war broke out. The first joint command, ABDA (American, British, Dutch, Australian), under General Wavell, fell to pieces in a matter of weeks and his command was soon enemy territory.[14] Other commands nearly all devolved on US generals or admirals, Nimitz in the Central Pacific, MacArthur in the South-West Pacific, save the later one (September 1943) of South-East Asia. Here the Supreme Commander was the status-conscious British Admiral (not a very senior one) Lord Louis Mountbatten, whose headquarters contained a strong US component. This engendered a complex situation centred on a simplistic anti-British personality, Joseph Stilwell, who was Deputy Supreme Commander, South-East Asia, Chief of Staff to Chiang Kai-shek in China, commander of the US forces in Burma, and in theory at the same time under the operational command of Lt.–Gen. Sir George Giffard, 11th Army Group commander, whose superior he was, in turn, as Mountbatten's deputy. He refused orders from Giffard, but accepted those of Giffard's subordinate, General Slim, commander of the XIVth Army. Only the merciful restraints of geography prevented these Lewis Carroll absurdities wreaking more havoc than they did.[15]

Conflict between arms was evident. The naval forces in South–East

Asia, under Mountbatten's purview, were commanded by Admiral Sir James Somerville, by far Mountbatten's superior in rank and seniority, who insisted on communicating directly with the Admiralty when he saw fit. This was only solved by Somerville's removal. Earlier still, in a civil–military conflict in Malaya before hostilities began, the prescient but difficult Secretary of Defence in Malaya, Vlieland, mortally offended the slow-moving military and naval commanders in Singapore who constrained the governor, Sir Shenton Thomas, to dismiss him and have him sent home. Shenton Thomas concurred, yet in the upshot Vlieland was proved to have been unerringly correct in his predictions about the Japanese offensive, its aims and directions. But he was an awkward civilian, and he went.

The Japanese were no more fortunate. The Navy was officered by men who had served abroad and had seen the industrial might of the United States at first hand, and knew perfectly well that ultimate victory against such an industrial giant was impossible. But according to one Japanese writer on the national character, the doctrine of 'harmony' (WA) was so inculcated into the naval staff that they preferred the risk of war to opposing the plans of the Army and thus destroying harmony between the services. The Army, with fewer overseas contacts, was more fanatical and more insistent on Japan retaining her military presence in China; and the navy caved in. Harmony made for smooth running between juniors and seniors, between departments, between services – at least that was the theory; but at the expense of Japan being dragged into a war she could not win and being incinerated before it was over.[16]

INTELLIGENCE

Long-range penetration should have been able to tie up with stay-behind forces and air-supplied guerrilla groups; but if we look at Burma and Malaya the story, though gallant, is not one of great strategic rewards. Force 136, the Asian version of Special Operations Executive, operated into Burma and raised guerrilla forces, particularly in the Karen hills on the border with Thailand. One British officer, Hugh Seagrim, stayed behind in these hills after the 1942 retreat, and ran a nucleus of armed Karens. But the Japanese military police organised a tōbatsu, or punitive expedition, against him and in order to save his men from torture he gave himself up.[17] Spencer Chapman stayed in northern and central Malaya for three years and made contacts with Force 136 agents who landed by submarine. But his activities (and theirs) were inhibited by the fact that the guerrillas were Chinese communists and organising themselves to take over post-war Malaya as well as confronting the Japanese.

The Japanese organised similar movements. They had an intelligence school, the Nakano School, which trained ardently patriotic young Japanese in espionage and subversion (*bōryaku*).[18] Using Nakano graduates, Major Fujiwara set up a *kikan* (organisation) to recruit disaffected Indians in Malaya and Burma, and later used surrendered POWs to found the Azad Hind Fauj ('Indian National Army') to fight the British. Its Japanese liaison body, *Hikari Kikan* ('Lightning Organisation') sent agents into India, without much success. Perhaps they might have been effective if Subhas Chandra Bose, the exiled Indian ex-colleague of Gandhi and Nehru, had been able to raise Bengal against the British in 1944 in the wake of Mutaguchi's Imphal offensive; but the 'Indian National Army' collapsed in the aftermath of that disaster.

None of this subversive activity in the end counted as much as the efforts of Richard Sorge on behalf of Soviet Russia in the months before the outbreak of war. He had sources close to the Japanese government, and was able to assure the Russians that the Japanese would not intervene in Manchuria on behalf of Germany after the German invasion of Russia in the summer of 1941. The claim is, of course, now made that the Russians knew this anyway through their sigint sources, but the repercussions of that episode are still heard in the Japanese press, partly because of the return to Japan some years ago of the communist Itō Ritsu, who is said to have betrayed Sorge's spy-ring under interrogation by the Japanese police.[19]

The sigint claim in this connection is characteristic of the re-writing of history that has taken place since 1974, when it became possible for the first time to discuss the impact of cryptography on the Second World War. Both Group Captain Winterbotham and Ronald Lewin (*The Other Ultra*) assure us that this impact was enormous, a claim which has recently been reinforced by the reminiscences of a British cryptographer, Alan Stripp, who worked on Japanese codes in Bletchley and Delhi.[20] That intercepted signals led to the Japanese defeat at Midway, and thus to a major turning point in the war, has long been familiar, not least to the Japanese themselves, some of whom in 1942 suspected that the Japanese navy codes had been broken and were ridiculed for their pains. It is also well known that intercepted signals helped the US fighter planes ambush the Japanese naval C-in-C, Admiral Yamamoto, during a tour of inspection in the South Pacific. Other claims are made: that MacArthur's knowledge, through Ultra, of the strengths of the Japanese garrisons in New Guinea, enabled him to discern which to take and which to bypass. Slim is said to have learned from Ultra that Mandalay was only defended by a weak force and that he could attack with sure knowledge of victory. Yet it took concentrated aerial bombardment to reduce Fort Dufferin before 19 Division succeeded in recapturing Mandalay. And if Ultra furnished Slim with accurate knowledge of Japanese strengths, dispositions and intentions in Burma (and from his own evidence, *pace* Stripp, it is not clear it did) it did not prevent him, nor his IV Corps commander Lt.-Gen. Scoones, from issuing orders to withdraw to the Imphal plain too late, or almost too late. 17 Division only narrowly escaped being cut in two by the Japanese in 1944 as it had been in 1942, through no fault of its own.

This brings us to consider not merely the role of intelligence militarily but also politically, and it is a constant theme of post-war Japanese historiography that, in both military and political spheres, where everyone assumed their espionage at any rate was widespread and effective, it was one of their weakest points.

Japanese historiography today freely – perhaps too freely – confesses to an inferiority in intelligence, if not in propaganda.[21] But the platform of race gave the Japanese a head start in Asia, which they might have kept had not military reverses and the blundering brutality of some of their soldiers (of all ranks) not lost them in many cases the favour their cause had initially gained, for instance, among the young Burmese revolutionaries of the Thakin movement and even, fleetingly, in some quarters least likely to be favourable to them, such as the Overseas Chinese in Singapore.

The value of intelligence sources differed from that which obtained in some other theatres. For instance, the use of Japanese POWs yielded very little information of value to the Allies. The low ranks captured – because of Japanese determination not to be taken alive – meant they had little information anyway (the highest rank taken in Burma was a captain). Documents were far more useful, and the plentiful supply of Nisei (second-generation Americans of Japanese descent) who served in US organisations such as the Allied Translation and Interrogation Service (ATIS) in the Pacific ensured a constant and systematic flow of documentary intelligence. The US Pacific commands even printed their own technical dictionaries. The British were far less well supplied with linguists, but in the battles in Arakan, Imphal, Meiktila, and the Sittang breakout, captured documents revealed Japanese intentions, numbers, weapons, routes.[22] It is a sad paradox that Nisei who served with the US forces and with the British in India and Burma were in many cases the sons of parents who had been herded in a panic by the US authorities from the West Coast of California to be 'relocated' in unpleasant conditions for many years.

Other bodies, like the Australian coast watchers on the Pacific Islands, provided intelligence in particularly dangerous positions, as did the V Force units operating behind the Japanese lines in Burma. These were dependent on the goodwill of local villagers but although the hill tribes in Burma (Chins, Nagas, Kachins, Karens) afforded great help, too much could not be asked of them because they were vulnerable to Japanese reprisals. The Burmans, on the other hand, were hardly reliable, in British terms, until March 1945 when they shifted their political allegiance from the Japanese back to the British.

Although intelligence-gathering was not its prime purpose, Special Operations Executive (Force 136) naturally provided military and political information wherever it operated, but it was subject, as in Europe, to the drawback of being essentially a subversive organisation, that is, one that attracted enemy attention, whereas an intelligence organisation should naturally do everything to avoid it. Clandestine warfare and the sabotage that accompanies it, and the gathering of intelligence, are mutually contradictory functions. It may perhaps be said that Force 136's greatest triumph was not in Burma (where its inheritance is still causing political dissension) but in Siam (Thailand), where it helped to organise an anti-Japanese underground, operating from Calcutta and Ceylon, centred round high army officials and politicians from the Regent down, with such success that its Bangkok representative, Victor Jaques, was able to drive round the streets of the Thai capital wearing British uniform, while it was still under Japanese occupation.[23] Hindsight indicates that that was intolerably foolhardy, but it does have a certain *panache*; as does the rash venture of Major Turrall, also of Force 136, who walked into a Japanese camp after 15 August 1945 to tell them the war was over. As throughout much of Burma, they were without radio news, did not believe him, and beat him for his pains. He was lucky to get away with his life.

On the Japanese side, the most spectacular product of the Nakano School was undoubtedly Lt. Onoda. Charged on Lubang Island with a duty to engage in guerrilla warfare and to hold out until relieved, he refused to believe the war was over, and treated every mission sent to recover him and every radio appeal as US counter-espionage devices meant to fool him (he had been trained not wisely but too well). One by one his comrades died or were shot while marauding the hapless Filipinos, until one day in 1976 he was tempted out of hiding by – of all unlikely people – a globe-trotting Japanese hippie, who convinced him the war had been over for some time. But Onoda had been given an order and would only desist from carrying it out if a superior officer withdrew it. Luckily for him, one was available, and was flown to the Philippines to give Onoda his *nunc dimittis*. Whatever one thinks of Onoda's *nous*, there is a certain mad nobility in his solitary refusal to give in. In this sense, he is a credit to the Nakano School, which trained so many of Japan's subversive agents and auxiliaries of the nationalist Asian liberation armies.[24]

The school did *not* train one of the weirdest figures in the history of the Pacific War, Colonel Tsuji Masanobu, a right-wing fanatic who was involved in every major Japanese army campaign since 1937, usually (as he saw it) in the foremost organising and battlefront roles – Nomonhan, Guadalcanal, North Burma, Meiktila, etc. To avoid being taken by the British for a particularly hideous war crime, he fled to Bangkok in 1945, disguised himself as a Buddhist monk in saffron robes and hid in a temple to avoid the British occupation. He then escaped after doing a deal with Chiang Kai-shek's secret service, General Tai Li's Blue Shirt Society, who shipped him into Chungking in time for him to act as anti-communist adviser to Chiang in the last days of the Nationalist government. He later returned to Japan and was elected to the Diet. The Laotians seem to have done for him in 1969.[25]

CASUALTIES: THE ROLE OF MEDICINE[26]

In a war fought by troops from urban industrial societies, in tropical or sub-tropical conditions, diseases can cause havoc. Men's bodies were subjected to constant rain and excessive heat, vulnerable to malaria, dysentery, beri-beri and scrub typhus. Disease caused more casualties than enemy action, but draconian measures by the Allies made inroads on apparently insoluble problems. Malaria was conquered in the British–Indian forces by the drilled use of mepacrine tablets to such an extent that it became a military offence to catch it; an order which became an embarrassment to its originator, General Slim, when he caught malaria himself and realised he should have put himself under arrest. Control of malaria made the tropics not merely liveable in but fightable in, hence Mountbatten's decision to fight through the monsoon in 1944 and 1945 and gain extra months of campaigning which would otherwise have been forfeit.

The process had begun in India Command before the war. Malaria figures were 218 per 1,000 men in 1919 but by 1933 were down to 103 and by 1938 to 50. Like much else, the key lay in the guarantee of air supply, which also ensured the rapid evacuation of wounded to rear hospitals (the major difference between the first Wingate expedition, in which wounded had to be abandoned, and the second, in which they were evacuated by light aircraft from jungle strips).

At least 50,000 Japanese died of starvation and disease in Burma in the spring and summer of 1944, through lack of aircraft and poor logistics. British ability to overcome the medical problems of the Assam front was a

Marshall gives the following breakdown of Japanese losses:

Theatre	Killed	Permanently disabled	Captured	Total
Central Pacific	273,000	6,000	17,472	296,472
South Pacific	684,000	69,000	19,806	772,806
India-Burma	128,000	38,000	3,097	169,097
China	126,000	126,000*	1,059	253,059
Aleutians	8,000	1,000	30	9,030
Total	**1,219,000**	**240,000***	**41,464**	**1,500,464**

*I assume this to be a misprint, which of course affects the subtotal.

major factor in their victory, though at first the conditions at the front had reversed India Command's peace-time achievements: Eastern Command had 300 malaria casualties per 1000 in 1943.

The other classical brake on the movement of armies is, of course, venereal disease. Under the impact of antibiotics, the impact of this was reduced. In 1944, the admission rate for British troops in India was 60 per 1,000. The figure may seem high, but it has been pointed out that half a century earlier, in 1890, the corresponding figure had been 500, that is, venereal disease towards the end of Victoria's reign incapacitated half the British troops in India. Malaria was conquered by discipline and mepacrine. For venereal diseases, the moral approach was tried as well, but the rate of venereal sickness among British troops was higher than that of Indian troops, who were also far from home and subject to similar temptations and pressures. In leaflets, the soldier was exhorted to be continent, illicit intercourse was morally wrong, 95 per cent of Indian prostitutes were infected, etc. Practically, condoms and preventive outfits were issued free, so caution went hand in hand with objurgation. The troops were not oppressive as far as local women were concerned: John Masters records only one case of rape in his entire division during the war in Burma.

The Japanese attitude was different. Brothels, or 'comfort stations' (*ianjo*), went everywhere with the troops. Sanitary precautions were strict, alcohol was forbidden, and condoms and the use of prophylactic solution were *de rigueur*.[27]

British battle casualties in the war against Japan were not desperately high. The total number of UK casualties was 90,332, less than one-fifth of the total Dominion and Indian casualties on all war fronts (490,768). With the figure of UK troops killed, 19,968, may be contrasted the Merchant Navy losses in killed throughout the war: 30,248; or UK civilian losses from air-raids: 60,595 killed, and 86,182 wounded. Of 142,319 POWs taken, 12,433 were killed or died in captivity, as contrasted with 7,310 deaths in the hands of Germans or Italians.

General Marshall's report gives interesting figures for US forces. Casualties for factors other than battle amounted to 7.2 per cent of troops in the American Civil War, only 1.3 per cent in the First World War, and a negligible 0.6 per cent in the Second World War, which implies, *inter alia*, a spectacular conquest of insect vectors of disease by DDT.[28] Battle casualties show a different trend:

US Deaths per Month

Civil War (Union and Confederacy)	3,845
First World War	2,658
Second World War	4,576

After an enquiry, dated June 1950, by the Demobilisation Board, the Japanese give an overall figure for the total serving in the Japanese forces as 2,746,073, excluding third power nationals, that is, puppet armies. If we take this as a basis, then the total Japanese casualty figures represent over half this figure.

In terms of treasure, Japan's total general wealth lost has been estimated at ¥65,300,000,000; her military wealth lost at ¥40,400,000,000; a total of ¥105,700,000,000, using the yen standard of 15 August 1945. But this represents only tangible wealth damaged, and does not cover losses of overseas assets and production efficiency. Hattori gives an approximate table of losses and comparisons of war costs using 1948 figures and a unit of one million dollars:

Allies		Axis	
USA	317,600	Germany	272,900
Soviet Union	192,000	Italy	94,000
Great Britain	120,000	Japan	56,000
Others	55,461	Others	46,039
Total	**685,061**	**Total**	**468,939**

RACE

In spite of William Rogers Louis's quite accurate statement that the issue of race '. . . rested at the heart of power politics in the Far East',[31] there was nothing in the war in Asia and the Pacific resembling the cold-blooded, rationalised and industrialised genocide of Hitler's war against the Jews. This remains true, even though the Japanese and their puppet governments made great play with the racial origins of hostility towards the West (the Burmese leader, Ba Maw, made embarrassing use of 'blood kinship' rhetoric in his address to the Great East Asia Conference in Tokyo in November 1943). In spite of the Japanese intention to show themselves, in the old Field Marshal Yamagata's terms of August 1914, as the leaders of the coloured people against the white races, there is nothing in the Pacific War like the Holocaust.[32] Millions died, through brutality, greed, ruthlessness, ineptitude and the hazards of military operations, but not as the result of a plan coldly calculated years in advance and based on the prejudices of centuries. Racial conflicts there undoubtedly were, and even now racial resentments survive, between Japanese and Koreans, Japanese and Chinese, British and Japanese, but they were never industrialised into a system of death-camps. That is why, in spite of the unspeakable suffering of Allied POWs on the Burma–Siam Railway, it is important to recall the deaths of far more thousands of helpless Asian labourers.

There are odd survivals of racial prejudice in some surprising Japanese quarters. Aida Yūji, formerly a professor of the history of the European Renaissance in the University of Kyoto, is convinced there was a plan by British authorities in post-surrender Burma to vent racial contempt on the Japanese who fell into their hands. He has never retreated from this verdict, expressed in his book *Prisoner of the British*, which was aimed as much at his own countrymen's newly discovered Anglophilia of the 1950s as at the British themselves: 'I was obsessed by the idea that in prison camp we had glimpsed the unknown soul of the British Army and of the British. We had seen it. To us it was a frightening monster. This monster had ruled Asia for centuries and caused untold misery. . . .'[33] Aida viewed the cold racial contempt of the British as far worse than the brutality to which British prisoners were subjected by the Japanese; but there is little doubt that if Japan had remained triumphant in Asia, she would have inflicted on other nations of that continent a harsh, fanatical and sacralised regime. The evidence for this was brought forward in 1981, when the Japanese press announced the publication of studies carried out in 1942 and 1943 by the Population and Race Study Department of the Research Institute of the Health and Welfare Ministry. Directed by the then Surgeon-General, Koizumi Chikahiko, the research was printed in a hundred copies for government officials and came to light 40 years later in a Tokyo secondhand bookshop. There is, for instance, an enquiry into Koreans in Japan, estimated at 1,190,000 in 1940 and described as emigrant workers not easily assimilable into Japanese society. And, on the edge of fantasy, there is a justification of Nazi persecution against the Jews and a call for strict anti-Jewish measures. It appears the documents had been kept secret to avoid possible proceedings during the Occupation. The contents seem on the other hand unlikely to surprise anyone except the more recent post-war generations in Japan, who have left all these things behind, and revisionist historians here and in the United States who speak of the International Military Tribunals of the Far East in terms of 'victors' justice'.[34]

THE WAR OF IMAGES

The 'real' war was paralleled by a war of images. Japan put forward, for internal as well as external consumption, the old image of herself as 'the friend of Asia', the shelterer of Rash Behari Bose and Prince Cuong De, the awakener of China to her responsibilities in the resistance to Euro-American aggression, and the creator of a 'Co-Prosperity Sphere' which should ensure the economic autonomy of large parts of Asia then under colonial rule. Temporarily, Japan might have to use force to establish herself in the countries of Asia; but she promised ultimate liberation. In the event, the liberation was patchy and slow in coming.

The Philippines and a very much truncated Burma were offered independence of a sort in 1943. Indonesia and Indo-China had to wait until
the summer of 1945 before Japan grudgingly let go, and the signs were
so much against her then that it was clear she would have had to let go
anyway, in a matter of weeks. Elsewhere her role as liberator was belied
by the slaughter of untold numbers of mainland Chinese, and such episodes
as the massacre of Overseas Chinese in conquered Singapore in February
1942, to say nothing of the reduction to slavery of hundreds of thousands
of Burmese and Javanese labourers.

The contrast between promise and reality is still, of course, a matter
for debate in the reinterpretation of the Japanese military occupation of
South–East Asia, and some Japanese scholars have put forward the theory
that however brutal the impact of military occupation, one gift the Japanese
left behind them was the creation of autonomous military forces, which
proved to be invaluable in the liberation wars of the late 1940s. The claim
is even made that without the Japanese-influenced 'Indian National Army'
under Subhas Chandra Bose, India would not have achieved independence in
1947; though those who make claim seem unaware of the mood of the British
people in 1945 and of the attitude of the newly-elected Labour government
to the Indian question.

The image spread by the Japanese about their Western enemies was that
the British, Dutch and French were decadent imperialists whose time in Asia
had run out. The odd thing about this view is not that the Japanese held it, but
that it was as strongly maintained by Britain's major ally, the United States.
Initial US reluctance to come to the aid of Britain against Japan was partly
the result of the sure knowledge that a large section of US opinion would be
hostile to the employment of American forces to shore up Britain's empire in
Asia. The same view was held about France, by Roosevelt personally, and
culminated in a refusal to help the French when the Japanese decided to
take over total control of French Indo–China on 9 March 1945. A recent
book on the origins of the Vietnam War suggests that British planes flying
over Indo–China to supply the retreating French were shot down by US
planes acting on orders from General Wedemeyer, the successor to Stilwell's
command in the China theatre.[35] And it was US support, mediated through
the Office of Strategic Services, which ensured that Ho Chi Minh, and not
the French representatives, took over Hanoi after the Japanese surrender. A
US officer, on whom the mantle of historical irony now lies heavy, said of
the Vietnamese leader in those halcyon days, 'Ho is an awfully sweet guy
. . .' who objected to the return of the French but who would 'welcome ten
million Americans'.[36]

The Allies' own verdict on themselves was an obvious one. They were
fighting to free native peoples from the cruelties of Japanese military
occupation and to return them to the prosperity of the pre-war British,

Dutch and French Empires; though in the event they were too tired to insist for very long on this role after the Japanese surrender in 1945. Indeed, the British commander-in-chief, Far East, at the start of the war, Sir Robert Brooke-Popham, saw quite shrewdly and with much inner disturbance that Britain had offered Japan a moral foothold by failing to win the minds of the peoples she ruled. He was thinking of Burma, but the implications were wider:

> . . . it is rather disheartening, after all the years we have been in Burma and the apparent progress that has taken place under our rule, to find that the majority of the population want to be rid of us and that some of the leaders, for instance the late [sic] Prime Minister, U Saw, were actually in communication with the Japanese at a time when they were our potential, if not our actual enemies. We pride ourselves on being worthy to be entrusted with mandates and talk of regarding ourselves as trustees for the advancement of backward peoples. If we are to prove ourselves worthy of this it is up to everyone, especially to those on whom the burden of Empire will fall after the war, to consider what was wrong in Burma.[37]

The self-perceived role of the USA was as fighter for democracy against military fascist aggression in China, Manchuria and South–East Asia. The net upshot of the assumption of this role was strong, indeed oppressive, interference in the internal affairs of wartime China, a campaign for the liberation of the Philippines resulting in the slaughter of thousands of Flipinos – as well as Americans and Japanese – which, arguably, need never have been fought; and the refusal of help to the French in Indo–China which, whatever the rights or wrongs of the case, led inexorably to the US taking up the role of the French a decade later in a war from which the American national psyche still shows no signs of recovering.

In terms of personalities, the two roles and images of Britain and the US are neatly enough summarised in the vision of Roosevelt on the future of Asia and that of Churchill on the past of Asia. In the upshot, neither prevailed. America imposed democracy upon Japan by decree, a process which earned her both the respect and the dislike of the conquered, who are now busily re-writing the history of the Occupation with an unrestricted freedom which they only enjoy because the Occupation did in fact take place.

THE PRISM OF FICTION[38]

The history of the war in the Pacific lives on in sound recordings in the BBC Archive or the Imperial War Museum, in documentary films and endless volumes of official and semi-official reminiscence. But its final impact will be made on people who never took part in it and may never see the countries in which it took place, through novels and the films based on them. For the British it was an updated colonial war; for some Americans a totalitarian war of the ugliest kind — the totalitarian element being on *their* side, in Norman Mailer's still immensely readable *The Naked and the Dead*; for some Japanese it was an opportunity to recreate the European literary trajectory of the First World War, from dithyrambic greeting of the new dawn to the dread horrors of defeat in Ōoka Shōhei's *Fires on the Plain*. Until his death in 1988 Ōoka remained haunted by the war in the Philippines, during which he had become a prisoner of war. The factual *Furyoki* (A Prisoner's Story) and the fictive *Nobi* (Fires on the Plain) derive from it, and the fruit of his post-war return visit was the magnificent account of the campaign in *Reite Senki* (The Battle for Leyte) which is tragedy, military history and political pamphleteering of a high order. Another Japanese novelist turned the Burma campaign into a children's Buddhist morality tale. Takeyama Michio's *Biruma no tategoto* (The Burmese Harp) is an account by a non-combatant who had never even seen Burma but had picked up a war story from a secondhand bookshop in Kamakura and used it to preach Buddhist piety towards the dead: a Japanese corporal refuses to be repatriated after the war's end and disguises himself as a Buddhist monk in order to collect the bones of the Japanese dead and give them proper burial. It was later made into a beautiful film by Ichikawa Kon, and Takeyama's instincts were sure: in later years many groups of Japanese returned to the battlefields of Asia — at least to those where it was politically feasible to go — in the form of *ikotsu shūshū dantai* (bone and relic collecting groups). Armed with maps and nominal rolls, they picked over the battlefields, gathering the rain-stripped bones of their dead for burning and for relics for shrines in Japan.

The Burmese Harp is more a Buddhist tract than a novel, just as Richard Mason's story of India and Burma, *The Wind Cannot Read*, for all its gripping scenes of the fighting at Imphal, is really a prose *Madam Butterfly* in uniform, in which a pretty little Japanese news-reader, working for the Allies in Delhi, dies of a brain tumour. Her lover, captured by her fellow-countrymen, hears her voice on the radio when he is taken prisoner, and escapes just in time to be with her when she dies, to the almost audible sound of violins in the wings. In spite of the sentimentality of the love affair, one distinguished Japanologist none the less saw in it the watershed in the slow and unwilling transformation of post-war British views about the Japanese people.

Grimmer by far, but with an air of despairing truth, is Walter Baxter's *Look Down in Mercy*, the best piece of English fiction to come out of the war in Asia. Like Robert Merle's *Weekend à Zuydcoote*, which describes the disintegration of the French Army round Dunkirk, Baxter's novel describes the moral breakdown of a British officer — and, it seems, of the entire army to which he belongs – in the ghastly retreat from Burma in 1942. It is unremittingly harsh and brutal, but convincingly so, and the hero passes through cowardice, murder and homosexual seduction before he finally commits suicide in the safety of India. The link with the ultimate breakdown of the very vestiges of humanity, in Ōoka's *Fires on the Plain*, is perhaps the only thing on the Japanese side which can match it.

But perhaps the most widely known work of fiction to spring from the war in the Pacific is Pierre Boulle's novel, *Le Pont de la Rivière Kwai*, first published in 1952, and later transmogrified for ever by the histrionic litotes of Alec Guinness into a quite fantastic alteration of reality. Ostensibly, the theme is the courageous resistance of a British officer POW to cruel Japanese pressures, and the ultimate victory of the British spirit against a barbaric enemy and an even crueller environment. The film made from it is not – of course – a faithful transcription of the novel. A part had to be found for an American actor, William Holden, and a role engineered for a crucial American intervention in what had been Boulle's exclusively British panegyric of British valour. The brutish Japanese camp commandant of the novel was inevitably more sophisticated in the hands of Sessue Hayakawa, and the film dealt with a stubborn spirit ultimately doing the wrong thing – helping the Japanese build a bridge – for the right reason: keeping British POWs alive by occupying them and giving them a psychological focus for survival outside their destructive captivity.

But the basis of it, which was more to do with an earlier paean of praise for the British, André Maurois' *Les silences du Colonel Bramble*, is, of course utter nonsense. POWs *did* build such bridges on the Burma–Siam Railway (and were often killed when Allied planes bombed them), there *is* a River Khwae (Khwae Noi); but the Japanese engineer ignorant of bridge-building technology is wishful thinking, however real the original brutal camp commandant may have been. In the film, even the landscape was wrong. As Ian Watt, the historian of the English novel and himself a former POW on the Railway, wrote after seeing David Lean's beautiful shots of Ceylon, 'These were not the narrow and confused landscapes where we had been tortured by disease and fear and exhaustion; a formless and colourless amalgam of a prison camp that was a chaos of sagging huts, foul latrines, and decayed bedding and a railway track that gored the earth with spoil-pits and made a desolation of nature'.

In Watt's view, the failure of both book and film, when matched against remembered reality, was to ignore that 'the commonest lesson of the prison camp, I think, is one that everybody really knows but does not like to admit: that survival, always a selfish business, gets more so when it is difficult; and that the greatest difficulties of the task are the result not of any exceptional cruelty or folly but only of the cumulative effects of man's ordinary blindness and egotism and inertia'.

CRUELTY AND THE TREATMENT OF PRISONERS

There remains an intractable problem in terms of Japan's relations with other peoples, and that is the behaviour of her armed forces towards the armies they defeated and the countries they occupied. Inevitably, a certain amount of hypocrisy enters into this. Ruthless, clumsy and brutal though they were, the Japanese had no genocidal master plan to obliterate whole peoples, as the Germans did. Moreover, countries which participated in the International Military Tribunal for the Far East (Tokyo, 1945–48) and passed sentence on Japan's leaders for preparing aggressive war and committing crimes against humanity later fouled themselves by genocidal behaviour in later conflicts, the French in Algeria, the US in Vietnam.

None the less, certain episodes have entered the realm of national myth (I do not mean by this that they have no basis in fact) and it is difficult to see them apart from the mythological aura which surrounds them: the massacres at Nanking in 1937, at Hong Kong in 1941 and Singapore in 1942, and the treatment of Allied POWs and Asian labourers on the Burma–Siam Railway are obvious illustrations. It is not that the facts about these have not been published time and time again in Japan, they have. But it is easier for the Japanese to see themselves as victims of the war rather than perpetrators of it, and to remind themselves every August of Hiroshima and Nagasaki, so that what their armies did on mainland Asia gradually slips into the background and becomes weakened when conveyed by euphemism in school textbooks.

Japan's philosophy on the shame of being taken prisoner is in part responsible for this.[39] But it also seems to be true that there was a brutalisation of her military training in the 1930s which made it easier to ill-treat prisoners. Some Japanese say this was the result of admiration of Nazi military methods. Others point out that the guerrilla warfare in which Japan became involved in China brought about demoralisation of the troops, much as Field-Marshal Viscount Montgomery claimed of the behaviour of British troops in Ireland in the 1920s. His soldiers turned into savage murderers, and he was glad when it was over. Those who only have experience of the Japanese soldiery in the Second World War are amazed to realise how the Japanese treatment of prisoners was held up as a model to the civilised world in 1904–5 in the Russo-Japanese War, and later, in the First World War, when Japan occupied the German ports on the China coast.

There was occasional cannibalism in the Japanese forces, as Ōoka Shōhei makes clear in his novel *Nobi* and his campaign history *Reite Senki*. There were also vivisection experiments on Chinese POWs (and, it is claimed, bacteriological warfare experiments, on British and American POWs) in plants set up for chemical and bacteriological warfare research in Manchuria by Major-General Ishii's notorious Unit 731. Unfortunately, the moral ground for criticism of this institution is removed from the feet of Allies who later acquiesced in the refusal to arrest Ishii and his confederates, in return for the handing over of bacteriological warfare secrets later used, it has been suggested, in Korea and Vietnam.[40]

THE EMPEROR'S RESPONSIBILITY

Related to this is the question of Imperial responsibility for the decisions and conduct of the Japanese armed forces: 'the supreme authority in military and naval affairs is vested in the Most Exalted Personage, and those affairs are subject to the commands issued by the Emperor'.[41] This issue was raised in 1945 when a decision had to be reached whether the Emperor was to stand trial along with his ministers before the International Military Tribunal for the Far East, and was raised at some later dates, notably in more recent times in the tabloid press in Great Britain in September 1988 when it seemed the Emporer was about to die, and in a BBC TV film early in 1989 and a book by the film's author, Edward Behr.[42] Both film and book leaned heavily on David Bergamini's conspiracy-theory work *Japan's Imperial Conspiracy*. But neither suffering nor indignation of themselves confer a knowledge of Japanese constitutional practice, and it seems reasonably clear that although the Emperor was kept informed of most of the war planning, and questioned details of it, as the records – so far available – clearly show, he did not take the planning initiative. His role was, by and large, to listen and concur. His apologists say much detail of horrific atrocities was kept from him; on the other hand, his own brother, Prince Mikasa, who served with the Japanese Army in China, was not only himself aware of army atrocities but saw a Chinese propaganda film based on them and was so impressed that he brought a copy of the film back to Tokyo and showed it to the Emperor himself.[43] So there can be no doubt that he was aware at any rate of *claims* of atrocities. But the decision not to put the Emperor on trial was a political one, decided upon in Washington, and based on an appreciation, fostered by the Supreme Commander, Allied Powers, General MacArthur, that to put the Emperor on trial would occasion widespread and possibly bloody and long-lasting resistance to what turned out in the end to be a remarkably peaceful Occupation; though – as he said himself – his absence from the tribunal naturally vitiated the verdicts imposed on those who had been his loyal servants.

JAPANESE VERDICTS

The Japanese have done more than write novels and histories about their war. They have, since 1945, indefatigably analysed it, militarily, politically and, more recently, from the point of view of business management. There is, of course, no single national verdict. One of the best-known English-language histories, Chitoshi Yanaga's *Japan Since Perry*,[44] speculates on the causes of Japan's defeat, usually from academic utterances. Some lay the blame on feudalistic sectionalism, on absence of press freedom, others on a lack of a scientific approach, on irrationalism, on inferior technology, on lack of public spirit. A member of the Diet blamed the monopolisation of government and economic affairs by a few, and the decadence and dereliction of duty by the civil service, a charge repeated by the *Asahi Shimbun*, which, to the bureaucracy's avarice, corruption and selfishness, added want of courage, competence and conviction.

Not all was breast-beating, of course. Hayashi Fusao's notorious *Dai Tōa Sensō Kotei Ron* (An affirmative view of the Great East Asia War),[45] not only employed the term forbidden under the Occupation (Great East Asia War instead of Pacific War), but insisted that it had been part of a 'Hundred Years' War' waged by Japan in defence of Asia, and that she had been provoked into it by the US support of Chiang Kai-shek and the cutting off of raw material supplies by the US embargo of 1941. The Americans wanted a 'White Pacific', whereas Japan insisted on a Co-Prosperity Sphere for *all* the nations of Asia. Japan wanted to save Asia from foreign imperialism, and had it not been for adverse conditions enforced on her by the war itself, she would not have committed against Asians the errors of which she was undoubtedly guilty. The result was that the Allies became 'liberators' instead of the Japanese, who rightly should have played that role. Japan had not been a one-party fascist power, and the army and fascism were criticised by the Emperor, the elder statesmen and the commercial cartels. There had been no collective conspiracy.

Hayashi Fusao's argument, for those versed in Japan's wartime propaganda, has few surprises. It is, as was pointed out at the time by Ienaga Saburō among others, a 'stupid and unscholarly' diatribe along lines made familiar by the militarists of the 1930s and their apologists.

At the other end of the political spectrum a group of left-wing writers has published a collective history of the war in several volumes, the conclusions of which do not basically differ much from those of Hayashi Shigeru's *Pacific War*.[46] This book, in a popular and widely-read series, makes it clear that for the Japanese the war must count as one of 15 years' duration, at the end of which their Great East Asia Co-prosperity Sphere vanished like a dream. Only Japan's defeat liberated the countries of East Asia, but she had, in the interim, destroyed the system of government of the former colonial powers. The Japanese armies were at first welcomed in Asia, but when the Asian peoples realised that Japan's advantage was the primary principle and was simply a form of aggression, their goodwill was rapidly lost. Whether called 'New Order in Asia' or 'Co-prosperity Sphere', it was not an ideology for the peoples of Asia but for the expansion of the Japanese state. In any case, Japan had not gone to war to put this ideology into practice. Hayashi Shigeru traces the causes back to the ideas of Ishihara Kanji and his army contemporaries that, to overcome the economic depression, Japan should expand overseas, particularly into Manchuria and China. Manchuria and Mongolia were to become Japanese territory. Once the Army took the first step on this road, the rest followed inexorably.

The left-wing group, under Imai Seiichi, sees the whole military adventure not just as a disaster for the mainland of Asia but also for Japan herself, in its restrictions on economic life, and the militarisation and regimentation of a whole generation of Japanese youth.[47] Their sixth volume deals with the San Francisco peace conference, and what is interesting about it is the space it devotes to querying casualty figures. Newspapers in 1973, they observed, celebrating the 'Memorial Day of the End of the War', put Japanese casualties at 3,100,000, based on military losses of 2,300,000, overseas civilian losses at 300,000, and 500,000 deaths during air raids on Japan. This is, says Imai, a much more realistic figure than the Japanese government saw fit to put out under the Occupation, when total military losses were put at 507,000 and deaths from bombing in the Japanese islands at 241,000. The low total of 748,000 was an accurate reflection of the nature of communiqués issued during the War by Imperial General Headquarters, which completely falsified Japan's predicament.

Imai notes that Colonel Hattori's *History of the Great East Asia War* (1953) boosted these bogus figures to a total of 2,517,406.[48] But he claims even this is too small. The dead at Hiroshima, for instance, in the immediate post-war *Report on the End of the War*, are given as 70,000. But in materials provided for the Hydrogen Bomb Materials Preservation Society they rise to 240,000, and in an investigation by the major local newspaper, *Chūgoku Shimbun*, they appear as 280,000. Imai also says that investigations into losses overseas were inadequate at the time of writing, and that his figure of 3,100,000 total may still be superseded.

But more than casualty lists are involved. Fifty-five per cent of Japan's dwellings were destroyed, and the scale of expense was enormous in comparison with the Sino-Japanese War and the Russo-Japanese War:

Sino-Japanese War:	¥ 2,000,000,000
Russo-Japanese War:	¥ 17,000,000,000
Pacific War:	¥755,800,000,000

The latter figure represents the spendings of a hundred years' budgets. And the net result of all this loss of national treasure? Cities turned to ashes, a merchant marine sent to the bottom, the earth of Japan turned into a desert, her people starving. And Japan did even greater damage to Asia than to herself. From Chinese sources, Imai quotes the number of Chinese military killed as four million, of civilians, 20 million. Koreans and Taiwanese were used as forced labour overseas, where many were killed in battle or died of starvation. More than half the Koreans conscripted into Japan's forces were killed, and many Korean girls became comfort girls and 'victims of the lust of Japanese soldiers' (Nihonhei no yokubō no gisei naru to iu). That is Japan's shame. 'There can be no adequate compensation for the size of the spiritual and physical damage done to all the peoples of Asia.'[49]

It would be a mistake to think that Hayashi Fusao's interpretation has slid quietly into the past. Not only is there still a brisk private publishing business in the production of expensive Japanese military history, in some cases even down to the level of individual battalions or companies, written by veterans whose associations meet on a regular basis. Some historians of a much younger generation have begun to reinterpret Hayashi Fusao's book not only as a necessary attempt to view Japanese history since the mid-nineteenth century as a hundred years' war to free Asia from the pressures of a predatory West, but also as an inevitable mode of affirming Japan's own identity. Hayashi was wrong, says a young woman historian, to accuse the Japanese people of glibly accepting the verdict of the Occupation authorities as 'the dementia of the defeated'.[50] The dementia was, in fact, the natural sagacity of the Japanese people re-asserting itself and refusing ever again 'to take up residence in the violent Western-style international community'.[51]

> Japan's plight is that it must live as if it were completely unaware that others calculate all their moves on the basis of power – in fact it must work actively to remain ignorant of such calculations. And when Japan unintentionally creates power or a power vacuum by its own actions, the Japanese can only wait in anxious suspension for the repercussions in the power equations of other countries.[52]

This attribution of a rather astonishing naivety to Japan's past rulers is certainly an interesting, if not very convincing way of looking at the Second World War.

A more piacular approach characterises Ienaga Saburō's case: 'Japan has a moral responsibility toward the millions of people killed and wounded, and to their families, when the Imperial Army triggered a fire storm of war across Asia.'[53] Of course Ienaga's case, like Imai's, has contemporary political overtones: the injustices against Asia of the Imperial forces have been compounded 'by an immoral military alliance with the United States, the new aggressor in Asia.'[54] But Ienaga recognises another side to the balance sheet, as far as Japan herself is concerned. Japan's defeat led to her internal liberation, although 'it was a shameful stigma on the Japanese people that liberation came from foreigners and not by their own hands.'[55] Ienaga has for years held the attention of Japan's academic circles as the focus of a case against the Ministry of Education for applying censorship tactics in an attempt to make his views conform to the Ministry's; and he has an aim in writing his history. It is to ensure that although 'nostalgia and time are eroding the reality of the war',[56] the consciousness of the horrors of war, which sustains pacifism and democracy in Japan, should not be lessened. Collective amnesia, he thinks, erases the costly lessons of the war, and his book is an attempt 'to halt that erosion of consciousness'.[57] Fifty years after those terrifying events, it seems a perfectly proper exercise for an historian.

NOTES

1. There are official multi-volumed British, American, Australian, Indian, Chinese, Russian and Japanese accounts of the Second World War in the Far East, but the best one-volume account is R.H. Spector's *Eagle Against the Sun* (1984, London: Penguin Books, 1987). John Toland's *The Rising Sun* (London: Cassell, 1971) has more graphic detail, and Bergamini's *Japan's Imperial Conspiracy* (London: Heinemann, 1971), though crammed with interesting facts and speculations, is ruined by gruesome mis-translation and a too overt polemical purpose. See also H.P. Wilmott *Empires in the Balance* (Annapolis, 1982), and A. Coox in Vol. 6, *Cambridge History of Japan*.

   Gordon Prange's posthumous books are the best introduction to Pearl Harbor: *At Dawn We Slept* (London: Michael Joseph, 1982 and Penguin Books), and *Pearl Harbor. The Verdict of History* (New York: McGraw Hill, 1986). The endless controversy over Pearl Harbor – did Roosevelt fail to warn his commanders in Hawaii of the coming Japanese assault, in order to ease the US into war on the wide of Britain? – is best summed up in the latter, but see also Roberta Wohlstetter, *Pearl Harbor; Warning and Decision* (Stanford, 1962) and D. Borg and S. Okamoto, *Pearl Harbor as History* (New York: Columbia University Press, 1973). The cryptographic aspect has been renewed by the announcement of a book using evidence from the Australian code-breaker Cdr. Nave, on which see C. Andrew, 'The Growth of the Australian Intelligence Community and the Anglo-American Connection', *Intelligence and National Security*, Vol.4, No.2 (April 1989), 213–56. See also S. Falk's excellent summary of the debate in 'Pearl Harbor: A Bibliography of the Controversy', *Naval History* (Spring 1988), pp.55–6.

   Arthur Marder, *Old Friends, New Enemies* (Oxford: Clarendon Press, 1981) gives the best view of deteriorating relations between the British and Japanese navies, leading to the sinking of the *Prince of Wales* and *Repulse* in 1941. As general accounts of the antecedents and narrative of the Malaya campaign, see L. Allen, *Singapore 1941–1942* (London: Davis-Poynter, 1977) and S. Falk, *Seventy Days to Singapore* (New York: G.P. Putnam, 1975). The two best Japanese accounts are, for the sea battles, Sudō Hajime *Marēoki Kaisen* (Sea battles off Malaya) (Tokyo: Shiragame Shobō, 1974) and, for the land battles, the official *Marē Shinkō Sakusen* (The campaign in Malaya) (Tokyo: Asagumo Shimbunsha, 1966) or the shorter version *Marē Sakusen* (The Malaya Campaign)(Tokyo: Hara Shobō, 1966); unfortunately the only translated account is the grossly egoistic and inaccurate Tsuji, *Singapore: The Japanese Version* (London: Constable, 1962, repr. Oxford University Press, 1988).

2. L. Allen, 'Japanese Literature of the Second World War', *Proc. Brit. Assn. Japanese Studies*, Pt. 1 (Sheffield: Centre for Japanese Studies, 1977), p.118.

3. 'Then he told me that he learned the contents of the Hull note only after the war had started. . . . Anybody who understood the mentality of the Japanese people would have known that such a proposal presented in such a manner would deeply injure their susceptibilities and might cause the breakdown of negotiations. He deplored anew the misfortune that the British government had not used its good offices at that critical juncture.' T. Kase, *Eclipse of the Rising Sun* (London: Jonathan Cape, 1951), pp.62–3.

4. On the battle of Midway, G. Prange, *Midway* is the best account, but there is an earlier work, from the Japanese side, which is still worth reading, M. Fuchida and M. Okumiya, *Midway: The Battle that Doomed Japan* (London: Hutchinson, 1957). The importance of Midway from the point of view of code breaking is shown in R. Lewin, *The Other Ultra: Codes, Ciphers, and the Defeat of Japan* (London: Hutchinson, 1982); Japanese Army suspicions that the Navy's codes had in fact been broken are referred to in General Sugita's recent memoirs, *Jōhō naki sensō shidō* (War leadership without intelligence) (Tokyo: Hara Shobō, 1987), p.240.

5. I. Morris, *The Nobility of Failure* (London: Secker & Warburg, 1975); Ch.10 is deeply interesting on the connection of the Kamikaze flyers to a certain Japanese tradition. T. Takagi, *Rikugun tōkubetsu kōgekitai* (Army special attack unit), 3 vols. (Tokyo: Bungei Shunjū, 1986), deals with the Army pilots.

6. The Literature on Wingate is extensive. See L. Allen, *Burma: The Longest War*, Chs.2 and 5, M. Calvert, *Prisoners of Hope* (London: Jonathan Cape, 1952, new edn., Leo Cooper, 1971), B. Fergusson, *The Wild Green Earth* (London: Collins, 1946), R. Rhodes James, *Chindit* (London: John Murray, 1980), S. Bidwell, *The Chindit War* (London: Hodder & Stoughton, 1979), P. Mead, *Orde Wingate and the Historians* (Braunton: Merlin Books, 1987).

7. On Ivan Lyon, see B. Connell, *Return of the Tiger* (London: Evans, 1960), and R. McKie, *The Heroes* (Sydney: Angus & Robertson, 1960).

8. There is an interesting sketch of Mutaguchi in A. Swinson, *Four Samurai* (London: Hutchinson, 1968). See also L. Allen, *Burma: The Longest War* (London: Dent, 1984), T. Takagi, *Inpāru* (Imphal) (Tokyo: Bungei Shunjū, 1975), N. Kojima, *Eirei no tani* (Valley of heroes) (Tokyo: Kōdansha, 1970), and the *Inpāru Sakusen* (Imphal Operation) volume in the *Senshi sōsho* series (Tokyo: Asagumo Shimbunsha, 1968).

9. On Meiktila, see Slim, *Defeat into Victory* (London: Cassell, 1956), and M. Smeeton *A Change of Jungles* (1962).

10. S. Morimura revealed the horrors of Unit 731 to the Japanese in *Akuma no hōshoku* (Devil's appetite) (Tokyo: Kobunsha, 1981), with supplementary vols. later. A Japanese medical officer described similar activities, on a far lesser scale, in Burma, in *Akuma no Nihon gun-i* (The devil's medical officer) (Tokyo: Yamanote Shobō, 1982). The latest work on the topic is P. Williams and D. Wallace, *Unit 731* (London: Hodder & Stoughton, 1989), and the first Soviet account is given in *Materials on the trial of former servicemen of the Japanese Army charged with manufacturing and employing bacteriological weapon* (Moscow: Foreign Languages Publishing House, 1950).

11. G. Thomas and M.M. Witts, *Ruin from the Air* (London: Hamish Hamilton, 1977), refer briefly to Japanese atomic bomb research; there is a detailed article by Y. Tsujimoto 'Genbaku seizō ni tazusawatta hitobito' (Men who participated in making the atomic bomb) in *Rekishi to jinbutsu* (Tokyo, Dec. 1973), 103–12. It has recently been suggested that information on US atomic research, obtained in June 1942 by a Spanish agent of the Japanese, persuaded Tojo to redouble efforts in this direction. Gerhard Krebs, 'Japanese–Spanish Relations, 1936–1945'. *Transactions of the Asiatic Society of Japan*, Vol.3 (1988), 21–52.

12. On the Indian Army, see P. Mason, *A Matter of Honour*; J. Masters, *The Road Past Mandalay* (London: Michael Joseph, 1961); J. Connell, *Auchinleck* (London: Cassell, 1959).

13. B. Prasad, *Official History of the Indian Armed Forces in the Second World War; Reconquest of Burma. Vol.1* (Calcutta: Orient Longmans, 1958), p.xxv.

14. On Wavell, see J. Connell, *Wavell: Supreme Commander 1941–1943* (London: Collins, 1969).

15. C.F. Romanus and R. Sunderland, *Stilwell's Mission to China* (Office of the Chief of Military History, Washington, DC, 1953); *Stilwell's Command Problems* (1956); *Time Runs Out in CBI* (1959), B. Tuchman, *Sand against the Wind: Stilwell and the American Experience in China 1911–1945* (New York: Macmillan, 1970). On Vlieland, see L. Allen, *Singapore 1911–1942*, Ch.X and Appendix III. On SEAC's command problems see P. Ziegler, *Mountbatten: The Official Biography* (1985); P. Dennis, *Troubled days of peace. Mountbatten and South East Asia Command, 1945–46* (Manchester: Manchester University Press, 1987); and E.J.K. McCloughry, *The Direction of War* (1955).

16. S. Watanabe, *Nihon soshite Nihonjin* (Japan and the Japanese), (Tokyo, 1980) (English trans. *The Peasant Soul of Japan,* Macmillan, 1989) Ch.I, Section 5.
17. On Seagrim, see I. Morrison, *Grandfather Longlegs* 1947; on SOE in Asia cf. C. Cruickshank, *SOE in the Far East* (1983), A. Gilchrist, *Bangkok Top Secret,* 1970 and T. O'Brien, *The Moonlight War* (1987).
18. L. Allen, 'The Nakano School' is a brief introductory sketch *(Proc. Brit. Assn. Jap. Studies,* Vol.10 (1985), 94–8). See also 'Japanese Intelligence Systems' *(Journal of Contemporary History,* Vol.22 (1987), 547–62, I. Fujiwara, *F Kikan* (English trans. Y. Akashi, Hong Kong: Heinemann, 1983), H. Toye, *The Springing Tiger* (S.C. Bose) (London: Cassell, 1959), J. Lebra, *Jungle Alliance* (Singapore: Donald Moore Press, 1971). On both Fujiwara and Suzuki see L. Allen, *The End of the War in Asia* (London: Hart-Davis, 1976), and 'Fujiwara and Suzuki: The Lawrence of Arabia Syndrome' in S. Henny and J.P. Lehmann (eds.), *Themes and Theories in Modern Japanese History* (London: Athlone Press, 1988), pp.230–242.
19. See F.W. Deakin and G.R. Storry, *The Case of Richard Sorge* (London: Chatto & Windus, 1966), and G. Prange, *Target Tokyo: The Story of the Sorge Spy Ring* (New York: McGraw-Hill, 1984); and Ozaki Hotsuki, 'Zoruge jiken to Itō Ritsu' (Itō Ritsu and the Sorge case), *Ushio* (Tokyo, Oct. 1980) (and other articles in the same issue).
20. Alan Stripp, *Codebreaker in the Far East* (London: Cass, 1989; see also E.J. Drea, 'Ultra and the American War against Japan: A Note on Sources', *Intelligence and National Security,* Vol.3, No.1 (Jan.1988), 195–204.
21. H. Iwashima, *Jōhōsen ni kanpai shita Nihon. Rikugun angō 'Shinwa' no hakai* (Tokyo: Hara Shobō, 1984). (Japan's defeat in the intelligence war. The destruction of the 'myth' of the Army codes.) And see J.W. Chapman, 'Japanese Intelligence, 1918–1945: A Suitable Case for Treatment', in C. Andrew and J. Noakes (eds.), *Intelligence and International Relations* (Exeter, 1987).
22. There is no account of the training of Japanese linguists in English, other than Stripp's book, which is confined to those specialising in Sigint; but a Japanese resident in London has researched a short history of the role of the School of Oriental and African Studies: Oba Sadao, *Sen-chū Rondon Nihon-go gakkō* (London's wartime Japanese language school) (Tokyo: Chuō Kōron, 1988).
23. C. Cruickshank, *SOE in the Far East* (Oxford: Oxford University Press, 1983); I. Trenowden, *Operation Most Secret* (1978); A. Gilchrist, *Bangkok Top Secret* (1970).
24. H. Onoda, *No Surrender. My Thirty-Year War,* trans. C.S. Terry (London: Andre Deutsch, 1975).
25. M. Tsuji, *Underground Escape,* trans. R. Booth and T. Fukuda (Tokyo: Asian Publications, 1952); L. Allen, *End of the War in Asia,* Ch.2; K. Miki, *Sanbō Tsuji Masanobu. Raosu no kiri ni kiyu.* (Staff Officer Tsuji Masanobu. Vanished into the mists of Laos) (Tokyo: Nami Shobō, 1985).
26. B.L. Raina (ed.), *Official History of the Indian Armed Forces in the Second World War, Medical Services. Preventive Medicine,* 3 vols. (1961); *Field Service Hygiene Notes: India, 1945* (Calcutta: Government of India Press, 1945); A.S. Walker, *Australia in the War of 1939–1945. Series (5) Medical. Middle East and Far East* Canberra, 1953. On the Japanese side, three interesting memoirs by Japanese MOs: S. Karube, *Inpāru. Aru jūguni no shuki* (Imphal, an MOs diary) (Tokyo: Tokuma Shotan, 1979); T. Hashimoto, *Ruikotsu no tani* (Valley of Bones) (Tokyo: Ōshisha, 1979); T. Machida, *Ōkan Senki. Ichi guni ni yoru Nampō kenbunroku* (A view across the battlefield. An account of things seen and heard in the Southern regions by a medical officer) (Tokyo: Kyōei Shobō, 1985).
27. On the comfort house system, see L. Allen, *Burma. The Longest War,* and K. Senda, *Jūgun ianfu* (Army comfort girls), 2 vols. (Tokyo: Futaba-sha, 1973, 1985).
28. *General Marshall's Report. The Winning of the War in Europe and the Pacific* (US War Department, 1945).
29. T. Hattori, *Dai Tōa Zenshi* (Complete History of the Great East Asia War) (Vol. ed. Tokyo: Hara Shobō, 1968), pp.10–17.
30. L. Allen, *Singapore 1941–1942* (Ch. XI 'The Factor of Race'), (1976); C. Thorne, *Racial Aspects of the Far Eastern War of 1941–45, Proc. Brit. Acad.,* LXVI (1980); C. Dover, *Hell in the Sunshine* (London: Secker & Warburg, 1942).

31. W.R. Louis, *British Strategy in the Far East* (Oxford, 1973).
32. R. Tsunoda, *et al., Sources of Japanese Tradition*, (New York: Columbia University Press/ London: Oxford University Press, 1958), pp.207–8.
33. Y. Aida, *Prisoner of the British*, trans. H. Ishiguro and L. Allen (London: Cresset Press, 1966), p.xii.
34. The reference is to R. Minear, *Victors' Justice: The Tokyo War Crimes Trial*, Princeton, 1971; but see also P.R. Piccigallo, *The Japanese on Trial: Allied War Crimes Operations in the East, 1945–1951* (Austin, TX: University of Texas Press, 1979). See also the international symposium *The Tokyo War Crimes Trial*, edited by C. Hosoya *et al.* (Tokyo: Kōdansha, 1986). The relative difficulty of consulting the English text of the Tokyo trials, copies of which existed in very few libraries and research institutes, is now merely a financial one, since R. Pritchard and S. Zaide have reprinted the entire text with extra volumes of finding aids: *The Tokyo War Crimes Trial: The Complete Transcripts of the Proceedings of the International Military Tribunal for the Far East* (New York: Garland), 22 vols., 5 supplementary vols.
35. P.M. Dunn, *The First Vietnam War* (London: Hurst, 1985); the case is rejected by T. O'Brien in *The Moonlight War: The Story of Clandestine Operations in South-East Asia, 1944–5* (London: Collins, 1987), p.87.
36. *The Reporter*, 27 Jan. 1945, in L. Allen, *The End of the War in Asia*, p.113.
37. Brooke-Popham Papers, Liddell Hart Archive, File V, No.7/18/2.
38. Ōoka Shōhei, *Furyoki* (A Prisoner's Story) (Tokyo: Kōdansha, 1971); *Nobi* (Tokyo: Shinshōsha, 1954), trans. I. Morris, *Fires on the Plain* (London: Secker & Warburg, 1957); *Reite Senki* (The Battle for Leyte) (Tokyo: Chuō Kōran, 1971); Takeyama Michio, *Biruma no tategoto* (Tokyo: Shinshōsha, 1956), trans. H. Hibbett, *Harp of Burma* (Rutland, Vermont and Tokyo: Tuttle, 1966); Richard Mason, *The Wind Cannot Read* (London: Hodder & Stoughton, 1946); Walter Baxter, *Look Down in Mercy* (London: Heinemann, 1951); P. Boulle, *Le Pont de la Rivière Kwai* (Paris: Julliard, 1952); Ian Watt, 'Bridges over the Kwai', *The Listener*, 6 Aug. 1959. It is difficult to select from the vast POW literature, but I would suggest an Australian version, E.E. Dunlop, *The War Diaries of Weary Dunlop* (1987), and C.P. Adams, *No Time for Geishas* (London, 1973).
39. T. Fukiura, in an article '*Sen-jin-kun* to Nihon-hei horyo' ('Battlefield Lessons' and Japanese POWs), *Rekishi to Jinbutsu* (Sept. 1984), pp.187–96, describes an interview with the Army Captain Shirane, who drafted the fatal phrase during the campaign in China: 'ikite ryoshū no haji wo ukezu' (do not have the shame of being taken prisoner alive).
40. P. Calvocoressi, *Survey of International Affairs* (London: Oxford University Press, 1950), pp.454–5; P.R. Piccigallo, *The Japanese on Trial* (Austin, TX and London: University of Texas Press, 1979), pp.150–57; and see Note 9.
41. A. Stead (ed.), *Japan by the Japanese* (London: Heinemann, 1904), p.36.
42. E. Behr, *Hirohito: Behind the Myth* (1989), and see review by L. Allen in *Japan Forum*, No.2 (1989), and S. Large and A. Stockwin, 'Hirohito' in *The Woodstock Road Editorial*, No.1 (Winter 1989), 7–8; and the March 1989 issue of *Bungei shunjū* on the Emperor's death, particularly K. Hayashi, 'Sensō sekinin to wa nani ka?' (What is war responsibility?), pp.154–65.
43. Mikasa no miya Takahito, *Kodai Oriento-shi to watakushi* (Ancient Oriental History and myself) (Tokyo: The Society for Near Eastern Studies in Japan, 1984), pp.18–19.
44. Hamden, CT: Archon Press, 1966, pp.622–3.
45. *Chūo Kōron* (Tokyo, 1963), in article form, 2 vols. 1964–65.
46. Hayashi Shigeru, *Taiheiyō sensō* (The Pacific War), Vol.25 of the 26 vols. *Nihon no rekishi* (A History of Japan) (Tokyo: Chūkō Bunkō, 1974).
47. Imai Seiichi *et al.*, *Taiheiyō sensō-shi* (A History of the Pacific War), 6 vols. (Tokyo: Aoki Shoten, 1973).
48. Hattori Torashirō, *Dai Tōa Sensō Zenshi* (A complete History of the Great East Asia War) (1953), 4 vols.; 1st vol. ed. 1965 onwards (Tokyo: Hara Shobō). (Hattori died in 1960.)
49. S. Imai, op. cit., Vol.6, p.30.
50. Hasegawa Michiko, 'Sengo sedai ni totte no Dai Tōa Sensō', *Chūo Kōron* (Tokyo, April 1983), pp.96–111, trans. as 'A Postwar View of the Great East Asia War', *Japan Echo*,

     Vol.XI (Special Issue, 1984), 29–37.
51. Hasegawa, loc. cit., p.36.
52. Ibid., p.37.
53. Ienaga Saburō, Taiheiyō sensō (The Pacific War) (Tokyo: Iwanamī Shōten, 1969), trans.
    F. Baldwin as *Japan's Last War* (Oxford, 1978), p.239.
54. Ibid., p.240.
55. Ibid., p.242.
56. Ibid., p.254.
57. Ibid., p.256.

INDEX